UNDERSTANDING HUMAN BEHAVIOR FOR EFFECTIVE POLICE WORK

UNDERSTANDING HUMAN BEHAVIOR FOR EFFECTIVE POLICE WORK

*

HAROLD E. RUSSELL

and

ALLAN BEIGEL

With a Foreword by George G. Killinger

Basic Books, Inc., Publishers

NEW YORK

Library of Congress Cataloging in Publication Data

Russell, Harold E.   1918–
    Understanding human behavior for effective police
work.

    Includes bibliographies and index.
    1. Deviant behavior. 2. Psychology, Pathological.
3. Mental illness. 4. Police. I. Beigel, Allan,
joint author. II. Title.
HV6080.R88   157'.02'43632   75-7261
ISBN 0-465-08861-9

TO

PAT AND JOAN

With deep affection and appreciation

for their support

Contents

Foreword   ix
Preface   xi
Acknowledgments   xiii

PART I

Introduction

1. The Changing Role of the Police Officer   3

PART II

The Origins and Complexities of Human Behavior

2. Foundations of a Professional Attitude Toward
   Human Behavior   17
3. Normal Personality Development   26
4. The Normal Personality in Operation: Conflicts
   and the Mechanisms of Defense   36
5. Abnormal Behavior: What It Is and What to Do   54

PART III

Understanding Mental Illness

6. Classification of Abnormal Behavior   73
7. Personality Disorders   79
8. The Neuroses   90
9. The Psychoses   110

PART IV

Assessing and Managing Abnormal Behavior in the Field

10. Psychopathic Behavior   129
11. Deviant Sexual Behavior   148
12. Delinquent Behavior   167
13. Drug Dependent Behavior   176
14. Paranoid Behavior   193
15. Violent Behavior   202
16. Suicidal Behavior   219
17. Behavioral Aspects of Disaster   240
18. Behavioral Aspects of Riots and Riot Control   250
19. Legal Aspects of Abnormal Behavior   266

PART V

Conclusion

20. The Police Officer as a Person   277

Index   295

Foreword

Understanding Human Behavior for Effective Police Work by Doctors Russell and Beigel is a contemporary and excellent addition to professional literature not only for police but also for corrections and social rehabilitation personnel. It fills an existing need for a text which will assist workers in the helping professions to respond appropriately to deviant and disturbed behavior in their encounters with the public and enable them to function optimally as an ally of medical and paramedical therapeutic professionals.

Inappropriate initial assessment of atypical behavior must be avoided by all who interface with behavioral abnormalities. In its extensive canvas of the spectrum of human behavior, with its origins and complexities, definitions, and insights related to evaluating and managing abnormal behavior *in the field and on the spot,* this book deserves to be required reading for today's students of human behavior. It is especially pertinent to all of us working in the area of criminal justice.

Extensive use of case reports generated from actual police experience add interest and clarify definitions. A final chapter on the police officer as a person is most appropriate.

The authors, eminently qualified by training plus years of psychological, psychiatric, clinical, and teaching experience have produced an outstanding text.

George G. Killinger, Ph.D.
Director, Institute of Contemporary
Corrections and the Behavioral Sciences
Sam Houston State University
Huntsville, Texas

Preface

SINCE the end of World War II there has been a concerted effort on the part of many police officials and organizations to make police work a "profession." Many colleges and universities presently offer programs which include the following: (1) a certificate for completion of thirty hours of college work; (2) an Associate of Arts Degree for completion of two years of college work in police science; (3) a four-year course in police science; and (4) graduate work in police science.

By the early 1970s, 10 percent of the police officers in the United States were going to school in one of these programs. Currently, there are approximately thirty-five hundred junior colleges and universities offering certificates and degrees in police science and some $40 million is being spent annually on the education of police officers.

Furthermore, there are approximately forty thousand police agencies in the United States. Many of them, particularly those located in large cities and state police agencies, have their own police academies offering recruits a minimum of sixteen weeks of mandatory training. Many states have enacted legislation specifying completion of a minimum number of hours of formal and field training before certification and employment as a police officer.

The importance of understanding behavior in the training of professional policemen is indisputable. Behavior is the major phenomenon that the police officer must deal with during his working day. He must deal with not only the behavior of criminals but also the behavior of the general public, the behavior of his family, and his own behavior. He can no longer regard the study of behavior as the sole concern of the psychologist and psychiatrist. He must learn more about behavior and the behavioral sciences in order to effectively and safely carry out his job.

In this latter regard, it is important to note that recent studies have demonstrated that as many as 13 percent of all police officers killed in the line of duty were involved in answering calls concerning a mentally deranged person. Additionally, FBI statistics indicate that 20 percent of police officers killed in the line of duty are fatally injured answering a family disturbance call and that 40 percent of all injuries to police officers occur during these calls.

During their college training or their police academy experience police officers may take courses and/or attend lectures in normal and abnormal psychology. These subjects are taught primarily by academic psychologists who usually use the same approach with police officers as they do with all their students, including those studying to be psychologists. In college courses, especially, little may be offered which is oriented to the special needs of the police officer; at the police academy, the lectures devoted to the recognition and handling of abnormal behavior often include outdated material.

Our extensive experiences with police officers indicate that they both welcome and need up-to-date theoretical and practical information regarding normal and abnormal behavior as applied to police work. This textbook is designed to meet that need by describing clearly those areas involved in the behavioral aspects of police work and by providing helpful hints which will be useful to the police officer in the field. We have directed our book especially to the officer on the street, the recruit in the academy, and the police science student.

Acknowledgments

MANY colleagues and friends, both from law enforcement and from mental health, have assisted us in the preparation and completion of this textbook. From the field of law enforcement, we have benefited immeasurably from the helpful comments of Special Agent Frank Sass, Inspector Marion Talbert, Chief Superintendent Brian Fairbairn (London), Dr. Andrew Crosby, and Mr. James Sterling, all of whom read the preliminary manuscript and contributed significantly to our task. We also appreciate the assistance of the following law enforcement professionals who reviewed the final draft: Dr. Robert Walker, Alan Harrington, Deputy Chief Don L. Daniel, and Chief Robert E. Kessler. The opportunities we have had to work with Chief William J. Gilkinson of the Tucson Police Department, former Sheriff Michael S. Barr, and Sheriff Coy Cox of the Pima County Sheriff's Department have presented us with a clearer understanding of the police officer's role in assessing and managing abnormal behavior in the field. We are also indebted to Dr. Walter Menninger and Dr. Alan I. Levenson for their assistance in helping us improve the quality of our book.

For editorial help, we thank Mr. Louis Hinshaw, Ms. Robyn Butler, Ms. Jeanne O'Flaherty, Ms. Helen Purcell, and Ms. Mary Schmidt. An extra note of appreciation must be given to Ms. Schmidt, who provided us with the most able secretarial assistance in typing the final manuscript.

We wish to thank Erwin Glikes and Herb Reich of Basic Books for assisting us in the preparation of this book, and Mr. Arthur Rosenthal, former Publisher of Basic Books and currently Publisher of Harvard University Press, for giving us the opportunity to go forward with our idea.

Finally, we wish to express our sincere thanks to the many policemen and policewomen by whom and for whom this book is written.

PART I

Introduction

Chapter 1

The Changing Role of the Police Officer

Police Work—1875

"Killers watched every move the ranger ace made. Slade [the Ranger] knew it. So he tensed to alertness as two shadowy figures approached in the poorly lit Juarez street. They wore hoods and the flowing robes of brothers of the mission. But under the shorter robe of one Slade spotted a pair of rangeland boots. Slade's guns streaked from their holsters as the 'brothers' wheeled to face him. The quiet street exploded with gunfire. A slug ripped the crown of his hat. Then a stunning blow to his midriff sent him reeling—but both his guns pumped their lethal hail in the last few seconds of a duel to death!" (Scott 1973).

Police Work—1975

"They had worked for more than two weeks tailing people in a numbers operation. Finally, the pick-up man who took the work into the bank where the office crew would run the adding machine was 'put' there. It was a three-story building in a neighborhood that was hotter than a pistol; a plainclothes cop couldn't hang around ten minutes without being spotted and the alarm going out through the entire area. They knew the building but that wasn't enough. Which of the three floors or basement was being used for the numbers bank was still a question. The lieutenant had one of the team bring his five-year-old boy to work with him so he would look like a father on his day off, an ordinary guy who would not be suspected of being a cop. He slipped into the building when the toot of a horn signaled that the numbers courier was coming up the street. That gave him time to get to the top floor and see the guy coming up the stairs go into the second-floor apartment. Each floor looked like a railroad flat of five rooms running one into the other in a row.

"Feeling rather good about the whole thing, Lt. Scaffardi had had search warrants sworn out. The Chief Inspector's squad raided the place and came up with the runner and two bookkeepers, plus all of the day's slips. The oldest bookkeeper, a fifty-year-old who looked like a minister, asked the captain if he could 'talk' to him. When the captain said he 'was listening,' the bookkeeper offered $5,000 to forget the whole thing. When the captain asked 'What $5,000?', the guy said, 'the five my brother will be here with in thirty minutes.' A phone call was made and the brother showed up with five big ones. So he got arrested for bribery and the other three for numbers" (Salerno and Tompkins 1969).

Newspapers, magazines, radio, television, movies, and drama perpetuate the idea that the police are "a body of men engaged in the exciting, dangerous, and competitive enterprise of apprehending criminals. Emphasis on this one aspect of police functioning has led to a tendency on the part of both the public and the police to underestimate the range and complexity of the total police task" (President's Commission 1967, p. 13). The apprehension of criminals has been and will continue to be an integral part of police work. But there is also a growing awareness among law enforcement officers and agencies that this is not the police officer's primary function.

As we shall see, the daily experiences of many police officers provide evidence that their role as "law enforcer" is undergoing rapid and extensive change. Protests and arguments are frequently heard in response to this process of change. There are those who do not regard this change as progressive and who are reluctant to turn from the methods and philosophies of the "good old days."

4

"The Good Old Days"

People who speak of the "good old days" in reference to police work are recalling the past, when often the only things a police officer needed were a badge, a gun, and plenty of guts. Actually, it is doubtful if these alone ever did suffice, and it seems reasonable to assume that then, as now, good police officers possessed other equipment and human attributes that contributed much to their ability to perform their assigned tasks.

Even back in the "good old days" police officers performed many social services, including distributing charity to the poor, helping the unemployed to find jobs, visiting homes to check on communicable diseases, and escorting drunks safely home. Whitehouse concludes that "it would appear that police traditionalists have not read their police history closely enough. The police officer's dual function of performing law enforcement duties and peacekeeping community services has apparently been present as long as there have been municipal police departments" (Whitehouse 1973, p. 92).

Sterling also shares the view that the public service component of police work has always been there. He states: "What is new in regard to this component of police work is research supporting this view and the *capability of the police* to admit that they really don't spend all their time in activities such as gunfights with the SLA." *

Nevertheless, the police officer was primarily perceived *by the community* as an enforcer of the law. He detected and apprehended criminals and his presence deterred others from engaging in criminal acts. There was emphasis on the physical and mechanical aspects of police work and police officers were usually selected for their size and general toughness. They received little, if any, formal training and had a low status in the community and even lower pay.

The common viewpoint of those days concerning crime and criminals might well be described by the old saying, "There is more justice in the end of a nightstick [or a gun] than in all the courts of the land." Crime was fairly rigidly defined as a function of the individual's will and its complexity as a social, economic, political, and psychological problem was appreciated very little by the general public. The officer was neither given nor expected to have flexibility in determining the enforceability of certain laws. Criminals were consid-

---

* J. W. Sterling 1974: personal communication.

5

ered to be men who, with malice aforethought and free choice, elected to engage in criminal activity. With this philosophy in vogue, enforcement of the law assumed first priority over other legal concepts such as civil rights, liberty, and sometimes even freedom. As far as law enforcement practices were concerned, the end justified the means.

Although the police officer performed an essential function in the society of the "good old days," he did not have the sole responsibility for preventing crime or apprehending criminals. The family, the church, the schools, and other social institutions usually exerted a strong influence upon people to live according to the generally accepted social and moral codes. Standards of conduct were explicitly prescribed by society's various institutions and adhered to by most people because to do otherwise would be to risk not only the penalty of the law but also exclusion from society itself. Individual citizens were expected to support personally the principles of law and order and were held responsible as well for their neighbor's conduct. "It was each citizen's duty to raise the 'hue and cry' when a crime was committed, to collect his neighbors, and to pursue a criminal who fled from the district" (President's Commission 1967).

The Changing Role

Today, a police officer patrolling a district in a large city is confronted with a variety of problems, few of which involve serious criminal activity. He probably recognizes criminal activity as the real essence of police work and may even succeed in convincing himself that this is really why he is there. But it is apparent that most of his duty hours will involve such activities as helping a drunk, finding a lost child, settling a family dispute, giving a traffic citation, preventing a suicide, taking a mentally disturbed person into protective custody, or helping a confused elderly person. During one recent typical tour of duty in a medium-sized city, two police officers handled the following calls.

Over the last decade, various studies have indicated that the majority of a police officer's duty hours are spent in noncriminal, social service tasks like many of those cited above. For example, Chief Bernard L. Garmire of the Miami Police Department notes that "a sam-

Officer #1

TYPE OF CALL	TIME SPENT
Accident (auto)	32 minutes
Family disturbance	17 minutes
Neighbor problem (noncriminal)	14 minutes
Juvenile problem (noncriminal)	7 minutes
Burglary	20 minutes
Disturbance (noncriminal)	29 minutes
Armed robbery	26 minutes
Traffic warrant	36 minutes
Accident (auto)	8 minutes

ple of all the calls for service in 1970 disclosed that 61 percent of calls did not involve either serious or minor crimes, i.e., they were calls in which a citizen wanted some kind of service not related to crime per se. This, incidentally, is a conservative figure" (Garmire, Rubin, and Wilson 1972, p. 25).

However, as noted before, many officers do not feel that this is really police work and argue that these services should be someone else's responsibility. Yet none can deny the relationship between these services and, at least, the preventive aspects of crime. Family disturbances may result in homicides and assaults; the drunk may be robbed and/or assaulted; and the association between suicidal behavior and homicide is seen on many occasions. Besides, there is no one else to perform these services—at least no one who is on the job twenty-four hours a day, seven days a week.

Another important factor is that people in the lower socioeconomic classes are accustomed to calling the police for assistance in dealing with a variety of problems. The police are seen as their first and sometimes only resource. Because of the present lack of specialized agencies and personnel to handle these kinds of situations, it is

Officer #2

TYPE OF CALL	TIME SPENT
Silent alarm	12 minutes
Accident (auto)	60 minutes
Family disturbance	19 minutes
Disturbance (knife fight)	7 minutes
Disturbance (noncriminal)	11 minutes
Lost child	14 minutes
Alarm (robbery)	11 minutes
Man down (noncriminal)	5 minutes

likely that police officers will have to function as social workers, psychologists, and family counselors for some time to come. Unfortunately, new police officers are, for the most part, rarely more prepared to handle these events than is the average citizen. While police training programs are much more sophisticated now than ten years ago, the provisions for providing training in these areas are virtually nonexistent in many departments. The veteran police officer is an exception because he has gained many psychological insights from experience.

The police officer must not only deal with a broad range of tasks but also is expected to exhibit an equally wide range of skills in performing them, further complicating his job. As a careful observer of the police role has noted:

Reviewing the tasks we expect of our law enforcement officers, it is my impression that their complexity is perhaps greater than that of any other profession. On the one hand, we expect our law enforcement officers to possess the nurturing, caretaking, sympathetic, empathizing, gentle characteristics of physician, nurse, teacher, and social worker as he deals with school traffic, acute illness and injury, juvenile delinquency, suicidal threats and gestures, and missing persons. On the other hand, we expect him to command respect, demonstrate courage, control hostile impulses, and meet great physical hazards. . . . He is to control crowds, prevent riots, apprehend criminals, and chase after speeding vehicles. I can think of no other profession which constantly demands such seemingly opposite characteristics (Levy 1966).

Increased complexity is but one aspect of the new reality which confronts the police officer in his changing role. Society itself is also changing and no longer appears to present the solid front against unlawful behavior that it once did. For example, what one segment of society may consider a serious crime, another may not. In addition, there has been considerable lessening in the influence exerted by the family, the church, and the schools in promulgating moral standards and encouraging people to live by them. We now have a society "in which parents fail to raise their children as law-abiding citizens, in which schools fail to educate them to assume adult roles, and in which the economy is not geared to provide them with jobs" (President's Commission 1967).

Furthermore, the general public takes less responsibility in dealing with serious criminal activity. There is little desire to "get involved." In contrast to the "good old days," the police officer now feels more alone in enforcing the law. He must perform his various tasks in the midst of usually apathetic, indifferent, and often hostile surroundings. He must face situations in which emotions are high and danger is a constant threat, situations in which he will have to rely upon every personal resource he possesses and not merely upon his nightstick or other weapon. In an oversimplified way, this is a measure of how the role of the police officer has changed.

The Core Element in the Policeman's Role

We have attempted to describe the increasing complexity of the police officer's role. This is not at all to suggest that he must now function by circling in endless confusion. It is our conviction that, seen from the standpoint of psychology, there is a single basic element in the police officer's role.

The one thing a police officer deals with—not just during his duty hours, but during his entire waking day—is human behavior. This includes the behavior of criminals, of citizens, of fellow officers, and last, but by no means least, of himself. Some of the behavior is criminal, some is not; some is sick, some is not; some is conscious, some is unconscious; some is simple, some is complex. Furthermore, he often deals with this behavior during conditions of emotional stress and in situations involving life-and-death decisions and personal danger.

He must be, therefore, like the psychologist, a devoted student of human behavior. But he must practice his psychology "on the street" rather than in a clinic, office, or university classroom. He must make in a minimum of time (sometimes only a few minutes or seconds) decisions that would baffle the academic behaviorist, decisions whose ultimate resolution may involve months or even years of debate and legal consideration. More importantly, errors in the psychologist's decisions are seldom critical; errors in the cop's judgment can be deadly.

The authors often tell recruits that they have a far tougher job than either of us. No one expects a psychologist to be a police officer, but a police officer is expected to be a psychologist—a practical, street-level psychologist.

Today's police officer must know as much as possible about human behavior. He can no longer regard this subject as the sole province of the psychologist.

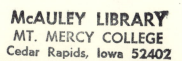

INTRODUCTION

The man who goes into our streets in hopes of regulating, directing, and controlling human behavior must be armed with more than a gun and the ability to perform mechanical movements in response to a situation. Such men as these engage in the difficult, complex, and important business of human behavior. Their intellectual armament—so long restricted to the minimum—must be no less than their physical prowess and protection (President's Commission 1967, p. x).

Bruce Terris, in his article "The Role of the Police," explains it this way:

The situations in which police officers most frequently find themselves do not require the expert aim of a marksman, the cunningness of a private eye, or the toughness of the stereotyped Irish policeman. Instead, they demand knowledge of human beings and the personal, as opposed to official, authority to influence people without the use or even threat of force (Terris 1967, p. 67).

He goes on to note, however, that "these characteristics are not commonly found in police officers because police departments do not consider these values as paramount" (Terris 1967).

Sterling's report, like many other recommendations made in recent years, urges a greater emphasis on the behavioral sciences in recruit training.

This knowledge can be of limitless value to police officers as they face a perplexing array of interpersonal problems which are always accompanied by confusion, distress, danger, and heightened emotions. . . . The police must act quickly, decisively, and lawfully often with only a partial knowledge of the circumstances. However, their action orientation does not in any sense obviate the need for understanding behavior. Rather, it reinforces the necessity for a greater understanding of the self and others (Sterling 1972, pp. 294–295).

Knowledge of human behavior is essential to the police officer not only to insure maximum effectiveness in his role but it is also essential for his safety. For example, statistics have indicated that approximately 20 percent of police officers killed in the line of duty were answering a family disturbance call. Another 40 percent of police officers' injuries occur on such assignments. Yet a group of policemen trained in certain basic psychological techniques managed to handle over two thousand calls involving over a thousand different families in a tough ghetto area without suffering even a scratch. Bard's work clearly demonstrates that, with proper training in certain psychological principles and techniques, the police officer can do his job *more effectively and safely* and, furthermore, can make a significant contribution to the care of others who live in his community (Bard 1970).

In addition, a knowledge of deviant behavior will be of great value to the police officer in the prevention and detection of certain types of crimes. For example, a knowledge of suicidal behavior will provide the police officer with an investigative tool to aid him in determining whether the deceased was actually a suicide or met death by accident or through the violence of others. A sadistic sex murder can point to either a psychopath or a paranoid schizophrenic. Knowing about these two disorders may significantly help the officer in his investigation. With a knowledge of alcoholism and drug addiction, the police officer will realize how alcohol can mask more serious neurological and psychiatric conditions which may cause death in a jail cell to a prisoner considered to be only "drunk and disorderly." These and other aspects of deviant behavior will be treated in subsequent chapters and certain principles applicable to police investigations will be offered to aid the police officer in dealing with these kinds of incidents. Finally, a better understanding of his own role and the psychological impact on himself of the stresses which he faces will enable the police officer to be more effective.

Summary

In this discussion of the changing role of the law enforcement officer, we have described the differences between the police officer's role in the late nineteenth century as viewed by police traditionalists and his present role, and the characteristics required of the officer in each. We have spoken of the changes in society itself and how these changes have affected the role of the police officer. Finally, it is argued that, regardless of the complexity of the police officer's role, he deals basically with human behavior and thus must be competently prepared in this area of knowledge.

That the role of the police officer in our society is changing should be obvious to all concerned—officer, recruit, and citizen alike. Our concern has been to briefly reiterate some of the prominent elements involved in this change. There are two distinct features in the development from earlier times to the present which should be reemphasized.

The policeman's role in the "good old days" was described as that of "apprehending criminals," while that of the present-day officer is seen as "controlling, directing, and regulating human behavior." Notice how the *kind* of activity described has changed—from *apprehension* to *acts of control, direction, and regulation.*

The object of these kinds of activities has changed from *criminals* to *human beings.* The important implications for the law enforcement officer in a hundred years of social change can better be appreciated by considering these two different descriptions of the policeman's role.

Today's officer must perform new, broader, more sophisticated tasks that require new skills and a wider knowledge base. He must function in relation to a more general objective, widening his concern from criminal activity to the larger area of human behavior. The greater complexity of the job facing the police officer today can be successfully dealt with by the individual who recognizes in himself a more complex person, as well-trained mentally as he is physically, as capable of using his mind as he is his hands. For this person, a knowledge of how human beings, including himself, behave is essential.

As we proceed with the discussion of human behavior, it will be with the goal of contributing to the development of the competent, professional, law enforcement officer.

REFERENCES AND ADDITIONAL BIBLIOGRAPHY

Bard, M. 1969. "Family Intervention Police Teams as a Community Mental Health Resource." *Journal of Criminal Law, Criminology and Police Science* 60:247–250.
———. 1970. "Training Police as Specialists in Family Crisis Intervention." In *Proceedings of National Institute of Law Enforcement and Criminal Justice.* Washington, D.C.: U.S. Government Printing Office.
———. 1971. "The Role of Law Enforcement in the Helping System." *Community Mental Health Journal* 7:151–160.
Garmire, B. L.; Rubin, J.; and Wilson, J. Q. 1972. *The Police and the Community.* Baltimore: Johns Hopkins University Press.
Kelly, C. M. 1973. *Uniform Crime Reports for the United States, 1973.* Federal Bureau of Investigation. Washington, D.C.: U.S. Government Printing Office.
Kreins, E. S. February 1974. "The Behavioral Scientist in Law Enforcement." *The Police Chief* 41:46–49.
Levy, R. 1966. Quoted in *Proceedings of Conference for Police Professions.* Lansing: Michigan State University.
National Advisory Commission on Criminal Justice. 1973. *Standards and Goals: Reports on Crime.* Washington, D.C.: U.S. Government Printing Office.

President's Commission on Law Enforcement and the Administration of Justice. 1967. *Task Force on the Police*. Washington, D.C.: U.S. Government Printing Office.

Salerno, R. and Tompkins, J. S. 1969. *The Crime Confederation*. New York: Popular Library.

Scott, B. 1973. *Killer's Doom*. New York: Pyramid Books.

Sterling, J. W. 1972. *Changes in Role Concepts of Police Officers*. Gaithersberg, Md.: International Association of Chiefs of Police.

Terris, B. 1967. "The Role of the Police." *The Annals* p. 10.

Whitehouse, J. E. 1973. "Historical Perspectives on the Police Community Function." *Journal of Police Science and Administration:* 187–92.

PART II

The Origins and Complexities of Human Behavior

N.Y. Daily News Photo

Chapter 2

Foundations of a Professional Attitude Toward Human Behavior

IN Chapter 1 we suggested that a police officer must perform as a street-level psychologist to function effectively as a professional. Before proceeding to a discussion of several fundamental psychological concepts and theories, this topic of a professional attitude toward human behavior must be considered at greater length.

The Professional Attitude and Personal Involvement

The professional police officer must learn to view behavior as the behavioral scientist does. He must develop a professional view of behavior to insure maximal efficiency in his handling of the many complex situations he faces. Although the recruit may interpret this as an admonition to remain aloof and uninvolved when interacting with others, this attitude is not desirable, especially when dealing with the noncriminal public.

For example, one police department received a "citizen's complaint" from a woman whose car had been stopped by an officer for speeding on a deserted street late at night. She was returning from a hospital emergency room where she had taken her sick baby. Her complaint was not that the officer had stopped her unjustifiably, but rather that he had shown no concern for the condition of her baby. As she said in her complaint, "He might have at least asked how the baby was."

The image of an aloof police officer is, in fact, a contradiction in terms. The police officer is involved during every moment that he is in contact with the public or with a criminal offender. He is even *personally* involved because often it is *his* life which is in danger and because always it is *his* action or decision which can avert a crisis or solve a problem. This kind of "personal" involvement must be contrasted sharply, however, with the behavior of an officer who personalizes the situation he faces and then reacts emotionally to it.

To further explore this distinction, the following analogy is pertinent. The psychiatrist does not get angry at the mental patient who calls him a pot-bellied quack, but rather accepts the remark as evidence of the patient's anger and hostility. He then directs his attention to the reason for the anger. Is it because the patient feels neglected on the ward or because his wife failed to visit him that afternoon? In doing this, the doctor is searching for the reason behind the behavior in order to understand it. Only with this understanding will he be able to alter or control it. The police officer as a professional must also try to understand the behavior he encounters so that he, also, may have the opportunity to alter or control it.

Personal involvement in another sense is inevitable for the police officer. He will often see behavior which is shocking, immoral, or degenerate. For example, he may encounter a father who has just beaten his four-year-old son to death, a rapist who has just violated and tortured a seven-year-old, or an armed robber who has beaten an old man and left him to die in the streets. In these situations and many others like them, the police officer cannot avoid experiencing feelings of anger, frustration, revenge, or disgust. The police officer is a human being with normal human reactions to deviant behavior. He cannot and should not stifle these personal reactions, but should develop ways of handling them and turning them to good use. The

18

police officer who learns to anticipate his reactions to offensive and difficult situations and who has developed ways of dealing with them has not only removed a serious barrier to the effective performance of his duty, but also has taken a first step toward the acquisition of a professional attitude toward behavior. He has discovered that, although personal involvement is unavoidable, emotional involvement is controllable.

As pointed out in Chapter 1, the contemporary police officer has as his primary task the regulation, direction, and control of human behavior. Usually, this is understood to refer only to the behavior of those persons, criminal and noncriminal, whom he comes in contact with during the performance of his duties. It should now be added that the officer's own behavior must also be under his control. To accomplish this, he must handle his own feelings, whatever they are and in whatever situation he encounters them.

Consider, as an example, the feeling of fear. Much was learned about the emotions experienced under conditions of stress and danger during World War II. Prior to that time soldiers were taught that the feeling of fear was an indication of cowardice and that a coward was a despicable individual. This attitude was exemplified by General George Patton when he scolded and slapped an enlisted man who had been hospitalized for *combat exhaustion.* In what was perhaps an overzealous attempt to spur the man to greater effort, Patton accused the soldier of cowardice and demanded that he not be treated (Farago 1963). General Patton was apparently unable to understand or admit the existence of the *normal* emotion of fear. The alternative, though entirely out of character for the General, would have been for him to have openly recognized the emotions being experienced by the soldier and to have assisted him in finding ways to cope with them.

General Patton's attitude was not shared by all American military authorities. Army psychiatrists and field commanders know that, in combat, fear is a constant companion. Everyone is afraid. The important thing is not whether the soldier is afraid, but how he handles that fear. If he can admit to his fear and use it positively (for example, fear can make one more alert or lead to a better effort), he can then perform his duties in an effective manner. Fear will not overcome and incapacitate him.

One study which compared military units where it was possible to admit and talk about fear with those where it was never admitted or talked about showed that the former experienced fewer casualties, both physical and mental, than the latter (Russell 1965). The professional police officer, like the professional soldier, cannot let feelings of fear interfere with effectiveness. This demonstrates how the goal of developing a professional view of behavior is clearly intertwined with the officer's own behavior, especially under conditions of emotional stress.

Thus, the first element in the foundation of a professional attitude toward behavior is the realization that, in all stress situations, every human being will experience certain normal emotional reactions. This is as true for the professional police officer as it is for the ordinary citizen. What, then, differentiates the professional from the citizen?

The professional enters into these situations not only anticipating his own emotional reactions but also those of the person or persons with whom he is dealing. By anticipating what he and others may be feeling, the professional police officer has reduced the number of unknowns inherent in the situation. This will enable him to direct his attention to other factors and to enhance his effectiveness.

As an added benefit, his knowledge of what to expect from his own emotions and those of others will permit him to achieve the second element of a professional attitude, namely, the ability to control his own behavior. For example, he will see that recognition and control of his own fear will contribute to his efforts to cope with a hostile crowd.

The Psychological Concepts of Motivation and Learning

These first steps in developing a professional attitude toward behavior will be cultivated by means of repeated experience in real-life situations. The next steps require a more theoretical and reflective approach. They involve knowing and thinking about two basic psychological principles of behavior, *motivation* and *learning*. The first states simply that all behavior has a cause and the second that learning plays a crucial role in personality development.

Motivation

All behavior is motivated. There is a reason for everything one does. Psychologists define behavior as anything the organism does. Since we are talking about people, we can say "anything the human organism does." Behavior may be *complex* (climbing Mt. Everest) or *simple* (reading a newspaper). It may be directed by the *central nervous system* (e.g., walking) or by the *autonomic nervous system* (e.g., breathing). It may be conscious (picking out a good book to read) or unconscious (a woman developing a headache without realizing that it is related to her not wanting to go to a party). Whatever its nature, all behavior is motivated.

In the examples given, climbing Mt. Everest may be motivated by an intense desire for achievement in the face of great danger. Reading a newspaper is usually motivated by the less complex desire for knowledge and information. Walking is motivated by a desire to go somewhere. Breathing occurs because of the body's need for oxygen. Some motives are physiological, based on the body's physical needs and drives such as hunger, thirst, sex, and pleasure. Others are psychological in origin, such as the desire for knowledge or the wish for privacy.

The value of this principle to the police officer, as a trained observer of behavior, is that it directs his attention to the underlying causes for human behavior. He should become accustomed to asking himself, when observing a particular behavior, "Why is this person doing what he is doing?" With this question, he demonstrates a grasp of the concept of motivation and adopts a professional attitude toward behavior.

Learning

Learning plays a crucial role in personality development. This psychological concept is a scientific way of expressing the popular belief that we are what we are today because of all the yesterdays we have lived. A somewhat overdrawn example from *Psychiatry for the Curious* by George Preston (1940) illustrates this principle effectively.

Visualize a table, a rock, a hammer, and a person. If a person places the rock on the edge of the table and strikes the rock with the hammer, it can be predicted, from basic laws of physics, that the rock will leave the table, travel a certain distance, and come to rest. The person can then take this same rock back to the table, place it in the identical position, strike it with another identical blow, and again, according to basic principles of physics, the rock will travel a certain distance and come to rest. This could be repeated indefinitely.

Since we are interested in behavior rather than physics, imagine that, instead of a rock, a little boy is placed on the edge of the table. When he isn't looking, we will hit him on the head with the hammer. Assuming that he is not knocked unconscious, it can be predicated that, according to basic laws of psychology rather than physics, he will leave the table, travel a certain distance, and come to rest. The difference between the boy and the rock is that the boy could not be placed on the table again to undergo the same experience. The rock does not change as a result of the experience, but the boy certainly does.

Boy-on-table is quite different from boy-hit-on-head-by-hammer. As a result of his initial experience, the boy will react negatively to any suggestion that he sit on the table again. He has *learned* something about tables, about hammers, and about people who use hammers. This learning has also effected a change in his behavior.

Something else is also likely to have occurred. Psychologists call it *stimulus generalization*. It is a tendency to invest other stimuli associated with a major stimulus with the same emotions and feelings that have already been accorded to the major stimulus. For example, since the table was elevated, he may begin to develop a fear of heights. If later other situations occur that are painful and/or frightening to him and also involve height, he may eventually develop such a fear of heights that he may not even be able to look over the edge of a one-story building without feeling afraid and becoming anxious. Or, if the person who hit him with the hammer had red hair and wore glasses, he may begin to develop a dislike for all people with red hair and glasses.

In later life, he probably will not remember the details of this early experience. However, suppose that this lad who, as a child, was hit on the head by a red-haired person wearing glasses grows up and becomes a police officer. Then suppose that one night, near the end of his shift, he encounters a juvenile with red hair and glasses who is causing trouble. As a result of his early experience and the associated learning, he might be less patient with this boy than he would have been with another boy who did not possess these specific characteristics.

From these examples, it is apparent how the principle of learning involves an objective view of behavior. An understanding of it provides the police officer with another cornerstone for maintaining a professional attitude toward behavior. The realization of the importance of learning in personality development forces the professional to view each individual as unique, since the experience, and thus the learning, of any one person is never identical with that of another.

This principle should not be taken by the professional as a sanction for emotionally sympathizing with all people he encounters. Rather, the police officer should use his awareness of the uniqueness of individual experience to recognize that the behavior he is facing is occurring as a result of learning. Wishing that the people with whom he deals were different is not part of a professional attitude toward behavior. They are what they are. Rather, the presence of a particular behavior is a fact and the professional attitude is to try and understand how it was *learned*.

The Professional Attitude in Operation

As described thus far, a professional attitude toward behavior rests upon several fundamental principles. The professional who deals with human behavior must maintain control of his personal emotional involvement in any situation. He must seek with scientific interest the motivations for that behavior and he must strive objectively to understand how it was learned before attempting to change it.

Unfortunately, this is easily discussed in the pages of a book, but difficult to put into practice. A personal example may make this clearer.

Several years ago, one of the authors (H.E.R.) was requested to perform a psychological evaluation on a young man who had spent an entire evening torturing a small boy (his stepson) to death. He was very angry because the boy's mother had gone away with another man that afternoon, leaving him with the children. In his extreme frustration and anger, he started drinking and, after becoming intoxicated, took both children in the bathroom where he slowly and methodically tortured the little boy to death while the ten-year-old girl was forced to watch. As part of the team ordered by the court to examine this man to determine if he was sane and could stand trial, the author could easily have allowed his own personal feelings of disgust and anger to interfere with the important task of establishing the good rapport with the prisoner necessary to complete the psychological testing. Had he allowed his personal feelings to take control of his behavior, the author would have lost his professional attitude.

The police officer will face situations like this daily. If he has to arrest a man for setting drunks on fire, he cannot judge and condemn him, he cannot allow his feelings to permit him to strike out or to handle him roughly. To do so would not only detract from his performance as a professional police officer, but also might provide the offender's lawyer with a means of gaining the release of his client because of a violation of his civil rights.

It is helpful to the police officer in these situations to remember that people *learn* to be the way they are and that in all probability the offender who beats and tortures his victim was himself subjected to similar treatment while growing up. This understanding will enable the police officer to be professionally more tolerant and accepting of behavior which would otherwise alienate him if he did not have the appropriate professional attitude toward behavior.

Summary

This chapter has discussed basic principles in the development of a professional attitude toward human behavior. It has been pointed out that since personal involvement is unavoidable, it must be recognized, accepted, and handled. The psychological principles of motivation and learning have been emphasized because of their value in stimulating a scientific inquiry into the reasons for behavior and an objective view of it.

It has also been suggested that a thorough understanding of these principles will contribute to a professional understanding and tolerance of human behavior, thereby increasing a police officer's effectiveness.

In the next chapters, a more detailed discussion of personality development, function, and malfunction will be presented as a means of amplifying what has been suggested to this point about human behavior.

REFERENCES AND ADDITIONAL BIBLIOGRAPHY

Banton, M. 1964. *The Policeman in the Community.* New York: Basic Books.

Danish, S. and Brodsky, S. 1970. "Training of Policemen in Emotional Control and Awareness." *American Psychologist* 25:368–369.

Farago, L. 1963. *Patton: Ordeal and Triumph.* New York: Dell.

Hilgard, E. 1962. *Introduction to Psychology.* New York: Harcourt, Brace and World.

Maslow, A. 1954. *Motivation and Personality.* New York: Harper.

Preston, F. H. 1940. *Psychiatry for the Curious.* New York: Farrar and Rinehart.

Russell, H. E. 1965. *Combat Psychiatry.* Fort Sam Houston, Texas: U.S.A. Medical Field Service School, Brooke Army Medical Center.

Chapter 3

Normal Personality Development

TO THIS POINT we have spoken about behavior—the police officer's concern with it and the professional attitude toward it. Attention will now be turned to personality—its basic structure, course of development, manner of function and malfunction, and its relationship to behavior.

The professional police officer who constantly encounters both normal and abnormal behavior must have some understanding of how personality normally develops. There are three major influences on normal personality development: constitutional or hereditary factors; situational factors which arise from the interaction between the individual and his environment; and developmental factors within the individual himself (Mezer 1960).

Constitutional Factors

Constitutional factors exist at birth and represent heredity's part in personality development. These factors include, among others, potential for growth in terms of height and weight, color of hair, intellectual potential, and sex. Less commonly, hereditary factors can include a predisposition for various diseases such as diabetes or a variety of anatomical defects such as harelip.

Each of these features or conditions may influence the development of personality along certain paths, helping in some ways and hindering in others. For example, whether one is born a male or a female has profound implications for personality development. Similarly, possessing a serious anatomical birth defect poses problems with which the developing personality may or may not successfully cope. Will the person become too dependent or feel inferior as a result of the defect or will he adjust to the situation and perhaps even compensate by a greater effort in other areas?

Hereditary factors can, therefore, be considered as the *physical* foundation for all subsequent personality development. These factors determine the outer boundaries within which the personality will develop. For the most part, they do not change in the course of life, although many congenital defects can be corrected surgically.

Situational and Environmental Factors

The influences of religious background, race, and economic status can be grouped in this category. The Constitution may state that all men are created equal, but this is only an ideal. Reality is very different. Even while in the uterus, the yet-to-be-born baby is affected by social, economic, and environmental conditions. If his mother lives in a ghetto, it is likely that she may not receive adequate prenatal care. Her diet (or lack of it) greatly affects the baby's development in the uterus. The incidence of complications during delivery may increase and the baby may suffer some type of brain damage.

After birth, environmental forces are also influential. Some people "belong"; others don't. Studies of prejudice and discrimination have shown that these practices adversely affect the development of the personality. The realization that one is not considered as good as other people can have a very negative influence on personality development. It may lead to a negative self-image in the person who is discriminated against.

The theories of Erik Erikson are helpful in understanding the influence of social and environmental factors on personality development. Erikson postulates that the first stage of personality development involves the formation of a basic *sense of trust.* He emphasizes the importance of adequate mothering during the first year of life and claims that, to be effective, it must move beyond the satisfaction of only physiological needs. Psychological needs must also be met; these include the need to be rocked, cuddled, sung to, comforted, and loved. If the mother adequately fulfills these needs during the first year of life, the infant will develop a basic sense of trust. If he does not receive this mothering, if his cries go unattended for long periods, and if he is not cuddled, then this basic sense of trust will not develop and the infant will perceive the world as hostile and ungratifying.

In Erikson's conceptual framework, the second stage of personality development is viewed as the time of the development of a *sense of autonomy.* This begins at approximately twelve to fifteen months of age. For the next two years, the child's energies are centered on proving that he is a separate person with a will of his own. In this stage, the child must be allowed to make choices in order to develop a sense of self-reliance. At the same time, he must be protected from exceeding the boundaries of self-determination of which he is capable. The interaction between child and parents will again determine the success or failure of the development of this sense of autonomy.

In Erikson's third stage, at four years the child begins to want to find out what kind of person he can be, to develop a *sense of initiative.* He observes others, especially his parents, and tries to imitate their behavior. At no other time in life will he be as avid to learn and to do. Parents should always encourage and support the child's initiative, but it is especially important that they do so during this time of life.

Very soon, the child moves into the fourth stage. He wants to be engaged in tasks which will give him a *sense of accomplishment.* During this period, the child acquires not only knowledge and skills, but also the ability to cooperate and to interact positively with others. If he encounters situations in which he is labeled too often as a failure, he will develop a sense of inadequacy rather than one of accomplishment. At this time in his life, the school and its personnel play an important interactional role with the child. By experiencing positive or negative reinforcement in the school situation, further groundwork is laid for the development of a healthy or unhealthy personality.

The fifth stage occurs as the child enters adolescence. At this time the central problem becomes the establishment of a *sense of identity*. Who is he? What will his role in society be? What job or profession will he seek? Will he marry? Can he make it even though he's black? Will he be a success or failure? He worries about his acceptance by his peer group. He worries about his future. He becomes fearful of his developing sexual desires and of the whole world of heterosexual relationships.

As the adolescent matures into adulthood, he must also be capable of developing a *sense of intimacy* with others (Erikson's sixth stage). This sense of intimacy is necessary for the mature emotional give-and-take essential to a successful marriage. Some people, because of inadequacies in previous stages of emotional development, can never get close enough to others to achieve this sense of intimacy. They tend to retire into psychological isolation and maintain interpersonal contacts on a formal level which is lacking in true warmth and spontaneity.

Positive movement through these stages is, in Erikson's view, the basis for normal personality development. As will be pointed out later, the influence of interpersonal interactions between the individual and his environment can be negative at any point in this process, leading to a variety of emotional problems, both minor and major.

Developmental Factors

As one of the earliest and most influential students of personality development, Sigmund Freud constructed a theory based on an assessment of those mental functions and malfunctions which he encountered in his adult patients. In his theory, Freud postulated a series of concepts concerning the workings of mental processes which, through their interaction, influence personality development. His concepts of the id, ego, and superego represent interdependent aspects of mental functioning which relate dynamically to influence personality and observed behavior.

The Id

From birth and throughout almost the entire first year of life, according to Freud, the newborn's mental processes are influenced entirely by the id. The id may be conceptualized as a *mental inheritance,* a complex of biological urges and needs (instincts). Examples include hunger and the instinct for self-preservation.

The newborn baby does not learn to be hungry. He is hungry because his biological need for food makes his stomach uncomfortable, leading to a behavior pattern which can be altered by the provision of food. Likewise, the instinct for self-preservation is common to all living things, ranging from the plant which turns to face the sun and sends down roots deep into the soil for water to the infant who reacts with a startle-withdrawal pattern to a painful stimulus.

Libido is a term which refers to the *energy* of the id. It may be compared to electricity flowing through a wire. Just as turning on an electric switch sends current through the bulb, so the libido finds expression when a connection is made between the needs of the id and a suitable fulfillment for them in the environment. Psychologists call this process *need gratification.*

The Ego

The ego, Freud's second basic mental concept, first makes its influence felt on mental processes toward the end of the first year of life. Until then, the newborn baby's psychological functions are influenced entirely by biological urges and needs (id) and the desire to gratify them. He is not aware of any distinction between himself, his needs, and the world outside. Nipple, breast, bottle, mother, and self are all mentally fused into one unit and experienced as such.

However, as he begins to grow older, he becomes aware that, unlike the situation that was present when he was in the womb, he is no longer protected from all outside stimulation. His hunger and elimination needs are no longer being *automatically and immediately* taken care of. Now when he is hungry, he begins to recognize that there is a delay when mother gets ready to feed him while she warms the bottle taken from the refrigerator. Bright lights and noises intrude when he wants to sleep, and elimination can produce uncomfortable, even painful, results if he is not changed promptly.

He slowly begins to realize that something outside of himself exists and that his own well-being depends on this outside person, usually mother, for gratification. As his recognition of her increases, he also becomes more aware of himself as a separate person. As this awareness of individuation grows, the ego begins to form and assumes a role in the mental processes.

To help understand the ego and its functions, an analogy to a corporation executive is useful. Just as the executive gathers information about all aspects of the company and its place in the total economy and then makes decisions on what corporate actions should be taken, the ego gathers information about the body, its needs, and its relation to the environment, and then decides which courses of action to take. The ego acts as the mediator or negotiator between the basic desires of the id and the outside world.

The ego should not be viewed as totally antagonistic to the id. Rather, the ego and id should be conceptualized as partners, since it is the function of the ego to find realistic ways of gratifying the id's desires. To return to the analogy, the corporation executive acts within the economy as a whole to serve the best interests of the corporation's stockholders.

Not only does the ego function to mediate the influences of the inner world through contact with the outer world, but it also serves a protective function to the individual. Should the ego fail in its protective and executive function, serious mental illness will ensue.

From this, it can readily be seen that an important function of the ego is to maintain a tolerable state of psychological equilibrium or balance. Psychologists refer to this equilibrium as *homeostasis*. Coined by the physiologist Walter Cannon, this term was first used to describe the system of physical checks and balances existing within the body helping to maintain a physiological equilibrium. For example, if a man goes out into the hot sun from a cool room, his body temperature does not change because there is a temperature regulating mechanism in the body which maintains a constancy of body temperature regardless of the outside environment, thereby preserving physiological homeostasis. This concept can also refer to the psychological state. The ego is analogous to the physiological temperature regulating mechanism and helps keep the individual in psychological homeostasis.

The Superego

In Freud's postulates, the third aspect of mental functioning is the superego, a psychological concept closely related to the concept of conscience. As the child grows up, he acquires from his parents a system of values—things he should do and things he should not do. At first, these are forced upon him from the outside (by parents, church, school, etc.), but eventually they become internalized so that, even in the absence of his parents or other authorities, he will follow them.

The values which he first learns from his parents form a rather primitive superego which views right and wrong in absolute terms. As he comes into contact later with the moral and social code derived from policemen, teachers, clergy, Boy Scout leaders, and other authority figures, a more mature, social superego develops. Finally, he becomes acquainted with the formalized laws and regulations of society. Thus the superego is reinforced and strengthened throughout his whole life.

However, some people fail to internalize these positive social values. Consequently, lacking the "policeman from within," they respond only to the "policeman from without." As an example, a common response by those arrested to the question "Why is it wrong to steal?" is "Because you get caught." They do not recognize that stealing in itself is wrong because they lack the "policeman from within."

The don'ts internalized by the child represent the conscience. However, Freud also described another part of the superego which he called the *ego ideal*. This represents the positive values and ideals with which the individual identifies. White defined the ego ideal as "the self that one wants to become." It may be an ideal of personal conduct (an upright citizen, a charming woman, a successful executive) or an ideal of desired accomplishments (to stand for honest city government or to protect the consumer). Furthermore, White observes that, from the time of his birth, the individual is proffered an array of ready-made ego ideals. He may reject most of them, but those accepted have an important influence on his life (White 1968).

When this ego ideal is threatened, anxiety, fear, and/or anger can occur. While some individuals may have a very poor ego ideal which is easily threatened, others may demonstrate an exaggeratedly superior ego ideal. This is often a defense against hidden powerful feelings of inferiority and inadequacy which would overpower the ego ideal if recognized openly.

The Three Levels of Mental Activity

Closely associated with Freud's functional approach to understanding developmental factors is his structural approach, which introduces the concepts of consciousness, preconsciousness, and unconsciousness. He described these three layers of mental activity as follows: (1) the *conscious*—our immediate experience; (2) the *pre-conscious*—that which is presently outside consciousness but which can be immediately recalled into consciousness; and (3) the *unconscious*—that which is made up of events and feelings which cannot readily enter into consciousness or preconsciousness.

The following analogy is useful in understanding these concepts. In the center of a room stands an individual with a flashlight. That portion of the room that is within the beam of the flashlight is the conscious (what you are now thinking, seeing, hearing). The preconscious is that part of the previously darkened room that can be illuminated by moving the flashlight. The unconscious is that portion of the room which is beyond the capability of the flashlight to reach either because of distance, objects which block portions of the room, or the inadequacy of the flashlight's capacity.

Of all behavior, that which is unconsciously motivated is perhaps the most powerful and significant. Although Freud postulated this concept in a new framework during this century, it actually reaches far back into history. Socrates, the early Greek philosopher, said: "In all of us, even in good men, there is a lawless, wild beast nature which peers out in our sleep" (Mezer 1960). Religious philosophers often warned that a "devil" lurks within each of us, awaiting the opportunity to destroy our souls.

Nevertheless, it was Freud who first formulated a clinically workable theory to explain the *dynamic* nature of the unconscious. He demonstrated that the unconscious is not merely a jumbled collection of past experiences, memories, and feelings, but rather a dynamic system of primitive needs and urges constantly seeking immediate gratification through entry into consciousness. Some of these unconscious thoughts are allowed expression only under certain conditions; others are never allowed into conscious expression.

The unconscious can also be compared to the larger part of an iceberg which lies unseen under the water's surface while the conscious part of behavior is the smaller tip of the iceberg that is visible to all. Evidence of unconscious activity include dreams, sleepwalking, symbolism, and the process of remembering and forgetting. Freud called these behaviors "the psychopathology of everyday life" and gave many examples from clinical histories to illustrate how some feelings of guilt, jealousy, and hostility which are usually unconscious can find expression in consciousness through these mechanisms.

For example, take the case of the woman who doesn't want to go out with her husband and another couple because she is unconsciously afraid and jealous of the other woman. She develops a severe headache which forces cancellation of the evening's plans. Or consider the worker who is hostile to a co-worker and who "accidentally" lets a pipe slip through his fingers which strikes and injures the other worker.

Slips of the tongue are also examples of unconscious motivation. For example, the fellow at the bus depot who approaches the buxom ticket seller and says "two pickets to Tittsburgh" does not need a psychologist to interpret his slip.

As we shall see in the chapter on suicide, some people who "accidentally" fall from windows, are hit by cars, or fail to make the curve on a lonely highway may be satisfying an unconscious urge to do away with themselves. They do not consciously intend to commit suicide, but their unconscious urges interfere with their ability to avoid such situations and/or to take counteractions which might save them.

Summary

As was pointed out earlier, the police officer with a professional attitude toward behavior must be able to assess and understand the behavior with which he is dealing. Why is the adolescent running away from home? Why are some individuals more prone to violent behavior? What causes abnormal sexual behavior? Why do some offenders always get caught so easily?

To answer these and similar questions, the officer must possess a frame of reference which includes an appreciation of what is necessary for healthy personality development. Comparing the background of an offender with these known needs for healthy personality development will enable the officer to evaluate more effectively the motivation of the offender with whom he is dealing.

The basic psychological terms and theories which have been presented in this chapter are part of the knowledge necessary to appreciate the complexity of human behavior and personality development.

In the next chapter we will continue our discussion of basic psychological principles by discussing the development of defense mechanisms and the part they play in both conscious and unconscious behavior.

REFERENCES AND ADDITIONAL BIBLIOGRAPHY

Cameron, N. 1963. *Personality Development and Psychopathology*. Boston: Houghton Mifflin.

Erikson, E. H. 1964. *Childhood and Society*. New York: Norton.

Kisker, G. W. 1972. *The Disorganized Personality*. New York: McGraw-Hill.

Mezer, R. R. 1960. *Dynamic Psychiatry*. New York: Springer.

Spitz, R. 1965. *The First Year of Life*. New York: International Universities Press.

White, R. W. 1968. *The Abnormal Personality*. New York: Ronald Press.

Chapter 4

The Normal Personality in Operation: Conflicts and the Mechanisms of Defense

Introduction

The previous chapter discussed normal personality development and some of the factors which influence it. In the ideal development, the id, ego, and superego work together to maintain a psychological balance which maximizes functioning. Before this discussion of the normal personality is complete, it is important to understand how daily stresses are handled by the ego. Upsetting events, nagging problems, both small and great, dreams which never materialize, and plans which go astray are experiences encountered by all. To insure that they do not disturb the balance between the id, ego, and superego, the ego employs psychological defense mechanisms to handle these stresses. It is the failure of these defense mechanisms to work effectively that often leads to emotional problems and mental illness. A complete understanding of defense mechanisms requires a knowledge of other psychological concepts including conflict and frustration. Involved in an understanding of these concepts is an awareness of the roles of sexuality, hostility, and aggression and of the need for status. Finally, an unsuccessful resolution of frustration and conflict can lead to the presence of anxiety or guilt.

Frustration and Conflict

The definition of the id in Chapter 3 referred to a group of biological urges and needs. These needs can also be called *motives* or *drives* because they supply the power that motivates or drives the earliest forms of behavior exhibited by the personality. Psychologists also refer to these early drives as *primary drives* because they are the basic inherited constituents of behavior. Other drives and motives which appear later in development are referred to as *secondary* or *learned* drives. These include love and a need for acceptance. Whatever the organism does is the result of the operation of either primary or secondary drives or a combination of both.

Within the scope of these two types of drives falls a vast number of biological, psychological, and social needs all seeking fulfillment. Not all of these needs or drives can be fulfilled. Everyone experiences the *frustration* of his drives. This experience of frustration is generally represented by a diagram that shows the individual (I) striving toward some goal or objective (G) with a barrier (B) intervening (Kisker 1972).

$$I \longrightarrow B \qquad G$$

The barrier may be *physical* (time, distance, space, confinement), *biological* (lack of intellectual ability, physical deformities, lack of strength), *psychological* (personality factors, feelings of fear, guilt, or anxiety), or *cultural* (group norms, pressures, and demands). At each barrier a solution must be found or an adaptation made.

Related to this concept of frustration is the concept of *conflict*. In these situations a choice must be made between alternative goals. Needs or drives are perceived as being incompatible with each other. This situation can be illustrated by showing the individual (I) who is simultaneously striving toward two goals (G_1 and G_2).

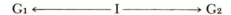

$$G_1 \longleftarrow \qquad I \qquad \longrightarrow G_2$$

He is torn between two goals of equal, or near equal, repulsion or desirability. He has difficulty in choosing. If the choice is of great importance, the conflict can be very disrupting to his psychological and even physical balance. If the conflict is resolved successfully, the probability of personality disturbance is slight. If this important conflict cannot be resolved, some form of personality breakdown is likely to occur.

Frustration and conflict are most likely to occur in three areas— sexuality, hostility and aggression, and the need for status.

Sexuality

The frequency of frustrations and conflicts arising in the area of sexuality is an indication of both how powerful sexual drives are and of how strong are the restraints put upon these drives by society. An individual is often unable to resolve these opposing forces satisfactorily, thus disturbing the state of psychological balance. For example, although childhood masturbation is normal, many parents get upset if they find their child "playing with himself." This creates a conflict situation for the child. Teenage girls often face a conflict between "putting out" on a date or staying home. More recently, it has been suggested that marital fidelity is out of date, or at least a matter of negotiation between husband and wife.

Hostility and Aggression

It is as difficult for the individual to learn how to handle his natural urges of hostility and aggression as it is for him to deal with his sexual feelings. *Aggression* can be categorized in a variety of ways. *Primary aggression* is a term used by Freud (1961) to describe an unlearned, inborn personality trait found in all cultures. It is part of the original id function characteristic of the newborn infant. There is also *learned aggression* (*secondary* or *compensatory* aggression) which is not inborn, but develops from the frustrations and conflicts that are a part of everyday experience. Depending upon various social factors, such as prevailing religious attitudes, legal restraints, and local customs, the individual can express aggression to a varying degree and in different ways. In this latter regard, aggression may be classified as *direct* or *vicarious*.

Society places the most restrictions on direct aggression. The physical expression of aggression (striking, wounding, or killing) is allowed only under certain conditions such as defense of property, life, or country. Direct verbal expression of aggression (swearing or calling names) is somewhat more permissible. Many people whom the policeman encounters have expressed aggressive feelings directly by killing someone, setting fires, destroying property, or other criminal acts of violence.

Born with aggressive drives, the child begins to express these urges early in life. At first, he thrashes about, then he learns to hit and bite and later to spit and call names. He also learns early that the direct expression of aggressive feelings is considered wrong. This belief is a barrier that produces frustration.

Although the child requires limits on his aggressive feelings, he must also be able to express them in order to learn how to control them. For example, all children have hostile and aggressive feelings toward their parents. A mother is always shocked to hear her five-year-old scream, "I hate you. I wish you'd die!" The family setting must provide the child with both the opportunity to express his basic feelings of hostility and aggression and with reasonable limits. This is a difficult task. However, if the child does not learn how to handle these feelings, he may later act them out through violence.

Parents are also often hostile and aggressive toward their children. When a parent has a problem with his own unresolved aggressive feelings, the child, who is both vulnerable and available, may be susceptible to this parental hostility. This is especially true if the parent sees the child as responsible for his own problems. The battered child is often a result of this situation.

Hostility and aggression may also be expressed indirectly or vicariously. When an executive feels uptight as a result of office pressure, he may go directly to a nearby driving range and hit a bucket of golf balls. He says it relaxes him. Hitting the golf balls enables him to work off feelings of hostility and aggression aroused by people and events in the office.

Teasing is another form of indirect aggression. Even when done affectionately, underlying hostility can be discerned. Wit and humor may also express aggression or hostility indirectly. Phrases such as "sharp wit," "biting humor," "poking fun," and "stop, you're killing me" illustrate this.

Spectator sports offer another way of expressing hostile or aggressive feelings vicariously. Not only can the spectator identify with the hockey player who throws a crushing body-check on an opponent, but he can also yell insults at the referee or at the opposing team without fear of retaliation. Many professional race-car drivers have expressed the opinion that fans attend racing events expecting and hoping to see a crash. Violence on television and in the movies is also a common source of release for indirect feelings of hostility and aggression.

The Need for Status

Status is very important in our society and the failure to attain it can often lead to severe frustration. Goals are often viewed with reference to status needs and conflict can easily ensue. The need for status and the accompanying frustration and conflict may also lead to serious crimes. After murdering several people on a weekend, Charles Starkweather is reported to have said he was sick of being a nobody (he was a garbage man). Sirhan-Sirhan is reported to have told one of his examining psychiatrists that he had achieved in a matter of seconds what it took Bobby Kennedy all his life to attain—fame.

These are extreme cases, but every child, because of his weakness and inferiority as an infant, wants to overcome these deficiencies and become more powerful and self-sufficient. As he grows older, enters school, and interacts with others, he desires recognition and achievement. He learns that society offers a competitive environment and that it is better to be a winner than a loser. Later, he may struggle to be in the "right" group, to attend a prestigious college, or to get the magic initials Ph.D. or M.D. after his name, although he lacks any real interest in the subject matter. He may elect to be "in" by becoming a hippie or by joining an anti-establishment group. Whatever his direction, the common thread is his need to be valued and to belong.

If there are birth defects, poor health, buck teeth, poverty, or racial handicaps, feelings of inferiority can be intensified. Imagined inferiorities can also be significant. Many men suffer from sexual impotency as adults because of imagined inferiority about the size of their penis as a boy. If the child's parents entertain expectations for him that are so high he can never satisfy them, he is also apt to feel inadequate no matter what his achievements actually are.

Reactions to Frustration and Conflict: Guilt and Anxiety

Psychologically, no one is immune nor insensitive to the frustrations and conflicts experienced in these problem areas or others. If each frustration could be easily overcome and every conflict quickly resolved, there would be no inner turmoil. Anxiety and guilt, the common reactions to frustration and conflict, arise when problems in the areas of sexuality, hostility and aggression, and the need for status cannot be quickly resolved. These feelings of anxiety and guilt seem to operate as signals, warning the ego that the psychological balance is being threatened.

Anxiety

Anxiety is an emotion with which everyone is familiar. If it is *normal anxiety*, the reasons for feeling anxious are probably obvious and the anxiety is in proportion to the cause. However, anxiety can also appear when there seems to be no obvious reason for it or can be manifested out of proportion to the cause. This is known as *pathological anxiety*.

Doctors first thought that anxiety occurred secondary to a physical dysfunction of the nervous system. Freud, however, postulated that anxiety is psychogenic, occurring secondary to mental processes rather than physical dysfunction. Erikson viewed anxiety as being secondary to the conflicts which the child, adolescent, or adult encounters in each stage of life. This is not to suggest that anxiety has no physiological components when it occurs. On the contrary, one of the ways in which anxiety is often noted is through changes in body functions.

Freud also pointed out the usefulness of anxiety. He postulated that anxiety can act as a signal to the ego, informing it of impending or present danger. With this signal, the ego is better able to anticipate or recognize situations which threaten the psychological balance.

How does anxiety differ from fear? Fear is a relatively well-defined response connected to a specific object, event, or person, while anxiety is a vague, diffuse response whose relationship to any specific object, event, or person is poorly defined. Sometimes it is difficult to make the distinction and it is accurate to say that fear and anxiety usually go together.

Anxiety-producing situations are also stress situations with physiological effects which manifest themselves through the autonomic nervous system and the endocrine system. Whenever the security of the individual is threatened, these physiological changes occur and help prepare him to meet the danger. This is why anxiety, uncomfortable as it is, is useful to the healthy person; it puts him on the alert physically by heightening his perceptions and reactions.

These physical changes vary. The heart may beat faster, blood pressure may go up, pain in the chest may occur, and respiration may increase. Digestion can also be disturbed with a loss of appetite, nausea, vomiting, or diarrhea. Shaking can occur or a sudden feeling of weakness may overcome him. Reactions may range from profuse sweating to cold and clammy hands and feet.

Psychologically, the expression of anxiety may also vary over a wide range from mild worry or a vague uneasiness to dread, apprehension, or panic. Associated feelings of gloom, depression, pessimism, inadequacy, helplessness, or hopelessness may also occur. The individual may be unable to sleep, have nightmares, or awaken easily.

In summary, anxiety may be both a normal signal of impending or present danger or a symptom of psychological imbalance. As a signal, it can serve the useful function of alerting the organism and getting it ready to fight or flee. As a symptom, it represents a reaction to frustration or conflict which, if not dealt with, can impair functioning and lead to more serious emotional problems.

Guilt

Like anxiety, guilt is also a possible reaction to frustration and conflict. It may be conscious or unconscious. When faced with two choices which are not acceptable but where one must be taken, individuals may often experience guilt feelings.

Guilt feelings are first instilled in the child by the parents, either as an aid in setting limits on behavior, as a form of punishment for misdeeds, or perhaps for not living up to their expectations. Even if they have no conscious intent to create guilt, the child may still experience these feelings because of his own interpretation. Guilt feelings are often associated with id strivings, particularly those sexual and aggressive urges described earlier. In our society, the creation of guilt feelings is used also to control the "base" nature of man. Kierkegaard, the noted Danish philosopher of the nineteenth century, stated that guilt "guides the individual and keeps the more violent tendencies of the personality in check" (Kierkegaard 1944; quoted in Kisker 1972).

When an individual feels guilty for something he did not do, it may be because he had an unconscious wish to do it but the superego would not permit that wish to come into consciousness. As an example, a woman who has had to care for an invalid mother for many years blamed herself for her mother's death. In treatment, it became apparent that her guilt feelings were largely due not to any lack in the care she had given her mother while alive, but rather to her wish, at first unconscious, that her mother would die so that she would be free from her responsibility.

Guilt feelings vary in intensity. One person may feel little guilt in a specific situation while another may feel very guilty. Some may even worry for years about something which others would easily forget. For example, it is not unusual for the Internal Revenue Service to receive guilt payments for tax omissions or evasions committed many years ago.

Police officers are also familiar with some of the variations of guilt. All have encountered the criminal who seems to want to be caught. The authors know of a burglar who broke into the snack bar at police department headquarters and was easily apprehended. The police officer may also encounter guilt in unusual ways. In the famous Black Dahlia murder, it was publicized that the police had no clues. In response, more than twenty-five men and women confessed to the crime.

Defense Mechanisms

We have followed the development of feelings of anxiety and guilt through three stages. We have seen (1) how the individual is always striving to achieve certain goals, either for conscious or unconscious reasons; (2) how these goals are frequently not achieved because of some barrier or because they are competitive, leading to frustration and conflict; and (3) how frustration and conflict can lead to anxiety and guilt.

It now remains to describe how the ego attempts to deal with these feelings of anxiety and guilt and to maintain psychological balance. Of the techniques used by the ego, two are overt, physical, and always employed consciously. The others are internal and dynamic, representing a psychological process which may be conscious or unconscious.

Fight and Flight

The two overt and physical mechanisms are fight and flight. When an individual resorts to fighting, he is trying to overcome his anxiety and guilt by aggressive behavior. This behavior is intended to destroy the source of danger, thus protecting the individual. However, there is also the danger that when aggressive, hostile behavior is allowed direct expression, it may arouse more guilt and anxiety which, in turn, may intensify the aggressive, hostile behavior and create a vicious cycle.

If the individual elects to flee rather than to fight, it may also be damaging. He may become passive and withdrawn or even resort to drugs or alcohol as a means of flight.

Internal Defense Mechanisms

It is the internal psychological mechanisms, however, which are of the greatest importance. Among these are: (1) displacement; (2) rationalization; (3) compensation; (4) projection; (5) reaction formation; (6) denial; (7) repression; (8) identification; (9) substitution; (10) fantasy; (11) regression; and (12) sublimation. It is most important to emphasize that these mechanisms are usually employed unconsciously, although occasionally they may become conscious through increased self-awareness or treatment.

Just as the body does not need to be told to evoke certain physiological mechanisms of defense, such as temperature regulation, when the physical equilibrium is disturbed, the mind does not need to be told to activate these psychological defense mechanisms when the psychological balance is threatened.

It should also be noted that, with the possible exception of repression, none of these mechanisms are necessarily pathological or harmful to the individual. All of us use these psychological defense mechanisms daily to protect us against guilt, tension, anxiety, inferiority, and other uncomfortable feelings. It is only when these mechanisms are employed indiscriminately and inappropriately or are not adequately developed that they become pathological.

DISPLACEMENT

In displacement, a strong emotion (such as anger) is displaced onto some other person or object as the recipient of that emotion rather than being focused on the person or object which originally aroused the emotion.

CASE EXAMPLE 1: OFFICER HUNT

Officer Hunt is sitting on his motorcycle observing traffic when he notices a car approaching the corner of First Avenue from Salina Street. There is a stop sign, but the car merely slows down before turning right onto First Avenue. Hunt pursues the vehicle and makes the stop. He intends to give the middle-aged driver a warning rather than a citation. However, when he approaches the driver, he is greeted with violent verbal abuse which ends with the driver's suggestion that he take his g.d. ticket and shove it.

Officer Hunt was a victim of displacement. The motorist's wife had announced, just before he left home, that her mother, whom he dislikes intensely, was coming for a three-week visit. Although Officer Hunt may never know the reason for the displacement, he does not need to. More importantly, Officer Hunt should be aware that a defense mechanism may be operating in this situation and recognize that the motorist is not really angry with him. In this way, he can avoid losing his own temper and responding to the motorist's hostility and aggression with his own. Knowledge of this mechanism may also help Officer Hunt become more introspective about his own behavior in situations where he loses control of his anger without sufficient cause.

RATIONALIZATION

Rationalization is the defense mechanism that enables individuals to justify their behavior to themselves and others by making excuses or formulating fictitious, socially approved arguments to convince themselves and others that their behavior is logical and acceptable.

CASE EXAMPLE 2: SERGEANT MALONEY

Sergeant Maloney is overweight. The chief has personally told him to lose pounds or face dismissal for physical unfitness. His own physician has advised him that his health is seriously threatened by his obesity. He is fully aware of his need to diet and has been trying to follow his doctor's orders. His wife nags him about losing weight but continues to cook many fattening foods because she feels the rest of the family shouldn't have to diet just because he has a problem.

The sergeant had been losing weight, but one night after a particularly exhausting and frustrating tour of duty, he opens the refrigerator door and notices a single piece of apple pie (his favorite) left over from supper and eats it.

However, Maloney could not have eaten that pie without feeling guilty and/or anxious (since his doctor told him dieting was necessary) unless he had first found a way to justify his actions. This was possible through rationalization.

How did he rationalize this action? He might have convinced himself that: (1) it is a fact that many people all over the world are hungry; (2) it is a sin to waste food; (3) if someone doesn't eat this piece of pie tonight, it will be too dried out by morning and will have to be thrown away; and (4) it is, therefore, not only excusable for him to eat the pie and thus avoid wasting food, but it is also his duty to do so even if he sacrifices his own welfare to do it.

With these rationalizations, Maloney can avoid feelings of guilt and anxiety. He is able to eat the pie, as he wanted to, and has justified his behavior to himself (and to others), thereby avoiding feelings of anxiety and guilt.

COMPENSATION

Compensation is the psychological defense mechanism through which people attempt to overcome the anxiety associated with feelings of inferiority and inadequacy in one area of personality or body image by concentrating on another area where they can excel.

CASE EXAMPLE 3: RECRUIT THOMAS

Recruit Thomas is the anchor man in his class as far as scholastic work is concerned, but he is at the top in marksmanship and judo. He spends every available extra hour either on the range or in the gym perfecting these two skills, in which he is already more than qualified, even though his classwork continues to suffer.

Compensatory behavior may be healthy and constructive. For example, Recruit Thomas compensates for his inferiority in the academic aspects of training by concentrating on judo and marksmanship in which he already excels. His excellence in these two

46

skills helps his ego cope with the anxiety generated by his marginal performance in the classroom.

PROJECTION

In projection, feelings and ideas which are unacceptable to the ego or the superego are projected onto others so that they seem to have these feelings or ideas, freeing the individual from the guilt and anxiety associated with them. This process is analogous to a motion picture projector. There is a picture on the screen, but the real image is on a small piece of film inside the projector.

CASE EXAMPLE 4: SERGEANT BUCKO

Sergeant Bucko was one of the first motorcycle officers in the department. He is not too smart and lacks even a high school GED. Things were going all right for him until a new lieutenant took charge of the squad. The sergeant had never had any trouble with other lieutenants who had been in command. This new lieutenant, however, places demands on the sergeant that have made his life miserable. Sgt. Bucko has informed the chief that he can't continue to serve under his new lieutenant because it is apparent to him that he does not like him. Although he has made no plans for retirement, could continue on the force for another ten years, and the Chief urges him to reconsider, Sgt. Bucko goes ahead and turns in his resignation.

Sgt. Bucko has been confronted with duties that he cannot perform. Bucko feels inadequate and inferior and harbors unconscious feelings of dislike and anger toward the lieutenant. He avoids dealing with these feelings and emotions by projecting the anger and dislike onto the lieutenant. Thus, it appears to Bucko that the lieutenant is angry with him and dislikes him.

REACTION FORMATION

This defense mechanism is defined as the development of a trait or traits which are the opposite of tendencies that we do not want to recognize. The individual is motivated to act in a certain way, but behaves in the opposite way. Consequently, he is able to keep his urges and impulses under control.

CASE EXAMPLE 5: MS. BREWSTER

Ms. Brewster is a middle-aged librarian who was raised in a strict Catholic family. She has never had a real date and considers sexual activity to be sinful and animalistic. She constantly calls her local police department with complaints about the goings on in lovers' lane, urging it to patrol the area twenty-four hours a day. She is the loudest voice in the community against smut and indecency, advocating strict moral censorship of all movies, plays, and books.

If Ms. Brewster's personal history were carefully examined, it could be learned that she was reared by strict, religious parents who regarded sexual activities as dirty and disgusting. However, they considered sex to be acceptable between married people, although they never explained how Ms. Brewster could accomplish a switch in her attitudes and emotions if she did marry. Even in marriage, her mother strongly implied that sexual relations were a duty which a wife had to endure. The idea that a woman might even enjoy sex was beyond her mother's comprehension.

Ms. Brewster grew up to be a physically healthy woman with a normal amount of sex drive. She is unable to entirely repress these urges. They emerge in dreams, threatening to break forth into consciousness. Her strict superego does not permit any direct expression of these urges.

Ms. Brewster seeks to reduce her own anxieties arising from her personal conflict by becoming overly concerned about the morals of the community. By badgering her local police department with complaints about porno movie houses and lovers' lane parkers, she can be preoccupied with sexual matters in such a way that quiet her own inner, unacceptable sexual urges and also give support to her superego.

DENIAL

When a person uses this mechanism, he refuses to recognize and deal with reality because of strong inner needs.

CASE EXAMPLE 6: PATROLMAN CLICK

Patrolman Click has been experiencing shortness of breath and occasional chest pains but he tells himself that these symptoms are probably muscular and of minor importance. One day, while riding in a patrol car with his partner, he suddenly experiences crushing chest pain. His partner rushes him to the nearest hospital where he remains for a week for tests. The doctor tells him that he has heart trouble, but that it is not that serious. He will have to lose some weight, give up smoking, and take medication. He will also have to leave patrol duty and transfer to a desk job. Officer Click doesn't believe the doctor and insists on returning to full patrol duty. He even goes to another doctor, at his own expense and without telling anyone. When he receives a similar evaluation, it does not alter his thinking and he persists in demanding a return to full patrol duty.

Click refuses to believe that he has heart trouble because it is too threatening to his self-image as a virile, active patrolman. He loves the duties of a patrolman and can't see himself in any desk job. To him, being on the streets is real police work. Therefore, he persists in his denial of the medical reality presented to him by two different and competent authorities.

REPRESSION

Repression is an unconscious process whereby unacceptable urges and/or painful, traumatic experiences are completely prevented from entering consciousness. Suppression, which is sometimes confused with repression, is a *conscious* activity by which an individual attempts to forget emotionally disturbing thoughts and experiences by pushing them out of his mind (for example, a person may attempt to forget grief by losing himself in his work).

CASE EXAMPLE 7: HELEN TROY

Helen Troy was brought to the police substation by a motorist who found her wandering, dazed and confused, on the highway. Her clothes were torn and she obviously had been beaten. A medical examination indicated probable rape. Ms. Troy could give no account of what had happened and was hysterical. Investigation revealed that she had left a local bar with a man, later identified as a habitual sex offender who had served time for rape and assault. Days later, Helen Troy could still not recall details of the incident and met all attempts to gather information with "I don't know. . . . I can't remember."

Ms. Troy has apparently repressed the entire rape incident. This may have occurred because the experience was too frightening for her to assimilate and deal with consciously. There is also the possibility of some feelings of guilt on her part. Perhaps she led him on, thinking she could control his passion and not imagining he would resort to force. The physical pain of the beating, the psychological terror of her experience, and the possible guilt over leading him on have created a traumatic experience which she can deal with only through repression. She is not lying when she says she can't remember, nor is she trying to protect anyone.

IDENTIFICATION

In this defense mechanism, an individual seeks to overcome his own feelings of inadequacy, loneliness, or inferiority by taking on the characteristics of someone who is important to him. You may recall that the child identifies with his parents who are seen as models of strength and competence.

CASE EXAMPLE 8

Police were called when the body of an unidentified man was found in a local swimming pool with his feet tied together. Investigation established his identity and also the fact that his wife had died by drowning a few days before while both were on a fishing trip.

In this case, we have a specialized form of identification, *introjection*. People have an unconscious tendency to assume (introject) characteristics of someone close to them who has died recently. When this man's wife died by accidental drowning, his grief and despondency drove him to employ introjection in his suicidal behavior (Kisker, 1972). A knowledge that this behavior exists could be of great value to the officer assigned to investigate whether this man's death was homicide or suicide.

SUBSTITUTION

Through substitution, the individual seeks to overcome feelings of frustration and anxiety by achieving alternate goals and gratifications. Unrequited loves, unfulfilled longings, unattainable plans and ambitions, and unacceptable urges and impulses will create feelings of anxiety and guilt unless some substitute gratification is attained.

CASE EXAMPLE 9: MARIE SMITH

Fifteen-year-old Marie Smith is arrested again as a runaway juvenile. She is found living with a thirty-eight-year-old man. This is the fourth time in two years that this has happened, each time with a different man. Each time she promises that it will not happen again. However, when it does, she is at a loss to explain why.

It can be postulated, however, that Marie is trying to find the love and affection she lacks at home by having sexual relationships with older men. If she had a father who had given her normal love and affection, she would not have to seek it by running away and engaging in promiscuous behavior with a father substitute. The officer who finds Marie Smith might be more helpful if he understood the reasons behind her behavior.

FANTASY

Fantasy is one of the most useful defense mechanisms. Its content is determined by unfulfilled ambitions and unconscious drives.

CASE EXAMPLE 10: OFFICER JEFFERS

Officer Jeffers sometimes has trouble keeping his mind on the academy lectures. He finds himself daydreaming that he will become the James Bond of the department and imagines himself overcoming all sorts of obstacles in solving the case of the century. Occasionally, these fantasies lead to inappropriate behavior, such as the time he tried to arrest a dangerous criminal by himself.

REGRESSION

When a person employs this defense mechanism, he reverts to a pattern of feeling, thinking, or behavior which was appropriate to an earlier stage of development.

CASE EXAMPLE 11: OFFICER RILEY

To most people, Officer Riley's wife seems mature. However, whenever she is denied something which she really wants (like a new dress for a department party), she throws a temper tantrum. Riley, even though he can't really afford it, finally agrees to her demands in order to stop her tantrum.

Ms. Riley never learned, while growing up, to deal maturely with denied gratification. She never had to learn because her father and mother gave in immediately whenever she started having a temper tantrum. Today, when denied something by her husband, she is only repeating the successful behavior learned in childhood.

SUBLIMATION

Sublimation is the diversion of unacceptable id impulses into socially and culturally acceptable channels.

CASE EXAMPLE 12: CHARLIE SMITH

Charlie Smith has always been hostile. Since early childhood, he has had frequent daydreams of hurting or killing someone. When he entered high school, Charlie did not enjoy the regular sports such as baseball and basketball. One day, a friend took him to the local gym and Charlie soon realized that he had found what he wanted—to become a boxer.

As a boxer, not only could he hit people and hurt them, but he could do so with social approval and the possibility of financial reward. Similarly, an individual with a strong sex drive and an urge to look at the naked body may become a photographer, or a man with strong homosexual feelings may become a masseuse or trainer. Sublimation is a positive and constructive mechanism for defending against otherwise unacceptable impulses and needs.

Summary

In this chapter we have pointed out that the dynamic interaction of the id, ego, and superego, occurring on both a conscious and unconscious level, can often lead to frustration and conflict. The most important frustrations and conflicts in our culture involve sexual and aggressive feelings and the need for status.

These frustrations and conflicts create feelings of anxiety and guilt. Psychological defense mechanisms (displacement, rationalization, compensation, and the others discussed) may operate automatically and unconsciously to protect individuals from these unpleasant feelings and to maintain psychological balance (homeostasis). When these defense mechanisms are used in a constructive and positive manner, the individual is acting in a healthy way; when they are employed indiscriminately and inappropriately, the individual is heading toward ill health. When they break down completely or have not been adequately developed, the individual is likely to become mentally ill.

The discussion in this chapter should once again impress upon the professional who must deal with human behavior that there is some motivation for every action of the individual and that, most likely, the person is not necessarily immediately aware of the reason for his behavior.

However, these basic concepts are only the starting point for understanding specific behaviors. Therefore, the professional must be cautious in drawing any conclusions regarding the underlying causes of a person's actions. If the person himself is unaware of why he acts in a certain way, the professional will come to understand this behavior only after thorough investigation and study.

Therefore, the police officer should not make instant diagnoses of the behavior he encounters. However, he may legitimately use his knowledge of psychology to assist him in forming preliminary judgments which will guide his actions, but he must also recognize that all may not be what it appears to be on the surface.

In addition, knowledge of psychological defense mechanisms should encourage the police officer to examine the effect of his own presence on the behavior of others. In many instances his presence will be perceived by others as a barrier to their desires or as presenting another element that must be taken into consideration before deciding upon further action.

The police officer himself can also be a source of frustration or conflict to the persons with whom he comes in contact. This emphasizes the importance to the police officer of knowing how the individual reacts and how he handles his inner feelings in these situations. Through this knowledge, he can better anticipate the behavior he is likely to see and, by anticipating it, control his own reactions and increase his effectiveness.

REFERENCES AND ADDITIONAL BIBLIOGRAPHY

Freud, A. 1946. *The Ego and the Mechanisms of Defense.* New York: International Universities Press.
———. 1961 (originally published in 1936). "Inhibitions, Symptoms and Anxiety." In Standard Edition, Vol. 20, ed. J. Strachey. London: Hogarth Press, pp. 87–172.
Kierkegaard, S. 1944. *The Concept of Dread.* Princeton: Princeton University Press.
Kisker, G. W. 1972. *The Disorganized Personality.* New York: McGraw-Hill.
Levi, L. 1967. *Stress: Sources, Management and Prevention.* New York: Liveright.
Storr, A. 1968. *Human Aggression.* New York: Atheneum.

Chapter 5

Abnormal Behavior: What It Is and What to Do

Introduction

In the preceding three chapters, concepts of normal personality development and functioning were presented. They constitute a body of knowledge basic to an understanding of the complexities of human behavior. It is now appropriate to consider some general concepts pertaining to abnormal behavior based on those concepts described previously.

In later chapters, those patterns of abnormal behavior which have special significance to the law enforcement officer in his work will be presented.

Definitions

What is abnormal behavior? Since *ab* means "away from," we conceive of abnormal behavior as behavior which is away from or deviating from normal behavior. However, to define normal behavior is not as easy a task as it may first appear since many variables are involved.

Some people regard their own behavior as quite normal and, therefore, conclude that people who behave as they do are normal, while those who do not behave similarly are abnormal. This personal standard of definition is illustrated by the old Quaker proberb:

> Everyone is queer
> Save thee and me
> And sometimes I think
> Thee a bit queer too.

Normal behavior can also be defined as the embodiment of an ideal (the ideal soldier, the ideal husband). Normal behavior is that which emulates this ideal model and abnormal behavior is that which deviates from it.

Normality can also be conceptualized statistically. This definition states that the average (mean) is normal. Significant deviation from this average is abnormal. A measure of central tendency (mean) is calculated and a measure of spread around this measure of central tendency (the standard deviation) is also calculated. The more one's score deviates from the center, the more abnormal one is. The deviation can be in a positive or a negative direction (for example, a child may be exceptionally dull or exceptionally bright depending on whether his IQ score is far below or far above the mean IQ). It should be noted that this approach does not lend itself particularly well to the study of the individual because there are always exceptions to the rule and because human behavior is too complex to be reduced to a curve or sets of curves.

Culture also plays an important role in determining what is normal or abnormal. According to Ruth Benedict, a noted anthropologist, normality, within a wide range, is culturally defined (Benedict 1934). One culture may approve of sex play among children; another may strongly disapprove. One culture permits homosexuality; another condemns it. Otto Klineberg, a social psychologist, has stated (1954): "Abnormality is embedded in the very structure of a society and can only be understood against the background of the culture in which it occurs." In this view, no behavior is intrinsically abnormal, but becomes abnormal only in relation to the whole range of social and cultural preferences.

In our own society, abnormal behavior most often refers to "sick" behavior. The professional judgment as to whether behavior is significantly abnormal is dependent on the presence of certain symptoms which are characteristic of mental illness. For example, is the patient hearing voices which are not there (hallucinations)? Does he have false beliefs which are strongly held despite all tests of reality (delusions)? Is he depressed?

In judging the seriousness of the illness, the professional observer also looks at the degree of ineffectiveness of the individual's behavior. Is he able to continue working or does his behavior interfere to such a degree that work is impossible? Is he or she able to fulfill his or her role as husband or wife, father or mother? In this view, behavior which is *ineffective, self-defeating, self-destructive, and which alienates* the individual from those who are important to him is regarded as abnormal.

Common Misconceptions about Abnormal Behavior

Regardless of these preferred technical definitions of abnormal behavior, it is usually associated by most people with the strange, the alien, the unknown. Consequently, abnormal behavior is frequently a cause of fear, repugnance, and misunderstanding. Attitudes toward it are shaped more often by rumor and popular stereotypes than by direct experience and sound information. The following misconceptions about abnormal behavior are common.

1. *There is something "evil" about mental illness and people who suffer from such illness are themselves evil, violent, and homicidal.* This misconception is a carry-over from the days when the mentally ill were regarded as possessed by evil spirits or as having willingly made a pact with the devil in return for certain favors. Many stories, plays, and movies have perpetuated this belief through tales about mad scientists, witches, maniacal killers, and sex fiends. A typical opening scene in many horror movies shows a state hospital or insane asylum sitting forlornly in the middle of nowhere. A violent thunderstorm is raging and, as the camera moves inside the in-

stitution, a Boris Karloff-type character is pacing to and fro along a darkened, eerie corridor. Is it any wonder that many people are afraid of mental institutions and of the people within them? They believe that all of them are violent and dangerous.

The truth is that there is nothing at all evil about mental illness and that the large majority of the mentally ill are neither violent nor dangerous. A better word to describe the majority is afraid. They are afraid of many things—of what is happening to them, of the people around them, and of the world in which they live. This is true even of the individual who is brandishing a knife and threatening to kill whomever comes near. If the police officer recognizes this fear, he can use it to his advantage when taking this person into custody by offering his help and protection instead of fighting him.

2. *Mental illness is an "all or nothing" affair.* The concept of mental illness is easily dichotomized. A person is often regarded as insane or normal. Nothing could be farther from the truth. Mental illness, like physical illness, is both a matter of kind and of degree.

Years ago, the Army made a training film whose purpose was to acquaint line commanders with different types of psychiatric casualties and how and why such casualties occurred. The title of the film was *Shades of Grey* and it opened with vignettes about various types of psychiatric disorders. The film begins something like this:

"It's a big day for the recruits on the grenade range. For the first time they are throwing live grenades. Suddenly, something goes wrong in pit #5. Private Smith pulls the pin on the grenade and then freezes with the grenade clutched tightly in his hands. The sergeant grabs the grenade from the recruit and throws it just in time." "What went wrong?" the narrator asks.

Another scene begins, "This soldier has been acting strangely recently, keeping more and more to himself. He seems suspicious of his buddies. Suddenly, while eating in the mess hall, he grabs the soldier next to him and accuses him of poisoning his food." The scene ends with the soldier being forcibly taken from the mess hall to the Mental Hygiene Consultation Center.

Another vignette depicts a soldier walking guard on a lonely, desolate post in the far North. "Suddenly," the narrator tells us, "this soldier is overcome by a wave of depression." He drops his weapon and leans against a stunted tree, staring blankly into the distance with tears in his eyes.

The film then goes into a discussion of mental health and mental illness. It points out that if physical examinations were given to every soldier in one of the most elite units, not one man in that platoon would be rated perfect. For example, a few might be coming down with a cold; others may have a minor stomach upset; and hardly anyone would have a perfect set of teeth. There would also be no one who would merit a completely negative physical rating. All would be a "shade of grey."

The same thing is true of mental illness. As no one is perfectly healthy, so no one is perfectly adjusted. Some may be too sensitive to what others say; some may worry too much about an overdue letter from home or unpaid bills; while others may feel without justification that they are not up to the standards of their peers and are inferior or inadequate. Even the chronic mental patient will have some area, no matter how small, of health. Mental health, like physical health, is not a dichotomy; it is not an all or nothing affair. It is a matter of degree.

It is also a matter of kind. For example, the man who has a common cold is not suffering from the same disease as the man who is suffering from a strep throat, even though both are ill. Nor is either of them suffering from the same kind of disease as the man who has terminal cancer.

In mental health, the individual who experiences mild feelings of inadequacy and tension when in social gatherings is not suffering from the same type of illness as the individual who has a strong and unrelenting fear (phobia) of crowds. Nor is either of them suffering from the same type of illness as the acutely disturbed individual who locks himself in a room all day to avoid all contact with people. Variations in kind are as critical as variations in degree.

3. *If a person is mentally ill, he will always be mentally ill and his condition will not vary significantly from day to day.* Illness, mental or physical, is like health. It is dynamic and does not remain constant. A person may show signs of emotional disturbance one day and not another. Even the sickest person in the state hospital has his good days and bad days, just like all of us. Mental illness can be treated and individuals can become functional again. Like physically ill patients, they may also get sick again, receive appropriate treatment, and recover again.

4. *The feelings and behavior of mentally ill persons have no relationship to the feelings and behavior of the mentally healthy.* Nothing could be farther from the truth. Have you ever had a day when you were down in the dumps, when everything around you made you feel more depressed? The manic-depressive patient experiences

similar feelings. The difference is that your feelings of ups and downs are usually connected with things that are actually happening while the manic-depressive patient is more often responding to inner feelings and thoughts unrelated to reality. While your depression could be immediately lifted if you were told that you had won $10,000 in a sweepstakes, the manic-depressive is not necessarily cheered by such news. He may even interpret his winning as another example of how unworthy he really is.

Consider another example. Some mentally ill patients experience delusions. A delusion may be defined as a false belief which is strongly held despite all tests of reality. All of us have experienced beliefs that later turn out to be false. The difference is that the mentally healthy individual is able to check his beliefs against reality and to modify his thinking based on the evidence presented. The delusions of the mentally ill person are not subject to the challenge of reality. Any attempt to convince him that his belief that all Masons are out to kill him is not true may turn him against you. He may conclude, because of his disturbed thinking, that you are either a fool for not believing him or that you are in league with those plotting against him.

These are some of the popular misconceptions about mental illness and the emotionally disturbed. Understanding these misconceptions is important because they tend to bias people against those who are mentally ill and prevent them from dealing with such persons in a more accepting, human, and professional manner.

Guidelines for Judging Abnormal Behavior

The officer on the street will often have to make a decision as to whether a person's behavior is or is not abnormal. If it is abnormal, he will have to decide whether it can be handled without police action or whether official intervention is necessary. This will involve a judgment as to how serious the abnormal behavior is, especially in terms of its dangerousness to the person himself and/or others.

To the trained law enforcement officer, the recognition and handling of abnormal behavior is, therefore, critical to the effective execution of his duties. The rest of this chapter will address itself to those general and specific characteristics of behavior which the police officer will assess in reaching a conclusion about the observed behavior and the individual manifesting it as well as in deciding how to handle it.

Appropriateness

Normal behavior tends to be appropriate to the situation; abnormal behavior tends to be inappropriate. The judgment of a behavior's appropriateness involves an assessment of not only the behavior itself, but also the situation in which it is occurring.

As an example, suppose you are standing in the foyer of a Catholic church during a noon Mass. Mr. Smith enters the church, comes up beside you, kneels, makes the sign of the cross, and starts to pray. This is appropriate behavior since it is taking place in a Catholic church during Mass.

However, suppose the locale, but not the behavior, is changed. It is Sunday noon at a busy intersection. You are in the center of the street directing heavy traffic. Suddenly, Mr. Smith appears, kneels by your side, crosses himself, and starts to pray. Not only is the behavior now inappropriate in this different setting, but it is also dangerous. Note that the behavior itself has not changed; only its appropriateness has changed.

Similarly, most of the time emotions are directly related to what is happening or what has happened. If an individual experiences great emotion after a major tragedy, that is appropriate. If, on the other hand, he comes apart following minor frustrations and conflicts, it may not be as appropriate. Perhaps you can recall a relative or acquaintance who became greatly upset under conditions that surprised you. Or, if you have been in military service, you may have noted some recruits who broke down and cried or went AWOL after only a minor reprimand.

In most instances, the degree of sadness or happiness is related to what is actually happening. The emotionally disturbed person, however, may be depressed to such a degree that he may want to kill himself even though another person with the same problems is neither as depressed nor as suicidal. Other kinds of mental illness may also show marked discrepancies between the degree or type of emotional response expected in a particular situation and the actual degree or type of emotion demonstrated.

Flexibility

Normal behavior tends to be flexible; abnormal behavior tends to be inflexible. Normal behavior, regardless of setting, tends to be flexible in that it is altered to fit the situation. As an example, the police officer's behavior toward the chief of police is flexible if he adopts a different approach when he is talking to him in the office on an official matter in comparison to a department picnic where they are both dressed in sports clothes and drinking beer together.

These criteria for examining behavior are closely related to appropriateness. However, while a person's behavior may be appropriate, it may lack the flexibility characteristic of healthy behavior.

Impulsivity

Abnormal behavior, since it is related in part to uncontrolled or partially controlled needs and drives, tends to be impulsive. Normal behavior is more likely to be a result of a consideration of its consequences, with important decisions being given careful thought before implementation.

One of the authors (H.E.R.) recalls a young man who was referred to the Mental Hygiene Consultation Service shortly after he entered basic training. He sat weeping in a chair, crying out with dismay and desperation how he could not cope with the army and how he had to get out. Asked when he had been drafted, he replied that he had enlisted. When asked why he had enlisted if he hated it so much, he related the following story.

He had never wanted to go into the service. He had been under the care of a psychiatrist for some time and had prevailed upon his doctor to write a letter which he could take to his draft board declaring that he was unfit for military service. He took the letter to his draft board expecting to be told that he would never be called. Instead, they told him that, when his number came up, this letter would be considered by the board in determining whether to draft him. This made him so angry that he went across the hall to the Army Recruiting Office and enlisted for four years.

In summary, when trying to determine whether a particular behavior is abnormal, examine it first from these three general dimensions before making a judgment.

In addition to these general guidelines for judging the abnormality of behavior, there are more specific criteria for determining whether a person is mentally ill, since not all abnormal behavior is indicative of mental illness. As stressed earlier, there are degrees of mental health and illness just as there are degrees of physical health and illness. If, however, a person's behavior is abnormal according to one or more of the three general dimensions discussed above, further analysis should be made to ascertain the necessity for additional action. In their book *How to Recognize and Handle Abnormal People,* Matthews and Rowland suggest the following specific criteria (Matthews and Rowland, 1974):

Big Changes in Behavior

Since behavior is dynamic, not static, everyone's behavior changes over time. However, one should be especially alert for sudden, big changes in an individual's life style. For example, if a man who always stays at home during his leisure hours, loves his wife and children, never quarrels with his neighbors, and works faithfully at his job suddenly becomes quarrelsome, misses work, spends his time in bars, starts drinking excessively, and is abusive to his wife and children, it is likely that he is suffering from a serious mental disorder. The officer should inquire about the individual's present behavior as contrasted to his past actions. Has this kind of behavior been noted before? If so, when and under what circumstances? When was this current change in behavior first noted?

Losses of Memory

All of us have losses of memory at one time or another. We may forget dental appointments, miss birthdays and anniversaries, or fail to recall material studied the night before. These memory losses are normal. However, if a person cannot remember who he is, where he is, or the day, month, or year; if a woman who has been raped cannot recall any of the details; or if a man who has been in an auto accident cannot remember anything after the crash, the possibility of brain injury or a psychological dysfunction based on serious conflict should be considered.

Feelings of Persecution

Policemen know that people do plot against other people. An individual who is realistically worried about being killed usually will be able to tell the officer who it is that might want to kill him and offer plausible reasons for the plot against him. The abnormal person, however, *imagines* that someone (or some group) is planning to kill him. He may specify that group but his choice is usually unrealistic. Furthermore, his reasons, if he is able to offer any, are likely to be bizarre and not readily understood by the officer. For example, he may say that "the communists" want to kill him because "they know my message to the President will end the war and dissolve the international conspiracy of communism."

Grandiose Ideas

An individual may reveal that he represents the second coming of Christ or that she is the Virgin Mary. In other situations, he may indicate how important he is by telling you that everybody is plotting against him. One must really be an important person if everyone is after him.

Or he may reveal how he has committed the world's worst sin and that he is the most miserable and unworthy human who was ever born. Even in these negative statements, he is emphasizing his importance.

However, it should also be recognized that some seemingly grandiose ideas may turn out to be true after investigation. A soldier, suspected of being somewhat paranoid, was talking about his father. He told the doctor that his father, who was retired, had been a German intelligence agent in World War I and that, during World War II, after immigrating to America, he had parachuted behind German lines for the OSS to make contact with and to escort to freedom a famous Dutch scientist who was being forced by the Nazis to work on V2 bombs. His story sounded like a James Bond novel. The doctor calculated that the patient's father would have been in his sixties during World War II and considered the whole story as delusional. Later interviews with the father revealed, however, that the boy's story was true.

Talks to Himself

All of us occasionally talk to ourselves, especially if we are angry or emotionally upset. Mentally ill people, however, can carry on entire conversations with imaginary people or animals for considerable periods of time.

63

Hears Voices

Occasionally, in talking with someone who demonstrates feelings of persecution or grandiose ideas, the police officer may note that the individual appears easily distracted and is not paying attention to what is going on around him. On further inquiry, he might determine that the person is hearing voices.

Actually, these voices are the person's own thoughts projected from himself to the outside (hallucinations). The voices may call him a sex pervert or degenerate and say other bad things about him. Some people who hear voices may tell you, however, that they do not know where they are coming from or who they are, while others may tell you they are coming from the radio (which is not on) or from someone who is not there.

Sees Visions, Smells Strange Odors, or Has Peculiar Tastes

Instead of, or in addition to, hearing voices (auditory hallucinations), the person may tell you he has seen his dead mother standing by his bed before he goes to sleep or that he has seen God or the devil. Unlike voices, however, these types of hallucinations are more often related to physical abnormalities such as the effect of alcohol on the brain or brain tumors.

Similarly, a person may smell strange odors (gas in the apartment) or complain of peculiar tastes (poison in the food). In these instances, physical illness should also be thoroughly investigated.

Thinks People Are Watching or Talking about Him

Sometimes an individual will complain that he is being watched or that people are talking about him. Because of his own conflicts, he has become, through the mechanism of projection (Chapter 4), supersensitive to other people. He sees two people talking and he is sure they are talking about him. He feels that he is being followed, but when he looks over his shoulder, no one is there. He interprets remarks made within his hearing as pertaining to him even though the person speaking may have no idea that he exists.

At first, he is not sure about these things. He tries to check them out. However, as he becomes more disturbed, he becomes more convinced of the accuracy of his perceptions and resists attempts to convince him that his beliefs are wrong. Finally, these *ideas of reference,* as they are called, become fixed delusions of persecution or grandeur.

Unrealistic Physical Complaints

All people have physical complaints at one time or another. The person who exhibits abnormal behavior or is mentally ill, however, often believes that things are wrong with, or happening to, his body that are not anatomically or medically possible. He may tell you, for example, that his brain is decaying or that half of his body is different from the other half. He will often tell you these terrible things with little or no emotion. If he is convinced that he has an incurable disease, he may try to take his own life. It is important to realize that these symptoms are very real to the person and that he can suffer as much as any individual with pain caused by a physical ailment.

Extreme Fright

Some people become frozen with fear while others panic. A person may tremble, speak haltingly, glance about in terror, or demonstrate a marked startle reaction at the slightest sound. The officer should protect him from any injury which may result from his efforts to get away from what he fears. He may also attack the officer if the latter attempts to stop him.

Dangerous or Destructive Behavior

As we shall see in a later chapter on the psychopath (Chapter 10), some emotionally disturbed persons will not show any of the symptoms mentioned above but will, time after time, do things which are destructive or dangerous to themselves or others. Although they may get hurt or hurt others, they do not seem either to learn from the experience or to show any emotion about it.

Depression

The officer should be alert for the individual who doesn't respond to his questions and seems very depressed. He may be a potential suicide or a suicidal risk.

How to Handle the Mentally Ill

The police officer must not only be able to recognize abnormal behavior and the mentally ill person, but also be prepared to guard, restrain, or take into custody someone whose behavior suggests the presence of mental illness. The following are suggestions for handling these difficult situations.

1. *Calls involving known emotionally disturbed individuals should be answered by more than one officer.* If it is not known that the call involves a disturbed person, the officer who arrives first on the scene should immediately ask for backup. Do not try to handle the case alone. Handling it alone does not prove you are a good policeman nor is your manhood threatened if you ask for help.

For many years psychiatric attendants, doctors, and nurses who have been working with very disturbed individuals, including both homicidal and suicidal persons, have suffered very few injuries. Even prior to tranquilizers, mental health professionals were able to work on a ward housing forty to fifty such patients without difficulty.

One reason for this is their ability to use effectively the *show of force principle.* For example, an attendant might approach Mr. Brown and tell him that he had to go to X-ray. He would, of course, try to convince Mr. Brown to go. If Mr. Brown showed signs of resistance and refused to go, the attendant would not argue or try to force Mr. Brown to go. Instead, he would withdraw and reappear with three or four more attendants and again tell Mr. Brown that, for his own welfare, the doctor had ordered X-rays and that he had to go to X-ray. He was told, without anger or threats, that he could walk down to X-ray under his own power or be carried to X-ray by the attendants. He was also told that more attendants could be called if needed.

Faced with this show of force, most patients usually elect to proceed under their own power. This show of force does two things for the disturbed individual: (1) it gives him a face-saving way out if he has been bragging how tough he is or that no one can force him to do anything he does not want; and (2) it shows him that many people are interested in him and that they care enough to insure that his treatment orders are carried out.

This process can work the same way on the street. If the disturbed person has been boasting that no cop is going to take him anywhere, he may feel required to put up a battle against one policeman. With two or three officers present as backup, he has a face-saving out. The officers can also use their numbers to assure him that they are able to offer him protection against any threat. As with the hospital patient, their numbers also give him a sense of importance and show him that somebody does care about him.

2. *Stay with the disturbed individual until additional help arrives.* If necessary, ask someone to phone for assistance rather than leave the person.

3. *Move slowly.* Resist the impulse to do something immediately. This may be difficult since most police training teaches the importance of quick decisions. With the emotionally disturbed, it is better to take time and to carefully assess the situation. Immediate action is only necessary when handling an *immediate* danger.

4. *Reassurance is important.* Remember that acutely disturbed individuals are generally very frightened.

5. *As a matter of policy, it is usually a good idea to send uniformed men.* "Cherry-tops" or sirens usually are not helpful since they tend to attract crowds that are not wanted. Keep spectators away if at all possible.

6. *Solicit help from friends, relatives, and others known to the emotionally disturbed individual.* The time spent in getting this help may make the task easier and prevent violence and harm from coming to the individual, yourself, or others.

7. *Don't lie to or try to deceive the emotionally disturbed individual.* If he is aware of deception, dealing with him will become more difficult. If you lie, you also create a barrier to his willingness to accept future help.

8. *Do not rely on your weapons.* The threat of a gun is quite meaningless to a person who is acutely disturbed. He may grab it and use it or you may be tempted to use it. A weapon should be used only in the very rare situation when it is necessary to save a life.

9. *Don't be fooled by the individual's size.* For the same reasons that some people are impervious to intense pain during periods of emotional stress, others may have unusual physical strength during these times. Experienced policemen are familiar with this phenomenon and can cite cases where several patrolmen have found it difficult to subdue a 125-pound senior citizen.

10. *Don't meet hostility with hostility.* This is often a natural reaction since a hostile person tends to elicit hostility in others. It is

important to maintain a professional attitude. Meet hostility and anger by being calm, objective, and accepting. Ask why he is angry or why he is afraid. If he will tell you, he may begin to calm down.

11. *Don't argue with delusions, but don't agree either.* Rather, try to steer him away from whatever subject is exciting him. If he demonstrates by his actions, facial expression, increased agitation, or bizarre behavior that the subject being discussed is making him upset, switch to another subject.

Try to bring him back to reality by asking concrete questions such as: "How long have you lived here?" "Who is in your family?" and "Where do you work?" By maintaining control of the discussion, you will reassure the person. Because he senses that you are in control of the situation, it will help him to gain control of himself.

12. *Don't be fooled by a sudden return to reality.* The emotionally disturbed individual can return to his delusions just as quickly. Consider him potentially dangerous because his behavior is unpredictable and remain alert even if he calms down.

However, you can remove any restraints that have been applied if, in your judgment, his behavior warrants it. However, be ready to reapply them if his behavior makes it necessary. Leather cuffs similar to those used in mental hospitals are best, if they are available. Agitated individuals have been known to pull tendons and cut wrists while in handcuffs. If handcuffs have to be used, check frequently to see that the circulation has not been cut off. When restraints are unavailable, safety devices can be made on the spot using pillows, mattresses, and belts or by reversing an ordinary coat or jacket.

13. *Take all suicidal behavior seriously.* Persons making threats, gestures, and attempts should be referred for professional psychiatric help. Do not excuse or gloss over a person's behavior just to reassure anxious relatives.

14. *Make sure the individual is not physically ill or injured.* Diabetic coma, fever delirium, brain tumors, convulsive disorders, and other medical conditions are often mistaken for drunkenness or combativeness. Head injuries often go unnoticed, especially if there is an odor of alcohol on the breath. If any doubts exist, get medical attention.

15. *Keep a record of a person's complaints regarding plots against him.* If his complaints change from a vague "they" to a particular person or small group of persons, it may constitute a threat to the safety of those named. Try to persuade someone who knows him

to take him to his family doctor, a clergyman, or a local psychiatric facility.

16. *Learn what facilities are available in the community* to help the mentally ill and their families, especially in an emergency.

17. *Remember that most disturbed individuals are afraid.* They experience extreme fear because they do not understand their feelings and because they are not certain how others will treat them. When an emotionally disturbed person becomes aggressive, it is almost always because of fear. Therefore, the officer should attempt to handle him in a calm, understanding, and humane way. This will often reassure the individual that the officer is there to help him.

18. *Don't make fun of other people's troubles.* It is easy to become callous, especially in dealing with a disturbed person.

19. *Maintain your sense of humor,* especially in stress situations. Many a day has been saved because someone did.

Summary

In this chapter, differences between normal and abnormal behavior have been presented and some of the misconceptions regarding abnormal behavior and mental illness discussed. Certain guidelines have been offered to assist the police officer in deciding whether the behavior he is dealing with at a particular time is abnormal and, if so, to what degree. It has been pointed out that abnormal behavior differs from normal behavior along three general dimensions (appropriateness, flexibility, and impulsivity). Certain specific signs and symptoms indicative of mental illness have also been discussed. Finally, various suggestions on how to handle individuals manifesting abnormal behavior have been presented to increase the officer's effectiveness and to decrease the chances of injury to him or others.

REFERENCES AND ADDITIONAL BIBLIOGRAPHY

Benedict, R. 1934. *Patterns of Culture.* Boston: Houghton Mifflin.
Blumberg, M. L. 1974. "Psychopathology of the Abusing Parent." *American Journal of Psychotherapy* 28:21–29.

Cochran, R. 1974. "Crime and Personality: Theory and Evidence." *Bulletin of the British Psychological Society* 27:19–22.

Eysenck, H. J. 1974. "Crime and Personality Reconsidered." *Bulletin of the British Psychological Society* 27:23–24.

Hafner, H. and Boker, W. 1973. "Mentally Disordered Violent Offenders." *Social Psychiatry* 8:220.

Klineberg, O. 1954. *Social Psychology*, 2d ed. New York: Holt, Rinehart and Winston.

Levine, D. 1972. "A Cross-National Study of Attitudes Toward Mental Illness." *Journal of Abnormal Psychology* 80:111–114.

Matthews, R. A. 1970. "Observations on Police Policy and Procedures for Emergency Detention of the Mentally Ill." *Journal of Criminal Law, Criminology & Police Science* 61:283–295.

Matthews, R. A. and Rowland, L. W. 1974. *How to Handle and Recognize Abnormal Behavior*. New York: National Association of Mental Health.

Sokol, R. J. and Reiser, M. 1971. "Training Police Sergeants in Early Warning Signs of Emotional Upset." *Mental Hygiene* 55:303–307.

PART III

Understanding
Mental Illness

Courtesy Herb Reich

Chapter 6

Classification of Abnormal Behavior

IN Chapter 5 the characteristics that differentiate abnormal from normal behavior were described. The ability to assess differences in abnormal behavior can enable the police officer to make important judgments regarding the seriousness of that behavior and his responses to it; for example, how strong a response must he make (does he take someone into custody for his own protection?), and what should be the character of his response (should his response to a suicidal person be different than to a psychopath?).

Finally, greater knowledge of abnormal behavior can enable the officer to better understand the approaches of other professionals such as the nurse, psychologist, social worker, or psychiatrist. This will increase the possibility of good communication and reduce confusion and misunderstanding.

Before proceeding to a detailed presentation of the types of mental illness and the common abnormal behaviors the officer may encounter in the field, it will be useful to review the general classification system for mental disorders. Although the officer may come in contact with some of these disorders only rarely, this classification will help him to place mental disorders (abnormal behavior) he observes into a proper perspective.

Historical Background

Long before there was any knowledge or understanding of the causes or nature of mental disorders, there were attempts to observe and classify their signs and symptoms. Hippocrates, a philosopher living in Greece during the fourth century B.C., described four basic temperaments—the sanguine, the choleric, the melancholic, and the phlegmatic—which he believed were derived from an interaction between the four bodily humours—blood, black bile, yellow bile, and phlegm. In presenting case histories, Hippocrates described many symptoms associated today with such well-known disorders as mania, melancholia, and dementia.

Belief in the supernatural also played an important role in the early systems of classification. For example, today's term *obsessive-compulsive* personality has its roots in the medieval belief that people who behaved in strange ways were possessed or obsessed by the devil.

The more modern classification system used in this text, while deriving some features from the influences of the Roman and Greek periods as well as the Middle Ages, has its roots in the late eighteenth century.

Pinel, a French psychiatrist, who is more popularly known as the first to "free the mentally ill from chains," devised a simple system based on observations rather than causes. Like Hippocrates in the fourth century B.C., he described melancholia; mania, both with and without delirium; dementia; and other forms of abnormal behavior.

It remained, however, for Kraepelin, a German psychiatrist, to recognize that mental illness should be classified not only according to symptoms but also according to its causes and course. In his system, introduced in the late 1800s, all mental illness was determined to be either *functional*, without physical cause and therefore subject to cure, or *organic*, having a physical cause and therefore not subject to cure. This basic format has been preserved in the present method of classification, although it must be pointed out that Kraepelin was unduly pessimistic in assigning some abnormal behaviors to the organic or incurable category.

Modern Classification

The modern classification system used in the United States dates back to 1917, when the American Medical Psychological Association prepared a classification based on a statistical probability model. In 1928, the American Medical Association adopted a standard and uniform nomenclature for all forms of illness including mental disorders.

In 1952, the American Psychiatric Association extensively revised the classifications proposed in these earlier models and developed the first Diagnostic and Statistical Manual of Mental Disorders (DSM-I). The current system of classification described in the remainder of this chapter is known as DSM-II and was published by the American Psychiatric Association (1968).

This Diagnostic and Statistical Manual of Mental Disorders, which is the coding system generally used by all mental health professions, classifies mental disorders into eleven major categories.

1. Mental retardation
2. Organic brain syndrome
3. Psychosis not attributed to physical conditions listed previously
4. Neurosis
5. Personality disorders and certain other nonpsychotic mental disorders
6. Psychophysiological disorders
7. Special symptoms
8. Transient situational disturbances
9. Behavior disorders of childhood and adolescence
10. Conditions without manifest psychiatric disorder and nonspecific conditions
11. Nondiagnostic terms for administrative use

Several of these categories are particularly pervasive and therefore relevant to the law enforcement officer. The brief descriptions presented here will be followed by a more detailed presentation with relevant case materials and helpful hints to the law enforcement officer in the following chapters.

Personality (Character) Disorders

This category includes those individuals who begin to develop a maladaptive behavior pattern early in childhood as a result of family, social, and cultural influences. As they become adults, these patterns become a part of their life style and the ways in which they relate to the world around them.

Unlike the psychotic, the individual with a personality disorder does not have difficulty in maintaining contact with reality. Unlike the neurotic, he is not overly anxious except under severe stress. Rather, these individuals tend to act out their emotional conflicts through behaviors which society often rejects.

Neuroses

The neurotic also demonstrates behavior that is often maladaptive. However, he is distinguished from the individual with a personality disorder by the presence of anxiety, which may be easily observable or controlled through defense mechanisms that may or may not incapacitate their functioning. While neurotics do not manifest gross reality distortion or personality disorganization as do psychotics, their symptomatology may be as incapacitating.

Neuroses are classified according to the predominating symptom such as anxiety, depression, or phobia. The assessment of underlying conflicts and their working through are essential components of treatment.

Psychoses

Psychotics have a serious distortion of reality which interferes with their ability to function adequately. They may experience delusions (false beliefs not subject to the test of reality) and/or hallucinations (false sensory perceptions not subject to the test of reality). Disturbances in thinking may be easily noted by the casual observer in conversation. There may also be difficulty in demonstrating emotions which are appropriate to events that are occurring. The psychotic may also demonstrate marked regression by displaying behavior more characteristic of early childhood.

Unlike the neurotic, the psychotic may often not be aware that his mental functioning is disturbed and will resist any attempts to point this out.

Organic Brain Syndromes

Organic brain syndromes are disorders caused by or associated with impairment of brain function as a result of some assault to the brain. Organic brain syndromes may also be a form of psychosis, since many who have them will also exhibit loss of contact with reality. Other important symptoms include impairments of orientation, memory, intellectual functioning, and judgment.

Organic brain syndromes may be characterized as mild, moderate, or severe according to the degree of impairment. They may also be viewed as acute or chronic, indicating the potential reversibility of the condition.

Psychophysiological Disorders

Psychophysiological (psychosomatic) disorders are illnesses in which the physical illness is considered to be highly associated with emotional factors. They generally affect organ systems (such as the gastrointestinal system or the cardiovascular system) whose functioning is involuntary. The individual may not perceive that his emotional state is contributing to his physical symptoms.

Since these disorders will not be discussed elsewhere, a specific example will be cited now. The duodenal ulcer is an example of the interplay between emotional and physical factors. Physiologically, a duodenal ulcer is a hole in the lining of the first part of the intestinal tract occurring as a result of excessive secretion of acid into the area over an extended period of time.

However, it has also been shown that strong emotions, for example, fear and rage, can cause acid to be released in considerable amounts. While this is part of a normal physiological response to fear or rage, some people are constantly subjected to these strong emotions and are unable to express them. They are in a state of constant physical alertness and have no way to release these emotions. Consequently, the individual literally "stews within himself"; the acid keeps secreting and eventually eats a hole in the intestinal wall, thereby creating an ulcer.

This example gives a clear illustration of how an organic condition can occur because of emotional stimuli. To treat the ulcer medically or surgically without also treating the emotional condition would offer little hope of long-term success.

Other conditions which often fall into the category of psychophysiological disorders are high blood pressure, tension headaches, asthma, and certain skin ailments.

Transient Situational Disturbances

Transient periods of abnormal behavior may occur in normal individuals as a reaction to overwhelming environmental stress. If the individual can adapt well, the symptoms will diminish. However, if the symptoms continue after the stress is removed, another type of mental disorder is usually indicated.

These disorders are classified according to the age of the individual and include adjustment reaction of infancy, adjustment reaction of childhood, adjustment reaction of adolescence, and adjustment reaction of adulthood.

Summary

This classification has been presented as a frame of reference for the law enforcement officer as he prepares to study in depth those mental illnesses and abnormal behaviors that are particularly relevant to the tasks which he faces in the field. It is not sufficient merely to distinguish between normal and abnormal behavior since the range of abnormal behavior is great and the responses called for on the part of the law enforcement officer are equally varied. The development of more sophisticated tools for the assessment of mental illness and abnormal behaviors will assist the officer in carrying out his professional role successfully.

REFERENCES AND ADDITIONAL BIBLIOGRAPHY

American Psychiatric Association. 1968. *Diagnostic and Statistical Manual for Mental Disorders.* Washington, D.C.

Shah, S. A. 1969. "Crime and Mental Illness: Some Problems in Defining and Labeling Deviant Behavior." *Mental Hygiene* 53:21–33.

Chapter 7

Personality Disorders

PATTERNS of normal and abnormal behavior originate during early development. Personality disorders result from aberrations in this developmental process leading to a maladaptive pattern of behavior that becomes a significant portion of the life style and interferes with functioning.

The path from normal personality development to personality disorder is *not* analogous to a divided highway where a normal personality becomes a personality disorder as soon as the center divider is crossed. Rather, the path is more analogous to a two-lane highway divided by a dotted line where an individual with certain traits may use them to his advantage at times (i.e., stay in the proper lane), but may also use them to his disadvantage (i.e., cross over into the traffic moving in the opposite direction).

Personality disorders are contrasted with neuroses by the absence of clearly defined neurotic symptoms such as anxiety and depression and with psychoses by the absence of a thought disorder, delusional thinking, and/or hallucinatory experiences.

In this chapter, following a general discussion of some common characteristics of all personality disorders, more specific descriptions of those disorders which the law enforcement officer is most likely to encounter in the exercise of his duties will be presented.

General Characteristics of Personality Disorders

There are many significant periods in childhood development during which a failure to receive appropriate input from parents and others can lead the child to develop maladaptive behavior patterns. These are intended to defend him against the increased environmental stresses. However, once adopted, they are very difficult to give up, especially if he does not receive input that supports change but is instead rewarded for the behavior. For example, if Johnny gets what he wants by having a temper tantrum, he may repeat this behavior because it has been rewarding.

Other negative early experiences may include the unreasonable demands parents sometimes place on their children by failing to accept excuses when the child's behavior does not meet the parents' expectations. Faced with this situation, a child may adopt a behavior pattern in which he quickly mobilizes energy to meet each demand, not necessarily with the goal of being successful, but simply to avoid punishment if he fails.

In people with personality disorders, *lack of flexibility* is often encountered in response to situational events. While the normal personality is flexible and responds with appropriate patterns of behavior to different environmental events, the person with a personality disorder cannot significantly alter or change his pattern of behavior to events which require different responses.

Following a description of some principal personality disorders which the police officer may encounter, we will offer certain helpful hints in handling the behavior associated with personality disorders.

The Passive-Aggressive Personality Disorder

The passive-aggressive personality disorder is a major cause of failure in jobs, school, and interpersonal relationships. There are three types: (1) the passive-dependent; (2) the passive-aggressive; and (3) the aggressive. They are considered together because their occurrence is most often related to disturbances in personality development during the earliest and most dependent phase.

The individual with a passive-aggressive personality disorder is usually found to have been overindulged, perhaps inconsistently, during his early years to the extent that he comes to anticipate that his needs will always be met and gratified. Consequently, in adult life he may evolve into the passive-dependent type who consistently anticipates that all of his needs will be met by others. Alternatively, he may evolve into the passive-aggressive type who, while also anticipating that all of his needs will be met by others, reacts with frustration and extreme anger directed against others or himself when these needs are not met. Finally, the individual who may evolve into the aggressive type will also have the same magical anticipation that all needs will be met. However, rather than waiting passively for these needs to be met, he adopts a consistently aggressive behavior pattern through displays of anger designed to draw attention to himself at all times. Some examples will help to illustrate these differences.

CASE EXAMPLE 1: VICTOR WILLIS

Victor Willis is a forty-one-year-old male brought to the emergency room by the police after they had been called to the home of his ex-wife because, reportedly, he was threatening to hurt himself. In talking with his ex-wife, the police learned that this was unusual behavior for Victor and had begun only recently.

Victor and his wife had been divorced six months previously after she "got sick and tired of taking care of him." Nevertheless, even after the divorce, she had allowed him to visit her home as often as he liked. Within the past month, Victor had been at the house daily for at least several hours.

During these frequent visits, Victor had begun to plead with his wife that they remarry. In recounting the events of the last month, Victor's wife admitted that she might have given him false hope since she was concerned that, if his wish was not granted, he might do something drastic.

Three days prior to the incident, she had even allowed him to move back into her home "to see how things would work out." However, she quickly recognized that he was the same old Victor, expecting everything to be done for him and unwilling to assume any responsibilities.

Three days later, she changed her mind and asked him to move out. At first, he left meekly, but later that evening he returned, banged on the door, and said that if she did not let him in, he would kill himself.

At that point, Mrs. Willis decided to get some help before something drastic occurred and called the police. She let Victor in the house and waited for their arrival.

CASE EXAMPLE 2: GREGORY MARTINEZ

Gregory Martinez, who is twenty years old, came to the police's attention one evening when his mother called the emergency number. She said that her son was lying on the bathroom floor and that his arm was bloody. Upon their arrival, the police administered emergency first aid and took Gregory to the hospital, accompanied by his mother.

While the doctor was treating the cut Gregory had inflicted on his arm, the officer obtained the following information. Gregory had just graduated from a vocational rehabilitation program after taking courses in automobile body work. He had entered the program after his parole. He had served one year for felonious assault on a boyfriend of a girl whom he had been dating. His mother said that he had been very upset recently because, even with his diploma, he couldn't find work. In the days prior to cutting himself, Gregory had been complaining bitterly of the prejudice he felt from others because of his past prison record and his Mexican-American heritage. In reality, however, it was a period of high unemployment in the community and jobs were scarce all over.

Gregory had been a spoiled only child and had never demonstrated any motivation to help himself until recently. Even his entrance into the rehabilitation program had occurred only after he had been cajoled by his parents, girlfriend, and other friends. Gregory's mother said, "He always seems to want everything to happen for him and when he doesn't get his way, he strikes out." When asked to explain further, she recalled how, as a teenager, he had many problems in school with both classmates and teachers because he would not accept direction when it was offered. His teachers had told his mother that he couldn't handle criticism, no matter how small, and that his typical response was to become more disruptive.

CASE EXAMPLE 3: ALLEN O'BRIEN

Allen O'Brien came to the attention of the police when they were called to the airport to calm a small disturbance in progress. On their arrival at a ticket counter, they found an enraged and screaming Allen and a somewhat frightened clerk who was, perhaps fortunately, separated from Allen by the ticket counter.

Investigation revealed that Allen had arrived at the airport with ticket in hand ready to board a flight to another city. However, he learned that the flight had been overbooked and that he, like ten other people, could not be guaranteed a seat until it was known how many passengers were going to appear. Unlike the others, Allen was not content to wait. Instead, he began an extremely loud, angry, and threatening tirade directed at the ticket agent. Furthermore, he refused to stop despite pleading from those around him and airline representatives.

When Allen saw the police, he switched the focus of his attention-demanding behavior to them, demanding that they put him on the plane because he had a guaranteed seat. When the police firmly told him that they could not do this and that, furthermore, Allen was not boarding any plane that day but instead was coming with them, he lost all control. He lunged at one officer but was quickly restrained by the other.

At the station, after being booked on charges of disturbing the peace, Allen calmed down somewhat and called his wife, who came to the station to post bond. She was not surprised that this had happened and told the officers that Allen had been arrested five times in the past four years after similar incidents. She said that this puzzled her since Allen was an excellent father and provider. She remarked, "He seems to have this one weakness which always gets him into trouble." She described how this weakness had already cost Allen three jobs in the past five years. In fact, he was at the airport that day because he was flying to another city for a job interview.

These examples of the three types of passive-aggressive personality disorders—passive-dependent (case example 1); passive-aggressive (case example 2); and aggressive (case example 3)—illustrate how an individual with a passive-aggressive personality disorder is unable to adapt to situations in which his needs are not instantly met and how he deals ineffectively with frustration.

The Hysterical Personality Disorder

People with hysterical personality disorders are easily excitable and possess an emotional instability characterized by a capacity to overreact to many situations in a dramatic (or histrionic) manner. This dramatic behavior is always attention seeking and usually seductive, which may account for its prevalence among females. Furthermore, these females are generally self-centered, immature, and have a tendency to sexualize all contacts with men.

Police often encounter them as victims of sexual attack, particularly in situations where it is not clear whether the victim was wholly "innocent." In presenting their stories of the attack, they are likely to embellish, in a very dramatic fashion, the details of the event, missing nothing in describing it to the investigating officer.

Paradoxically, despite sexualizing most relationships with men, they are virtually incapable of forming mature heterosexual relationships and generally have a history of frequent divorces and promiscuous behavior. They may also have many physical complaints which are utilized to gain attention. An example will illustrate some of these common characteristics.

CASE EXAMPLE 1: HILDA DAVIS

Hilda Davis is a twenty-two-year-old and has been divorced twice. She was brought to the emergency room after she had reportedly fainted on a local street corner. She told the doctor that, since arriving in the community one month ago, she had been living in a rooming house. She had been unable to look for work because of persistent headaches. They had apparently begun several months before, when the events which led to her departure from home had occurred.

She had been living with her sister and her husband and children in a small trailer following her most recent divorce. She remembered feeling nervous almost as soon as she had moved into their house and the headaches had begun shortly thereafter.

On further questioning, Hilda revealed that she had had an affair with her brother-in-law several years ago. Although not seeing any connection between this event and the feelings of nervousness which she had in their home, Hilda did reveal, perhaps inadvertently, that the headaches were worse at night when she was alone with her sister and her brother-in-law was working and they got better during the day when he was there and her sister was working.

Hilda was given some tranquilizers and asked to return to the clinic the next day. When she appeared, the doctor immediately noticed a remarkable change in her appearance. Instead of the disheveled young woman he had seen the night before, Hilda was now seductively dressed with somewhat overdone make-up. When invited into his office, she immediately said, "I'm so glad to be here. That medicine you gave me last night made me feel so much better."

Although it may appear that the primary interest of the hysterical personality is to have a sexually based heterosexual relationship, this is not the case. The inability to attain this type of relationship suggests that such individuals are really seeking a more basic type of love, namely, attention. When this attention has not been received during childhood, they learn to get it by dramatizing behavior or feelings. If this is not successful, they may seek other routes, such as feigning illness.

The Paranoid Personality Disorder

Hypersensitivity, rigidity, unwarranted suspicion, jealousy, envy, and feelings of excessive self-importance coupled with a tendency to blame others for any failure which they encounter characterize the paranoid personality. Projection is often used as a defense mechanism leading to an attitudinal set in which the entire world is seen through a very personal set of references. Any frustrations which are encountered are used to further justify their suspicious view of the world.

Furthermore, this is often accompanied by an exaggerated sense of importance in which the individual sees himself as the focal point of all activities surrounding him, whether or not they concern him. An example will help illustrate this.

CASE EXAMPLE 1: MARY RUTHERFORD

Mary Rutherford is twenty-six years old and single. She is employed as a secretary and is the leastliked woman in the office. She is impossible to get along with because of her constant jibes at others for "picking on her," giving her too much work, and "not treating her properly." However, this is puzzling because she appears intelligent and ambitious.

The woman who used to share a corner of the office with her remembers one encounter that she had with Mary which illustrates why she is not well liked.

One day, when this fellow worker was called into the office of one of the men for whom they worked, Mary and she had been proofreading a manuscript. When she got up to go into the office, she said, "Be back in a minute." Unfortunately, her return was delayed because the man had a lengthy task to explain.

When she finally returned to her desk, Mary was enraged, sarcastic, and jealous. Without provocation, Mary immediately lunged into a tirade accusing her of trying to seduce the boss. Attempts to quiet Mary down were unsuccessful and both the conversation and the accusations ended only when she excused herself, went to the powder room, and remained away from Mary the rest of the day.

Paranoid personalities usually grow up in a home filled with parental conflict. One parent is usually domineering and the other submissive. Not only is the child unable to deal with the domineering parent, but he or she does not receive help from the submissive parent.

As one way of handling this devastating situation, the child adopts a behavior pattern in which he or she reacts defensively to almost any situation in which a threat is felt from the domineering parent. The child becomes constantly vigilant to individuals and situations, realistic or not, which he fears. Feelings of rejection are exaggerated and become further justification for this vigilant attitude.

The Compulsive Personality Disorder

Excessive concern with conformity, adherence to strong standards of conscience, an inability to relax and to tolerate ambiguity, and a characteristic rigidity which makes it impossible for them to change their minds after having arrived at decisions characterize the compulsive personality. He or she is often encountered at work as someone who initially draws the positive attention of superiors because of an ability to organize thinking and to conduct affairs in an orderly fashion. However, these positive traits quickly become obscured by behavior which tends to be their undoing. An example will help illustrate this disorder.

CASE EXAMPLE 1: MIKE MORRIS

After several years as a patrolman, Mike Morris was promoted to sergeant. While complimented in the past for his attention to detail, his excellent reports, and his seemingly appropriate attention to rules and regulations, he was a total failure as a supervisor.

Those who had been his peers and were now his subordinates quickly found it impossible to work for Mike. With his new responsibility for enforcing rules and regulations rather than following them, he made life miserable for his men. His attention to detail, while admirable as a patrolman, interfered with the ability of his men to perform their work. His demands for more and more reports and his tirades when his subordinates did not "go by the book" were unacceptable.

While his excessive attention to orderliness was ignored by his peers when he was at their level and was complimented by his superiors, it now became obstructionistic and antagonistic. Initially, his men tried to please him, but soon found that they could not succeed. Finally, they gave up and began to devise ways of getting around him and "knocking" him behind his back. The situation deteriorated and finally the men felt forced to go to Mike's superior and ask for his removal or their transfer.

Mike's compulsive personality disorder nipped a promising career in the bud. However, he never came to psychiatric attention, nor do most compulsive personality disorders. Rather they often function effectively, provided they are placed in a suitable environment.

This need to maintain rigidity is an outgrowth of early developmental problems involving parental controls. Faced with the necessity of complying with them and overly threatened with the danger of loss of love if he does not, the child will either be overly compliant and compulsive or become rebellious. The latter alternative is often given up quickly because of the parents' demands and the child's need for love. The child learns quickly that parental approval and love comes if he is compliant. By paying scrupulous attention to detail, he avoids the dangerous feelings of fear and anger that would otherwise be directed at the parent for enforcing this standard of behavior. In attempting to gain control of his anger, he pays the price of giving up opportunities to express these emotions. If he encounters a stressful situation in which these emotions are overwhelming, the compulsive behavior pattern can break down and a psychotic reaction with severe depression can occur. Even in this decompensation, he may continue to pay attention to detail, as exemplified by Lady Macbeth who, while psychotic, focused on a spot of blood, causing her repeatedly to state, "Out, damned spot!"

Helpful Hints to the Law Enforcement Officer

The interpersonal relationships of those with personality disorders present a unique problem for the law enforcement officer. It is not uncommon for a police officer who is called into a situation involving an individual with a personality disorder to find behavior out of control and violence threatening. The officer should remember that this individual has adopted this maladaptive behavior pattern to protect himself from life's stresses. When this pattern is threatened, he may become potentially dangerous and apt to act impulsively in a desperate attempt to protect himself.

In handling these situations, law enforcement officers should work in teams. The team approach enables officers to assess the situation quickly and to divide up those responsibilities which will help to bring the situation under control rapidly. When one individual is in tense conflict with another person, the officer should remember that it will not be enough to direct all attention toward the individual with the personality disorder even if it is obvious which one he is. Since he is reacting to a stress from another individual, he will be reassured if the officers also direct their attention to the other person.

It is important to remember that since those people with personality disorders may do poorly under an acute stress, they will respond positively to any activity that helps remove that stress. This does not mean that the officer should give in to any magical expectations. Rather, he can remove the stress by indicating to the person involved in forceful, clear, and tactful terms that there is no way that his wish can be granted. This direct confrontation with reality, in clear and nonargumentative terms, can have a calming influence because it helps the person to reestablish contact with a reality which has temporarily been lost as emotions have gained control.

Summary

In this chapter, we have described those personality disorders that police officers encounter most often in their work. The passive-aggressive personality disorder, the hysterical personality disorder, the paranoid personality disorder, and the compulsive personality disorder may be encountered in a variety of situations. Appropriate police action can be taken if the officer is aware of their characteristics and modes of behavior.

Although the clinical examples utilized in this chapter tend to focus on noncriminal aspects of law enforcement, individuals with personality disorders can readily be found involved in the criminal aspects as well. This will be seen more clearly when we take up the subjects of psychopathic behavior, deviant sexual behavior, delinquent behavior, and drug abuse.

REFERENCES AND ADDITIONAL BIBLIOGRAPHY

Berne, E. 1964. *Games People Play*. New York: Grove Press.

Cameron, N. 1963. *Personality Development and Psychopathology*. Boston: Houghton Mifflin.

Redlich, F. C. and Freedman, D. X. 1966. *The Theory and Practice of Psychiatry*. New York: Basic Books.

Sokol, R. and Reiser, M. 1971. "Training Police Sergeants in Early Warning Signs of Emotional Upset." *Mental Hygiene* 55:303–307.

Chapter 8

The Neuroses

HAVING REVIEWED the major personality disorders, we will now focus our attention on the next major category of emotional disturbance—the neuroses. Whereas abnormal behavior in personality disorders is characterized by maladaptive behavior patterns which have become a life style, neurotics constitute a group whose abnormal behavior is usually characterized by the presence of anxiety in one form or another. The neurotic, unlike the psychotic, is not divorced from reality. He lives in the same world as we do. Instead of "acting out" his conflicts, as those with personality disorders do, the neurotic "suffers out" his conflicts by developing symptoms.

Before discussing the specific symptoms of each of the major neuroses, it will be helpful to understand some of their general characteristics.

General Considerations

The most important element in the development of symptoms is the presence of an impulse, generally coming from the id, which is likely to create anxiety if allowed into consciousness. If it becomes conscious, symptoms may also occur if it is not dealt with appropriately. Defense mechanisms are used to ward off anxiety, but symptoms may occur if the defenses do not work effectively or if the defenses work so well that the behavior resulting from them impairs functioning.

This is a simplified description of the process of symptom formation and does not do justice to its complexity. Part of the complexity is a result of childhood experiences. Consequently, a specific impulse that creates anxiety in one person may be warded off by another. Similarly, the way in which one person wards off anxiety may be different than another person's method.

An illustration will help clarify this point. Suppose that the unacceptable impulses coming into consciousness are sexual. It may be handled by one woman through sublimation by choosing a job, such as modeling, which helps her successfully channel her unacceptable sexual impulses. Another woman may use projection and channel unacceptable sexual impulses into a belief that others are looking at her on the street and thinking about picking her up. Why one chooses sublimation and the other projection to handle the same unacceptable sexual impulse may be a reflection of early development factors, including those defense mechanisms which the child used to handle the positive or negative reactions from parents.

Both women could develop neurotic symptoms if their defenses come under attack. Suppose that the first loses her modeling job or the second is one day picked up on the street. Both events could generate great anxiety, just as emergence of the original impulse would.

While neurotic symptoms may be disturbing, they also can serve a positive purpose. Freud called these advantages *secondary gain,* referring to the benefits obtained from being sick when others may pay more attention and do things that they would not ordinarily do for you if you were well. Although secondary gain may not play a major role in the onset of neuroses, it may support its continuation. If it is great, there is less motivation to give up the neurotic symptoms. The pursuit of secondary gain is not conscious. When it is, it is called *malingering.* Sometimes it is difficult for the professional to distinguish between conscious malingering and unconscious secondary gain.

Classification of the Neuroses

According to DSM-II, neuroses are classified according to the predominant symptom. If it is general anxiety, it is an anxiety neurosis. If the predominant symptoms are depression, obsessional thinking and compulsive behavior, conversion symptoms, phobic symptoms, or disassociative symptoms, the syndromes are termed depressive neurosis, obsessive-compulsive neurosis, conversion neurosis, phobic neurosis, or disassociative neurosis, respectively.

Although this classification is useful in identifying the subgroups, in reality the behaviors are less clearly differentiated than what is suggested by the classification system. This will become clearer as examples of each of these neurotic syndromes are given.

Anxiety Neurosis

An anxiety neurosis (also referred to as an anxiety reaction) is defined in DSM-II (see pp. 5–13) as a neurosis in which the anxiety is diffuse and not restricted to definite situations or objects. It is not controlled by any psychological defense mechanism as in other psychoneurotic reactions. It is characterized by anxious expectation and is frequently associated with physical complaints, but should be differentiated from normal apprehensiveness or fear (DSM-II, p. 39).

Historical Background

Anxiety neurosis has been used by many psychiatrists and psychologists in their attempts to explain the dynamics of personality development, abnormal behavior, and emotional disturbance.

In his early theory, Freud viewed anxiety as resulting from an inability to discharge physical tension. In his later theory, however, he adopted a more psychological orientation and made an important contribution to our understanding by recognizing the protective function of anxiety. In his concept of *signal anxiety*, he described a state in which the individual first perceives danger and then uses signal anxiety to mobilize defense reactions to avoid the danger. If these attempts to avoid danger are not wholly successful, anxiety may increase and become a diffuse state which affects all behavior, thereby contributing to the development of an anxiety neurosis.

Sullivan, a later theoretician, stressed the early mother-child relationship in the origin of anxiety neurosis. In his formulation, he proposed that the original model for adult anxiety could be found in the child's fear of mother's disapproval. This early anxiety is related to the child's knowledge that maternal approval is essential to his own comfort. It can also serve as an *alerting mechanism* to the child in situations where maternal disapproval might be forthcoming.

Characteristics

The individual with an anxiety neurosis usually has a history of chronic anxiety, not necessarily related to any specific situation. This anxiety can become more acute in some situations, but there is usually not any particular pattern observable by the casual observer. Physical complaints can be wide ranging and involve almost every organ system of the body. Headaches, nausea and vomiting, shortness of breath, palpitations, menstrual dysfunction, and insomnia are often associated with anxiety neurosis. In addition to these specific physical complaints, general uneasiness may be present, characterized by statements such as "I feel uptight," "I can't sleep," "I don't like to be by myself," or "I'm always worried." The following example will help illustrate the characteristics of the anxiety neurosis.

CASE EXAMPLE 1: HAZEL NEWTON

Hazel Newton is a twenty-one-year-old college senior who was brought to the hospital after the police were called to the campus. Her roommates had found her apparently unconscious with a half empty pill bottle by her bed. After receiving medical attention, she told the following story to the psychiatrist who interviewed her.

Although she had never gone for help, she recognized that she had not been her normal self for at least two years. During the summer between her freshman and sophomore years, she had broken up with the fellow she had been dating since her sophomore year in high school. He was the only man she had ever dated.

Since then, she said, "I have been uptight all the time." Upon further questioning, she told the doctor that she had had insomnia for two years. She had made many visits to physicians because of vague physical complaints. She had many tests to find the cause of these symptoms but without success.

Furthermore, her grades, which had been excellent during her first year of college, had gone steadily downhill. When asked about the suicide attempt she revealed that, several days previously, she had been called into the Dean of Women's office and told that, if she did not pull her grades up, she would not be able to graduate.

Hazel stated also that she no longer felt comfortable with men and that no man she had dated in the past two years had asked her out a second time. She commented, "I just can't seem to relax on dates."

Underlying Factors

Hazel's anxiety is consistent with the definition of an anxiety neurosis, since it is "diffuse and not restricted to definite situations or objects." Her case also illustrates another common characteristic, namely, the inability to link the onset of the neurotic behavior with any single precipitating factor. In Hazel's case, the breakup with her boyfriend two years previously and the prospect of failure and rejection conveyed to her by the Dean several days before her suicide attempt were critical factors in the original onset and recent worsening of her anxiety neurosis.

As previously suggested, events in early childhood serve as the focus for the development of an anxiety neurosis. In Hazel's case, her mother's long absences from home because of work and illness may have been an important underlying factor. Prior to breaking up with her boyfriend two years ago, Hazel had been able to cope with her fears of abandonment and rejection through a close and clinging relationship. However, after they split, she could no longer handle her fears of abandonment and the pattern of anxiety grew and grew, finally snapping like an overextended rubber band with the suicide attempt.

Depressive Neurosis

Depressive neurosis is a neurotic condition in which depression is the predominant symptom. It is differentiated from a psychotic depressive reaction (Chapter 9) in that the person with a depressive neurosis does not experience either the distortion of reality or the behavioral disorganization noted in the psychotic depression.

Historical Background

Theoreticians during the past seventy years have paid much attention to the differences between the various types of depression, specifically those seen in a neurotic and those in a psychotic. These differences have become more critical since the advent of medication because it appears to have a varying effect on different types of depression.

Characteristics

The primary complaint is a disturbance of mood. This may be reflected through a variety of descriptive phrases such as sad, blue, miserable, and depressed. In association with this alteration of mood, the individual may display other symptomatology, such as a general loss of interest in his environment, including his home, his family, his work, or his schooling; a tendency to be more self-critical without apparent reason or justification; and an increase in physical symptoms such as a sleep disturbance, loss of appetite, and a marked change in weight.

Similar to the anxiety of an anxiety neurosis, this depression is pervasive. While the depressive neurosis is in full force, the depressed mood is related to all life events. Unlike the anxiety neurosis, however, the individual can generally pinpoint a specific precipitating event following which the depressive neurosis began. Another clinical example will illustrate this syndrome.

CASE EXAMPLE 1: MARTIN DINE

Martin Dine is a twenty-six-year-old police officer who had recently been divorced. He took twenty-five Nembutal after drinking beer for several hours. He phoned the police just prior to passing out and they took him to the emergency room. After receiving medical attention, he was interviewed.

He had been depressed for some time after his wife told him that she was involved with another man, did not love him anymore, and wanted a divorce. When she was interviewed later, she said that Martin seemed to take the news very well initially, saying that he

95

recognized their marriage was on the rocks and that perhaps a divorce was for the best.

However, shortly after the divorce became final and six weeks prior to his suicide attempt, he became very depressed. His fellow officers noticed that he was paying less attention to work and occasionally taking unnecessary risks. Furthermore, he was obviously losing weight since he was not eating when his team took a dinner break.

On the day prior to his suicide attempt, he was called into the sergeant's office and told that his poor work was noticeable and that, if it did not improve, he would have to be put on leave and possibly be subject to a disciplinary hearing. Later on that same day, his former wife called him to say that she could not care adequately for their two children on the alimony payments he was making. Feeling more depressed and seeing his situation as hopeless, Martin decided to take the easy way out and tried to kill himself.

Underlying Factors

Those with a depressive neurosis, like those with an anxiety neurosis, have usually encountered difficulties in early childhood which contribute to a personality foundation highly susceptible to the development of a neurosis when an appropriate precipitating event occurs.

These early factors may include a poor self-image which develops either as a result of a lack of positive parental reinforcement or the presence of overcritical parents. People with depressive neuroses usually have very strict superegos developed as a result of an identification with the overcritical parent and thus become overcritical of themselves.

When faced with failure, as Martin was when his marriage ended and his job was threatened, they perceive these events as a natural consequence of their own inabilities, a point of view consistent with their underlying poor self-image.

Prior to the event which produces the stress that precipitates the neurosis, they often attempt to compensate for their poor self-image by being extremely organized or entering a profession with a good image. Consequently, when they encounter significant failures, they also experience guilt because they have been unable to live up to not only their own expectations, but also those of their parents and their profession.

In a depressive neurosis, one of the principal underlying factors is an inability to handle feelings of anger appropriately. The unexpressed hostility which Martin felt toward his wife at the time she told him about her extramarital affair and requested a divorce was an important contributing factor to the onset of his depressive neurosis. In treatment, Martin learned that one of the reasons he was unable to express this hostility was because of the nonacceptance of hostility in his early childhood surroundings. He was forced to hold back these feelings unless he was willing to run the risk of further criticism and rejection from his parents.

Obsessive-Compulsive Neurosis

The obsessive-compulsive neurotic is characterized by ideas or thoughts which are repetitive in nature (obsessions) and by actions which are repeated for unexplained reasons in a patterned form of behavior (compulsions). When these obsessions and compulsions have progressed to the point both quantitatively and qualitatively where they are significantly interfering with all functioning, an obsessive-compulsive neurosis exists. This gross impairment of functioning distinguishes the obsessive-compulsive neurosis from the compulsive personality disorder described in Chapter 7.

Historical Background

Observations of obsessional thinking patterns and compulsive acts date back to medieval times when these individuals were often viewed as being under the devil's influence. Consequently, many early theories about the origins of obsessive-compulsive neurosis dealt with spiritual forces or witchcraft.

By the nineteenth century, however, theorists began to view obsessive-compulsive neurosis differently. Pierre Janet was the first to assume a more modern view of this emotional disturbance, describing a biological base in which the central disturbance was the result of a lessening of mental energy.

However, it was Freud who, because of his recognition of the importance of the unconscious and conflict, devised the modern theory. He viewed obsessive-compulsive symptoms as related to three defense mechanisms—isolation, undoing, and reaction formation.

He saw obsessive thinking as an attempt to remove any associated feelings from consciousness. Only after these feelings were successfully isolated could the individual allow the previously unconscious and dangerous thought into consciousness.

However, there is also a price to pay for this, since the amount of energy required to keep the emotional component *isolated* often involves the entire personality in the process. In the preneurotic state, this defense mechanism of isolation is beginning to break down and the emotional component of the thought or impulse is constantly threatening to break through into consciousness and escape the controls placed upon it.

Other defenses must then be employed to counter this threat. The defense mechanism of *undoing* is a behavioral attempt to handle the obsessional thought which makes him anxious. This leads to the compulsive act. For example, a mother's compulsion to check the baby's room three times before going to bed might be her way of unconsciously undoing a death wish which she has toward the baby.

Reaction formation is used as a third defense as the individual tries to handle unwanted thoughts and emotions by channeling them into a pattern of behavior that is the opposite of the behavior associated with the underlying impulse. For example, the overprotective mother may really be a rejecting mother who deals with this unacceptable impulse by becoming involved in the organization of community child-care centers.

These formulations will be clearer as we talk about the characteristics of the obsessive-compulsive neurosis and present an example.

Characteristics

As described previously, the hallmarks of the obsessive-compulsive neurosis are the presence of obsessional thinking accompanied by a pattern of compulsive and ritualistic behavior. Kleptomania (compulsive stealing) and pyromania (compulsive fire setting) are variants of the compulsive neurosis occasionally encountered by the police officer. These behaviors protect against the release of even more dangerous impulses that are usually aggressive.

This aggressive content may not be recognized or accepted by the neurotic because it is too threatening, but it is usually clearly seen by a trained observer. Likewise, the neurotic who is experiencing the compulsive behavior pattern designed to ward off the obsessional thoughts is not able to make the connection between the acts and the thought pattern. The following case will illustrate this.

CASE EXAMPLE 1: MICHAEL MONROE

Michael Monroe was eighteen years old when he was admitted to the hospital's psychiatric unit because he felt he was going crazy. He told the interviewing psychiatrist that, for the past three months, he had been constantly preoccupied with thoughts about cleanliness and, more recently, had been spending great amounts of time washing himself and his clothes. His mother confirmed his story and also said that she had noticed other changes in his behavior, including an increase in his nail biting, a willingness to only eat certain foods, and a peculiar pattern of leaving notes all over the house to avoid talking with family members.

Several days prior to admission, a new behavior pattern emerged in which Michael, whenever he left the house, would walk out the door three steps and back up four steps into the house. This would be repeated four or five times before he could leave the house.

When questioned, Michael was unable to present any reason for this behavior. He could only state that his behavior had completely interfered with his school work and was seriously threatening his expected graduation from high school in June.

Underlying Factors

In Freudian theory, obsessive-compulsive neurosis has its origins in early childhood, particularly during the period of toilet training. In this theory, there is a marked degree of ambivalence and uncertainty during this phase of development. This early ambivalence, a type of not knowing what to do accompanied by a frequent changing of one's mind, can evolve into a ritualistic pattern of compulsive behavior when stresses are great enough. This ambivalence is exemplified by Michael's inability to make up his mind whether or not to leave the house. He must go through a compulsive behavior pattern before he can give himself permission to go.

Exploration of the neurotic conflicts underlying the obsessive-compulsive neurosis often reveals an inability to deal with rage, leading to the ambivalence and the obsessive-compulsive neurosis.

When obsessive-compulsive patterns begin to fail, regression may become the last defense available as an escape from the ambivalent bind. This regression is illustrated by the observations of Michael's psychiatrist. Although Michael reported being obsessed with cleanliness, he appeared as a dirty, sloppily dressed young man who had not paid attention to his personal hygiene for at least several days.

Michael's mother revealed that, just prior to the onset of this obsessive-compulsive pattern, his father had been seriously injured in an auto accident. Later, in treatment, the therapist was able to identify that this precipitating event had been a magical carrying out of Michael's previous unconscious hostility to his father. The accident had served as the trigger which brought many of these formerly successfully repressed hostile impulses to the surface. The obsessive-compulsive neurosis represented Michael's frantic attempt to prevent these hostile, aggressive impulses and thoughts from breaking through to the surface.

Phobic Neurosis

The phobic neurosis can be distinguished from the preceding three neuroses because its symptomatology is usually limited to a specific situation commonly referred to as either the *phobic object* or the *phobic situation.*

The earlier observation that neuroses are often more easily separated from one another in theory than in practice is exemplified by phobic neurosis, since it often coexists with other neurotic symptoms such as anxiety and depression.

Historical Background

The term *phobia* did not appear in the literature until the nineteenth century. In 1872 Westphal, a German theoretician, reported on three male patients who had specific fears of open places, a condition which he labeled *agoraphobia.* Today, we recognize a variety of phobias which are generally named after the particular fear the individual has. Other examples include *claustrophobia,* a fear of closed in places, and *acrophobia,* a fear of high places.

Characteristics

A phobia must be distinguished from a normal fear. In fact, phobia has often been referred to as a *morbid* fear of a particular object or situation. This adjective is designed not only to distinguish it from a normal fear but also to call attention to the fact that a phobia generally refers to a fear of something which normal persons do not perceive as any great threat or danger.

However, this distinction is not always entirely clear since some phobic objects or situations may create normal fear. When this occurs, we have to look at the quantitative nature of the individual's reaction to the object or situation and make a judgment as to whether a phobia is present by the degree of fear.

When anxiety about a specific object or situation cannot be handled appropriately, it is *displaced* in a phobic neurosis onto a previously neutral object or situation which then becomes the phobic object or situation. Phobias are always accompanied by anxiety when the individual is in the presence of the phobic object or situation. However, this anxiety is secondary and is not the original anxiety.

In the phobic neurosis, displacement is used as a defense, with the unacceptable feeling or thought being *unconsciously* transferred from its source to a less threatening substitute. Through displacement, the neurotic combats the original anxiety and, if he avoids the phobic object or situation, can function effectively.

Occasionally, however, the phobic neurosis becomes more severe because the anxiety generated becomes so great that the individual becomes phobic for almost every object or situation, or one or more of the phobic objects or situations becomes so important to the individual's life style that it cannot be avoided. The following example illustrates this.

CASE EXAMPLE 1: JUDITH ROSENBERG

Judith Rosenberg is a forty-three-year-old female who was accompanying her husband when he had an auto accident. Mr. Rosenberg told the investigating officer that his wife made him so nervous when he drove that she really caused the accident. In response to the officer's questions, he said that his wife was much less nervous if she drove the car. The officer suggested that Mrs. Rosenberg might seek some professional help about her nervousness. She did not do so at first but when her anxiety became so great that it was almost impossible for them to go anywhere unless she drove, she agreed to go.

The psychiatrist learned that Mrs. Rosenberg's aged mother (Mrs. Schwartz) had died six months ago after a twelve-year illness. During the terminal phase of her illness, Mrs. Schwartz had been in a nursing home. Prior to that, she had lived with the Rosenbergs for close to twelve years, during which time Mrs. Rosenberg had the principal responsibility for caring for her mother.

Underlying Factors

Those who are prone to phobic neuroses as adults have a history of observed anxiety, even as a child, in association with certain impulses. The common impulses with which early anxiety is associated are sexual and aggressive. In normal personality development, the individual develops appropriate defense mechanisms which channel these unacceptable impulses.

Mrs. Rosenberg, prior to devoting all of her energy to her invalid mother, had spent much time doing volunteer work for the sick. Consequently, it was natural for her to assume the responsibility of caring for her ill mother. At the outset, before her mother moved into her home, the physician had told Mrs. Rosenberg that he anticipated that Mrs. Schwartz had only a year to live. However, Mrs. Schwartz lived for twelve years with Mrs. Rosenberg devotedly caring for her every day.

Through this attention, Mrs. Rosenberg could continue to channel through sublimation and reaction formation many of her unacceptable aggressive impulses. She had begun this pattern with her volunteer work and continued it through her care for her mother. Only when her mother became so ill that she was unmanageable at home was she moved to a nursing home. This was done several weeks before her death against Mrs. Rosenberg's wishes, but at her husband's insistence. In treatment, it became clear that the onset of Mrs. Rosenberg's phobic neurosis was directly related to her failure to develop adequate mechanisms for handling her unacceptable aggressive impulse. When her mother died, her mechanism for sublimating this aggressive impulse was lost.

Her choice of the car as the phobic object was related to the corollary phobia of an accident. This latter phobia represented both a displacement and projection of her hostile impulses. She could feel more comfortable if she was in control of these impulses by driving the car, but was more anxious when she was not in control with her husband driving.

Conversion Neurosis

In the conversion neurosis, also referred to as hysterical neurosis or conversion hysteria, the unacceptable impulse which threatens the individual with overwhelming anxiety is converted into a physical symptom associated with parts of the body which are under voluntary control. These symptoms lessen anxiety and are often symbolic of the underlying conflict.

The conversion neurosis is both similar to and different from the phobic neurosis. The similarity is in the use of the defense of displacement and the difference is in the displacement to a part of the body rather than to an outside object or situation.

The conversion neurosis is also differentiated from the psychophysiological disorder (Chapter 6). In the latter, the physical complaints are generally related to parts of the body which are *not* under voluntary control.

Historical Background

Similar to obsessive-compulsive neuroses, the unusual symptoms of conversion neuroses contributed to an intense mythology during the Middle Ages, the seventeenth, eighteenth, and early part of the nineteenth centuries. Only in the latter part of the nineteenth and the early part of the twentieth century was a psychological basis for these symptoms recognized and their causative mechanisms worked out by Freud and his predecessors, Charcot and Bernheim.

In Freud's theory, the emotions associated with a specific psychological trauma cannot be expressed directly because they would lead to unacceptable impulses and behaviors. Consequently, these feelings and impulses are displaced and converted into physical symptoms. Furthermore, they are so well blocked that the individual displays a characteristic indifference about his physical symptoms. If he is hysterically blind, for example, he will not display the emotional concern most of us would.

Characteristics

The physical symptoms associated with conversion neuroses are either motor or sensory. Motor disturbances usually take two forms— impaired movement and paralysis. In both cases, complete neurological examination will not reveal any organic basis for the symptoms. Furthermore, the symptoms are often inconsistent with known anatomical pathways. In sensory disturbances, the areas affected will also not be consistent with known anatomical pathways (for example, in *stocking anesthesia* the patient's insensitivity will cover the same area of the leg that a stocking would, an anatomical impossibility).

CASE EXAMPLE 1: OFFICER KANNER

Officer Clarence Kanner had been transferred to Vice from SWAT (Special Weapons and Tactics) about six months prior to his admission to a hospital with the complaint of blinding headaches and his fear that he might have a brain tumor. Thorough medical and neurological examinations were negative. A consulting psychiatrist was called in and he established the following sequence for the development of the symptoms.

Officer Kanner had led a rather protected life as a youth and had dated only one woman since high school. Shortly after graduation, they were married. After several short-term jobs which did not interest him, he joined the police department. After he had been in patrol for about four years, he was transferred to SWAT, an assignment he enjoyed and was good at.

About six months prior to his hospitalization, he was transferred to Vice. Here he was thrown into association with many young women who, despite their lack of an acceptable moral code, were physically attractive to him. It was evident that a number of them found him attractive also.

When he came home from work to his wife and family (he had two small children), the boredom and problems of family living were in sharp contrast to the night life environment of his job. Furthermore, his wife had become careless in her appearance and a little heavy. His own strict moral code and sense of responsibility as husband and father were in conflict with the role he had to play on the job, a role which he did not exactly hate. Unable to resolve this emotional conflict, he developed a blinding headache, sometimes on the job (perhaps when temptation was becoming too great for his unconscious desires) and sometimes at home (when family pressures built up). He began to suspect that he had a brain tumor and this aggravated his symptoms. His emotional conflicts were thus converted into physical symptoms that had no real organic basis.

Underlying Factors

In contrast to other neuroses which have their origins in conflicts surrounding very early stages of development, the roots of the conversion neurosis are related more directly to the sexual conflicts which the child encounters between ages three and five. As in Officer Kanner's case, conversion neuroses and conversion symptoms occur as a result of the displacement of unacceptable sexual impulses which, if allowed to come into consciousness, would cause overwhelming anxiety.

Dissociative Neuroses

The dissociative neuroses are especially important to the law enforcement officer. For example, it is in this category that hysterical amnesia fails. This psychological forgetting is often difficult to distinguish from a true amnesia based on organic injury or disease.

Historical Background

In reviewing early theories, it is difficult to separate the dissociative neuroses from the conversion neuroses. Both were included under the general label of hysteria. However, later theoreticians, including Freud, differentiated between the two on the basis of the physical symptoms present in conversion neuroses.

Characteristics

The dissociative neuroses form a complex group of emotional disturbances because of the many forms they take. These include hysterical amnesia, the multiple personality, the sleepwalking trance, and, of special interest to law enforcement officers, the phenomenon of *highway hypnosis*.

All are related by the phenomenon of *dissociation*, in which material which is originally blocked from consciousness because of its unacceptable nature becomes so overwhelming that the only way to deal with the problem is to dissociate completely from the environment. A case of highway hypnosis will be presented as an illustration.

CASE EXAMPLE 1: JOHN VINCENT

It was a clear day when John Vincent, twenty-seven years old, died at 2:14 P.M. in a single car accident on an interstate highway in northwestern Arizona. The investigating officer reported that a thorough perusal of the highway on which John Vincent had been traveling just prior to crashing into a telephone pole did not reveal the characteristic pattern of weaving associated with falling asleep at the wheel or the skid marks commonly noted when the brakes are applied abruptly after the victim awakens. The death of John Vincent was probably a result of highway hypnosis.

Underlying Factors

In highway hypnosis, the victim becomes dissociated from the environment as a whole, losing track entirely of the passage of time and place. Mild cases of highway hypnosis are known to all of us. When we emerge from our dream state, we recognize that we have been driving for seconds or minutes and have passed several familiar landmarks without realizing it.

In serious cases, such as that which led to John Vincent's death, this trance state leads to complete immobilization at the wheel. Because of it, the driver is often unable to negotiate a curve after long, straight, monotonous stretches of turnpikes where curves are few and far. This offers little challenge to the motorist to pay attention to the road.

Helpful Hints to the Law Enforcement Officer

In handling someone with overwhelming anxiety, it is important to provide reassurance in order to help that person regain control over his or her panic. It is not helpful for the police officer to attempt to persuade the person that the anxiety or panic is unrealistic or unwarranted.

Even if the officer readily perceives the reasons for the anxiety and considers them ridiculous, it is important for him to recognize that they are not ridiculous to the person experiencing them. Instead of making light of the person's symptoms, he should offer reassurance and try to remove the person to a protective situation where he can begin to talk with someone about his anxious feelings.

When the police officer encounters an individual who is depressed, he should be alert to the seriousness of this condition. Even though he may not perceive any realistic cause for the depression, he should try to put himself in the shoes of the depressed person and identify with his depression by recognizing how painful it must be and by empathizing with his pain. After all, it is not how the officer sees it but how the depressed person sees it that will determine what a depressed person will do.

If it is determined that the depression is so great and the presence of suicidal ideation so extensive that a suicide attempt is possible, the person should be placed in a hospital immediately and watched very carefully until the depression has lifted. However, a word of caution is in order here since many people commit suicide at a time when it looks as though they are improving. It is thought that this *false improvement* is actually due to the neurotic's having made his final decision to commit suicide. Having done so, he is able to put on a happy face because he knows that all worries will soon be over. This happy face will sometimes fool even the professional, who may decide that the danger has passed.

The officer who has responsibility for prisoners should know that many depressed persons are encountered in jails, since the stress of incarceration is likely to precipitate a depressive neurosis in people. The officer must be alert for the depressed inmates so that he can make a judgment regarding suicidal potential. He should always be especially sensitive to the inmate who, several days before, was profoundly depressed but now has undergone a remarkable mood alteration unrelated to any significant external event, such as his imminent release. This person may have made the decision that life is no longer worth living. The observant officer should then summon appropriate medical help.

When encountering someone with severe obsessional thinking or a ritualistic compulsive behavior pattern, it is important for the officer to recognize that this individual is disturbed and should not be passed off as crazy. It is easy to assume the latter since compulsive acts, in particular, are often nonsensical and funny to the casual observer.

The officer as a professional observer of behavior should recognize these obsessive thought patterns and compulsive acts for what they are—symptoms of an emotional disturbance. Knowing this, he will be able to guide the person toward a therapeutic setting. Because of the seeming craziness of the behavior, and in most instances its apparent harmlessness, it is often easier to ignore this behavior rather than to take the trouble to refer the individual to an appropriate facility. However, it can be equally rewarding to suggest or make such a referral because this neurotic is generally very receptive to the suggestion that he seek help. He is in full contact with reality and recognizes that his obsessional thoughts and compulsive behavior are symptoms of illness. His ambivalence stops him from seeking help on his own but the influence of the officer will generally help him overcome it.

When the officer encounters someone who is experiencing an *unreasonable* fear (phobia) in relation to an actual situation, he can be of help by reducing the individual's panic through supportive intervention.

Summary

The neuroses include many examples of emotional disturbance with which the law enforcement officer is likely to come in contact. Awareness of the various types, their characteristics, and some of the underlying factors will enable him to assess their severity, the necessity for immediate intervention, and, most importantly, his own response to the individual who is experiencing the symptoms. Without this knowledge the law enforcement officer may respond to neurotics inappropriately. With it he is more likely to function as an ally of the medical and nonmedical therapeutic professional by evaluating neurotics correctly, responding appropriately, and referring them for treatment if needed.

REFERENCES AND ADDITIONAL BIBLIOGRAPHY

American Psychiatric Association. 1968. *Diagnostic and Statistical Manual for Mental Disorders.* Washington, D.C.

Fenichel, O. 1945. *The Psychoanalytic Theory of the Neuroses.* New York: Norton.

Freud, S. 1961 (originally published in 1936). "Inhibitions, Symptoms and Anxiety." In *Standard Edition*, ed. J. Strachey, Vol. 20, pp. 87–172. Hogarth Press.

Redlich, F. C. and Freedman, D. X. 1966. *The Theory and Practice of Psychiatry.* New York: Basic Books.

Chapter 9

The Psychoses

AS WE pointed out in Chapter 6, psychoses are either functional or organic in origin. If functional, the disorder is believed to be secondary to developmental and situational factors. If organic, it is usually a result of injury to, or involvement of, the central nervous system.

This chapter will focus primarily on functional psychoses. A discussion of their characteristics with several case examples and the developmental and environmental underlying factors will be presented. Helpful hints to the law enforcement officer in handling psychotic behavior will be given.

Common Characteristics

The diagnosis of psychosis depends on the types of symptoms present and the extent to which these symptoms interfere with effective functioning. The common theme in the psychoses is a significant *loss of contact with reality.* Each of the six major areas of psychotic symptoms (disturbances in thinking, disturbances in thought content, disturbances in perception, disturbances of mood and affect, disturbances in judgment, and regression) will be accompanied by a mild to severe loss of contact with reality.

Disturbances in thinking may occur in many forms as thought moves away from the rational, logical, and goal-directed thinking which we call normal. Many terms are used to describe these types of disturbed thinking, ranging from the least serious, *circumstantiality*, to the most severe, *loosening of associations*. As an officer listens to someone, an understanding of these terms will help him judge the seriousness of the emotional disturbance.

In circumstantiality, thinking remains goal-directed, but the goal is only reached after a series of digressions en route to it. For example, the person will go all around Robin Hood's barn in answering a question. By the time he gets to the answer, you may have forgotten the question. This is in contrast to *tangential thinking*, in which the goal is never reached, but the thoughts still have logical connections. In contrast to both of these, *loosening of associations* occurs when the goal is not reached and the connection between the thoughts is no longer rational.

Other forms of disturbed thinking affect the flow of thought in addition to the pattern of associations. These include *flight of ideas*, in which the person goes so rapidly from one connecting thought to another that you become lost trying to follow him. In contrast to this increased flow of thought, *blocking* refers to a slowing down or complete cessation of thought expression because of threatened anxiety.

In addition to the disturbances in the form and expression of thinking, another important characteristic of psychosis is *disturbances in the content of thought*. The most common form is the *delusion*, a false belief that arises without appropriate external stimulation and that is maintained more or less unshakably in the face of all reason and logic. Furthermore, these false beliefs are generally not shared by other members of this individual's peer group. Delusional thoughts may be either persecutory or grandiose. Their presence may be related to the patient's mood, with the depressed patient more likely to experience delusions of persecution ("the Mafia has put out a contract on my life") and the hyperactive person more likely to experience delusions of grandeur ("my father was Jesus Christ and my mother was the Virgin Mary").

Closely related to disturbances of thought content are *disturbances in perception*. In many psychoses, disturbances of thought content (delusions) are accompanied by disturbances in perception (hallucinations). A hallucination is defined as the apparent perception of an external object (for example, a voice) when no corresponding real object exists. In most functional psychoses, these hallucinations are auditory ("I hear my mother telling me I'm no good"); but, in the organic psychoses, visual, tactile, gustatory (taste) and/or olfactory (smell) hallucinations are more common.

The loss of contact with reality is also commonly associated with *disturbances in judgment.* If judgment is a mental function whose purpose is to insure reality-oriented action, then the psychotic is invariably going to demonstrate impairment in this area. The degree of impairment may be assessed by the police officer by posing hypothetical problem-solving situations ("What would you do if you smelled smoke in a theater?") or by simply observing ongoing behavior.

Disturbances in emotions are also seen in psychoses. In the psychoses, these disturbances are usually more severe than in the neuroses and interfere with effective functioning to such an extent that hospitalization is often necessary. These disturbances may include sudden changes in mood without accompanying changes in the person's situation or the complete absence of mood change despite major changes in the environment which would normally result in a change of mood.

Finally, the psychotic may also show *regression,* a condition in which the ego returns to an earlier state of development in an attempt to avoid the present tension and conflict (Chapter 4).

The degree to which some of these signs and symptoms are present can assist the police officer in deciding what type of psychosis is present. Disturbances in thinking primarily characterize the schizophrenias, while disturbances of emotions are most characteristic of the affective disorders. This does not imply, however, that disturbances of emotions do not occur to some extent in schizophrenia or, conversely, that disturbances in thinking do not occur to some extent in the affective disorders. Furthermore, the other disturbances described in this section are commonly associated with both types of psychoses.

Schizophrenias

Historical Background

Although observers have recognized many symptoms and signs of schizophrenia prior to the time of Christ, it was not described as a disease until the end of the nineteenth century. In 1898 Emil

Kraepelin was the first to combine many of these previous observations into a single entity.

In his famous paper "The Diagnosis and Prognosis of Dementia Praecox," he included many of these symptoms and signs as having in common their apparent lack of external causes, their occurrence in young and previously healthy individuals, and their impact which led to an ultimate deterioration of the personality as the disease progressed.

Although Kraepelin was the first to bring together the signs and symptoms of schizophrenia, it was Eugene Bleuler who, several years later, substituted the term *schizophrenia* for dementia praecox. He did this when he took issue with Kraepelin's concept of the disease's incurability and associated deterioration. He pointed out that only some patients deteriorated while others recovered.

To Kraepelin's descriptions of hebephrenia, catatonia, and paranoia, Bleuler added the concept of simple or undifferentiated schizophrenia. These four are the basic schizophrenic syndromes and will be discussed later in this chapter. The two types most commonly encountered by the police are, in either their acute or chronic forms, simple schizophrenia and paranoid schizophrenia.

Underlying Factors

There have been many theories regarding the cause of schizophrenia. Various genetic, biochemical, physiological, psychological, and sociocultural factors have been described, but none of them has been shown to be the sole cause, and the cure for schizophrenia is still unknown. However, a brief summary of these theories will provide insight into current thinking.

Some researchers believe that the origins of schizophrenia lie solely in developmental processes and, specifically, in the early interactions between the child and family. Disturbances in the mother-child relationship are given great weight. These predispose the child to a weak ego which, in later life, is not able to withstand stress. Consequently, the personality disintegrates, causing the signs and symptoms of schizophrenia.

Others have believed that physical conditions are responsible for schizophrenia. Endocrine (glandular) problems, brain damage, and toxic poisoning have been offered as causes. More recently, researchers have concentrated on certain biochemical functions while looking for substances in the body fluids which, when present in excessive amounts, might cause schizophrenia. To date, however, these theories are unproven.

Others suggest a strong genetic (hereditary) factor. Studies completed with identical twins indicate a higher incidence of schizophrenia noted in monozygotic twins (born from the same egg) compared with dizygotic twins (born from two different eggs). Although these data support the hypothesis that genetic factors may play a role in the development of schizophrenia, the mechanism is unknown. Whether this genetic factor operates through a physiological defect, such as the absence of an enzyme, or through some broader gene mutation is unknown.

The importance of sociocultural variables in the development of schizophrenia has also been stressed. In these theories, attention is directed to the greater prevalance of schizophrenia among the lower socioeconomic classes. Whether this finding is related to the cause or the result (through the *drift* of individuals suffering from schizophrenia into the lower socioeconomic brackets as a result of poor functioning) of schizophrenia is not known.

In conclusion, our current knowledge is inadequate to account for the development of schizophrenia. Despite many years of research, sufficient data are not available to determine conclusively the relative importance of the psychological, physical, genetic, and sociocultural factors that are possibly involved in predisposing an individual to schizophrenia.

SIMPLE SCHIZOPHRENIA

Simple schizophrenia is characterized by a gradual deterioration of drive, ambition, and the ability to function, reflected in the absence of social relationships, the inability to work effectively at a job, or difficulty in functioning above a marginal level in school. This gradual impairment is usually not accompanied by delusions or hallucinations. While disturbances of emotions are noted, primarily depression, the major sign is the thought disorder. An example will illustrate.

CASE EXAMPLE 1: FLOYD BROWN

Floyd Brown is thirty-two years old and single. The police were called to his home one evening by his mother following a violent outburst. When they arrived, Floyd's mother told them that Floyd had recently been very difficult to live with, spending most of the day sleeping and then remaining awake at night, pacing and yelling. On the evening she called the police, he had hit her for the first time. The police officers obtained the following information as they attempted to determine what to do. Should they take Floyd to the hospital or refer him and his mother to a community mental health facility?

Following graduation from high school, Floyd entered the local university and did well the first year. However, during his second year his functioning began to deteriorate. Not only did he slowly lose interest in his studies, which led to his dropping out of school, but he also began to become preoccupied with many bizarre ideas concerning science and the meaning of life. Totally preoccupied with the quest for "truth," he began to withdraw and spent most of his time at home despite the family's urging to go out. He lost interest in his personal hygiene and the family found it more difficult to cope with him because, as his mother put it, "We couldn't talk to him and he didn't make sense."

Floyd's first hospitalization occurred when he was twenty, one year after the onset of his illness. At that time, his deterioration had progressed to where he was spending all of his time indoors, refusing to take meals, and furiously writing down his ideas about the meaning of life.

This hospitalization was brief since he seemed to improve. After discharge, he entered a vocational rehabilitation program and later obtained a job as a hotel desk clerk. After six months, he lost his job and began a pattern of frequent job changes because he either failed to show up for work or got into minor arguments with his bosses.

During the last twelve years, Floyd had required hospitalization on two other occasions when his behavior got so bad that his family could no longer tolerate or manage him. In each case, his hospitalization had been brief, shortened by the helpful effects of medication. Following each discharge, however, he returned home and, shortly thereafter, usually discontinued both his therapy and his medication. Communication between Floyd and his parents became nonexistent.

Both parents found it difficult to listen to him because of the vagueness and bizarreness of his thinking. His mother commented, "He talked in riddles and we couldn't understand him."

With this information, the officers were able to recognize that Floyd was not in immediate danger if he was able to recognize that he needed help again. They talked with Floyd and his parents and he agreed to go to a community mental health clinic the next morning.

PARANOID SCHIZOPHRENIA

Paranoid schizophrenia is characterized principally by delusions of persecution and/or grandeur. Hallucinations, usually auditory, are often present. Prior to onset, the typical paranoid schizophrenic displays a suspicious and guarded attitude toward everyone. The paranoid does not generally show any marked regression at the outset nor any significant disturbances in emotions. A case example will illustrate.

CASE EXAMPLE 2: JUDY EDEN

Judy Eden is a twenty-eight-year-old single female who called the police to her home. When the responding officer arrived, Judy told him that she had a problem she wanted to explain. She began by saying that there were bottles of liquid in her home killing her and her dog and that the dog was already very ill. She took a wad of Kleenex from her purse and asked the officer to smell the odor. He did so and found no odor. When he did not confirm her suspicion, she told him that another officer had been to her home before and had told her to throw away the bottles. She said she had done this, but both the bottles and odors had returned. In addition, she mentioned that her air-conditioning system was spreading the odors throughout the house.

On further questioning, Judy revealed that lately she had received messages from the television set. She told the officer how most of the people on the television were talking to her and telling her that she was going to die if she did not mend her ways.

The officer learned also that Judy had been widowed six months ago when her Air Force husband was shot down in Vietnam. Initially, she had seemed to make a good adjustment to this tragedy, but several months afterward, her bizarre behavior began. She mentioned that her friends had seemed concerned, but she soon realized that it was because "I have a pension and they want my money."

Although Judy did not demonstrate evidence of violence, the officer recognized that Judy's illness had been rapidly progressive and that this was an eventual possibility (Chapters 14 and 15). Consequently, he asked her if she would accompany him to the hospital and talk to someone else. She refused. The officer left but immediately notified the local mental health center which sent a social worker to see Judy the next day.

HEBEPHRENIC SCHIZOPHRENIA

Although far less common than simple or paranoid schizophrenia, knowledge about hebephrenic schizophrenia is important to the law enforcement officer because of the severe disintegration of the personality. This disintegration may not be immediately noticeable because of the prominence of inappropriate giggling and smiling which the untrained observer may dismiss as childish playfulness. The presence of facial grimaces and the use of bizarre language which does not make sense should alert the officer to the seriousness of the situation. Hospitalization should be arranged as soon as possible.

CATATONIC SCHIZOPHRENIA

The catatonic form of schizophrenia is also rare. Its importance to the law enforcement officer lies in the extreme violence which may be associated with one of its forms—catatonic excitement—in which there is excessive motor activity, grimacing, talkativeness, and unpredictable emotional outbursts. When these symptoms are not present, the individual is usually in a stupor, a state in which total silence is present and the posture is often bizarre, with the individual remaining in a single position for hours, seemingly not paying attention to anything and responsive to no one. This lack of verbal or physical response is accompanied, paradoxically, by an increased awareness of what is going on. This helps to explain why, without warning, he may fly into the rage of catatonic excitement during which he is extremely dangerous.

Affective Disorders

In contrast to the schizophrenias, the affective disorders are psychoses in which the primary signs and symptoms are related to *disturbances of emotions* rather than to *disturbances in the form of thinking* (circumstantiality, tangentiality, and loosening of associations). However, disturbances in the flow of thinking, thought content, perception, judgment, and regression are also seen.

The affective disorders may be classified into three types: (1) manic-depressive reactions; (2) psychotic depressive reactions; and (3) involutional psychotic depressive reactions. Recent research suggests that, although they are grouped together because of the primary disturbance in emotions, there also are major differences between them.

Historical Background

Theories about affective disorders go back to the early writings of Hippocrates in which he described the interaction of the four bodily humours (blood, black bile, yellow bile, and water) as closely related to the occurrence of mania (a state of unusual elation) and melancholia (a state of unusual depression). Following the Middle Ages, during which there was an emphasis on demonology, the modern classification of affective disorders emerged, primarily as a result of the work of Falaret, Kahlbaum, and Kraepelin.

In 1854, Falaret published a description of an illness which he called *La Folie circularie*, the first description of the *circular* syndrome associated with manic-depressive psychosis. Kahlbaum, in 1882, was the first to view mania and melancholia as different stages of the same psychosis rather than as two different illnesses. Kraepelin first proposed the diagnosis of manic-depressive insanity for this entire group of disorders. Although they are more commonly referred to today as the affective disorders, *manic-depressive psychosis* is still sometimes used as an all-inclusive term representing the three primary classifications in this disorder.

Underlying Factors

Current research into the causes of affective disorders is at a similar level to research on the schizophrenias. A genetic (hereditary) factor has been recently suggested. Affective disorders occur with significantly greater frequency in the children of parents with affective disorders as well as in children of alcoholic parents. However, the presence of one or the other in a family does not necessarily mean that an affective disorder will occur in any or all children. Similarly, many biological changes are noted in those with affective disorders, but whether they are causative to or symptomatic of the illness has not been clearly demonstrated.

Earlier work focused primarily on developmental and psychological factors. For example, Abraham, in the early twentieth century, drew attention to the obsessive-compulsive personality structures of those who were most likely to develop an affective disorder in later life. Freud added to our understanding of this illness by pointing out the similarities and differences between normal mourning after the loss of a loved one and melancholia (depression). He viewed mourning as a period of appropriate grief. However, if the loss is not successfully resolved, melancholia occurs. The loss is no longer confined to the loss of the loved one, but is also turned against the self through a loss of self-esteem.

Conversely, mania, the opposite of melancholia (depression), is viewed as a flight from, and defense against, depression into a state of unrealistic and unusual elation. The involutional psychotic depression occurs at or about the time of menopause and is related primarily to the intense conflicts surrounding the threatened loss of sexuality.

An examination of families in which affective disorders occur has revealed that these families tend to place a high premium on strict conformity to accepted values, show considerable parental manipulation of children with a notable inconsistency in discipline, and evidence of a high degree of competitiveness.

MANIC-DEPRESSIVE REACTION

In manic-depressive reaction, either severe psychotic depression or an acute manic episode characteristically occurs when the person is in his late twenties or early thirties.

If the psychotic depressive episode occurs first, it is often difficult to make the diagnosis until it has been followed by a manic episode. Sometimes it is also difficult to distinguish an acute manic episode from an acute schizophrenic episode.

In contrast to schizophrenics, manics are more apt to have flight of ideas rather than loosening of associations. In addition, the presence of unusual elation, hyperactivity, and increased sociability are more characteristic of an acute manic episode. An example will help illustrate (contrast this with Floyd Brown and Judy Eden).

CASE EXAMPLE 1: MIKE FARR

Mike Farr is twenty-seven years old and came to the police's attention in an unusual manner. He had been under a physician's care for his manic-depressive psychosis for several months and had been placed on medication. One evening, he found himself out of medication and planned to return to the hospital the next day to get more. However, he postponed his visit for several days because he did not have transportation and, as time elapsed, became increasingly manic. As he began to recognize the impending recurrence of his illness, he began to panic.

Consequently, one evening he left the house and began walking. He passed a police officer on patrol and accosted him, demanding to be taken to the hospital so that he could get his prescription. When the police officer refused, indicating that this was not within his line of duty, Mike, who at the time was standing in a gas station, took a book of matches out of his pocket. He lit one and dropped it into a small puddle of gasoline on the ground. It immediately ignited and Mike was placed under arrest for arson. He was taken to jail where, without his medication, he became increasingly manic. He was eventually transferred to the hospital. Prior to his transfer from jail, the detention officers noted in their log the following comments about Mike's behavior: "Won't stop talking, constantly making jokes, seems on the verge of losing control, doesn't sleep."

In the hospital, he was placed back on medication and his manic behavior subsided after a week. For a period of several weeks, he appeared normal. Then the gradual onset of depression was noted, with increasing withdrawal and slowness of thinking. It gradually worsened until he was no longer responsive to the staff's questions. He spent most of his time in bed, had a poor appetite, lost weight, and began to have suicidal thoughts.

PSYCHOTIC DEPRESSIVE REACTION

In contrast to the manic-depressive psychosis, where the onset of either the manic or depressive phase may occur without reference to a significant external event, a psychotic depressive reaction generally begins after a clearly recognizable loss, with a failure to recover from the loss after a normal period of grief. As the person goes from grief to psychotic depression, severe disturbance in both emotions and thought content appears.

Both physical and psychological signs and symptoms are prominent, with marked agitation, restlessness, and depression. The person has no appetite and his sleep is disturbed, the characteristic pattern being early morning awakening and an inability to get back to sleep. Many physical complaints are present also.

Disturbances in thought content include delusions involving sin,

120

guilt, and unworthiness. Suicidal and paranoid thoughts are common. Delusions may also develop around somatic complaints. For example, the person may show an unrealistic concern over cancer. Hallucinations are less common. When they occur, they are usually auditory and have a condemning quality consistent with the delusions of sin, guilt, and unworthiness. A clinical example will illustrate.

CASE EXAMPLE 2: KAREN BRAGEN

On a Friday morning, police were called to the residence of Karen Bragen, age twenty-four, by neighbors who had heard gunshots. They found Karen sitting quietly in the living room with her face buried in her hands. In the bedroom, they found the dead body of her three-month-old son who had been shot twice in the head.

From their interrogation of Karen, her husband, and family they obtained the following information. She had had an uneventful pregnancy and, in fact, her husband commented how much happier she had seemed when pregnant. However, shortly after the baby's birth, she began to be depressed. Initially, both she and her husband attributed this depression to the commonly known *postpartum blues*, typically seen within several days after a baby's birth.

However, her blues did not go away after a week or two as is common in postpartum cases. Instead, she began to have bizarre thoughts which initially occurred in the late afternoon or early evening, particularly when she was alone. These thoughts consisted of fleeting mental images in which she saw herself with a gun, killing her baby and husband.

She tried to get them out of her mind by keeping busy. When this failed, she began a compulsive pattern in which she sat with a book, reading for several hours in the late afternoon and early evening while the baby was left in the bedroom. When this did not stop her violent thoughts, she began to lock the bedroom door so that she could not reach the baby.

This was also unsuccessful. One week before the murder, Karen began to hear the voice of her mother, with whom she had always had a poor relationship. The voice began to condemn Karen, saying she was a poor mother and accusing her of not taking care of her baby. She began to hear her mother's voice coming from the television set.

Her husband told police that, during the two weeks prior to the baby's death, Karen became increasingly withdrawn and was constantly "knocking" her capabilities as a mother. He tried to reassure her, but to no avail. She never told him her violent thoughts.

On the day of the murder, she heard a voice telling her to kill the baby. The voice said that then her problems would be solved because she would no longer have to be a mother. To Karen, in her psychotic state, this seemed to be a perfect solution. In response to the voice's continued urging, she took her husband's gun from the closet, walked into the bedroom, and fired two bullets into the sleeping baby.

This tragedy is presented to underline the serious homicidal and/or suicidal potential associated with this mental illness. If the possibility of psychotic depressive reaction exists, an officer should always try to get the person to a hospital or a doctor.

To the nonprofessional observer, it may not seem that Karen had encountered any specific loss prior to the onset of her psychotic depression. However, in later treatment, it became apparent that the end of her pregnancy was perceived by Karen as a significant loss because, during pregnancy, she had felt worthwhile for the first time in her life.

INVOLUTIONAL PSYCHOTIC DEPRESSION

Involutional psychotic depression is a variation of psychotic depression which may occur in men and women in their late forties or early fifties who are undergoing a *change of life*. Although men do not generally show overt physical signs of this change of life as women do in the menopause, involutional psychotic depressive reaction can occur in both sexes.

In this illness, the psychotic episode usually occurs during this crucial time of life without there being any prior history of mental illness. The specific loss for the woman is her loss of child-bearing ability. In the man, the loss is often associated with the realization that certain ambitions, principally at work, will never be reached. A period of grief may begin which, if unchecked, may lead to an involutional psychotic depression.

Symptoms are similar to those found in the psychotic depressive reaction described previously. Consequently, the diagnosis of involutional psychotic depression is usually made on the basis of the person's life history. An example will illustrate.

CASE EXAMPLE 3: MARGARET GERRARD

Margaret Gerrard is a forty-eight-year-old widow with four children ranging in ages from sixteen to twenty-eight. The police were called to her home by her youngest child who had found her in the bedroom, semi-conscious, with a half-empty bottle of pills at her side.

After calling the rescue squad and successfully reviving her, they obtained the following information. Two years ago, Mrs. Gerrard's husband had died suddenly of a heart attack. Shortly thereafter, her third child had married, leaving her with only one child at home. At the same time, she began to have difficulty concentrating, leading to poor work and conflicts with her bosses. After her husband's death, her job became her sole means of support. When her employer indicated that he was going to let her go, Margaret plunged into a severe depression.

Within two months, she became afraid to leave the house, spending most of her time in the bedroom. Her sixteen-year-old daughter had to do all of the chores. Several months prior to her suicide attempt, she began to complain of stomach trouble. Urged by her family to see her physician, Margaret underwent a series of tests, which were negative. However, she did not accept this and began to talk openly about "the cancer growing inside of her." Despite intensive efforts to convince her that her health was good, her preoccupation with cancer increased. In the suicide note, she said she was taking her own life because she could not bear the pain which the "cancer growing inside" was causing.

This case has been chosen to point out the association of violent behavior with involutional psychotic depressions. Although homicidal behavior is not common in the involutional psychotic depression, it can also occur. Suicidal behavior, however, is more frequent and is generally noted either as the individual is heading toward the bottom or when recovery is beginning.

Helpful Hints to the Law Enforcement Officer

Because of the confusion, the bizarreness of associated behavior, and the capacity for violence of the psychotic, the police officer is often the first one called to the scene when a mentally disturbed person displaying signs of psychosis is involved. The officer's ability to handle the psychotic person appropriately is not only important for his own safety and the safety of others (Chapters 14–16), but also to the psychotic person himself since he is probably experiencing tremendous fear. In addition, the ability of the officer to form a trusting relationship with the psychotic person may be very important in determining the outcome of further efforts at treatment.

The mental confusion, distortions of thought content, and disturbances of perception increase the possibility that the psychotic will distrust any person, even those attempting to help him. He may then react with violence to this perceived threat.

It is important for the officer to remember to approach the psychotic in the most nonthreatening manner possible. Any display of force, including guns and restraints, should be avoided unless the officer suspects that his own safety or the safety of others is threatened.

In the psychotic, sensory awareness is heightened. Consequently, it is important for the officer to reduce the sensory input to the psychotic in order to reduce his fear. This might include removing all nonessential people from the psychotic's environment, the use of a slow, soft voice by the officer, and the reduction of other sensory stimuli such as police sirens, bull horns, and other equipment. By reducing sensory stimuli, the officer helps the psychotic to gain control of himself, making him more approachable.

The individual suffering from depression is frequently in an ambivalent mental state in which he is unable to make decisions, vacillating between the pros and cons of any decision. Consequently, he may argue the opposite of whatever the officer suggests. For example, should the officer suggest hospitalization, the psychotically depressed person may immediately resist the suggestion, saying that he doesn't need to be in the hospital and/or offering all sorts of reasons to the officer why he can't go. The officer should stick firmly to his decision regardless of the person's pleading.

It is, therefore, important for the officer to make up his own mind as to what must be done before revealing his decision to the individual concerned. Once he has verbalized the decision, he must act as if there is no other alternative. Surprisingly, officers will find their firmness is reassuring and the person may change from a debating, argumentative person into someone resigned to following the dictates of the officer.

The officer's approach to the person who demonstrates delusional thinking is also important. He should not argue with the delusions, but neither should he agree with them. Rather, he should listen and hear out the person's concerns. He can then suggest that there are others who would like to talk with the person about his concerns and who can do more to help him. Mention of going to a hospital or a clinic may disturb some individuals, but they are more likely to go with the officer who handles the situation in a tactful and firm manner than with one who does not.

Summary

The police officer frequently comes in contact with psychotic behavior because the psychotic is acting in a strange or violent manner. Consequently, the officer should be aware of the strategies he can use so as to minimize the danger to others, the psychotic, and himself. He should also be cognizant of the signs and symptoms of these disorders so he can distinguish them from less serious illnesses such as personality disorders and neuroses.

In Chapters 7–9, descriptions of each of the major classifications of mental illness have been presented. Since one of the law enforcement officer's primary responsibilities in the field is to assess and manage deviant behavior, the next nine chapters (10–18) will take a closer look at the most common forms of deviant behavior that the officer is likely to encounter.

REFERENCES AND ADDITIONAL BIBLIOGRAPHY

Bleuler, E. 1950. *Dementia Praecox or the Group of Schizophrenias.* New York: International Universities Press.
Freud, S. 1955. "Mourning and Melancholia." In *Standard Edition.* Vol. 14. London: Hogarth Press.
Kisker, G. W. 1972. *The Disorganized Personality.* New York: McGraw-Hill.
Redlich, F. C. and Freedman, D. X. 1966. *The Theory and Practice of Psychiatry.* New York: Basic Books.

PART IV

Assessing and Managing
Abnormal Behavior
in the Field

Winston Vargas / Photo Researchers, Inc.

Chapter 10

Psychopathic Behavior

PSYCHOPATHIC BEHAVIOR is of particular importance to the police officer. A Dallas, Texas, police department study states that, although psychopaths comprise 40 percent of the criminal population, they are responsible for 80–90 percent of all crime (Dallas Police Department 1973).

Alan Harrington, a specialist in this area of abnormal behavior, claims that there are about ten million psychopaths in our country (Harrington 1972). They include unprincipled businessmen, crooked lawyers, high-pressure salesmen, unethical physicians, imposters, and a great assortment of criminals. The terms *sociopath* and *antisocial personality* are also used to describe these persons.

The cases that will be presented are examples of the wide variety of varying abnormal behaviors associated with psychopathic behavior. The sexual psychopaths, a variant of psychopathic behavior, will be explored in more detail in the chapter on deviant sexual behavior. These cases will serve as a focus for a discussion of the psychopath's characteristics, the underlying factors, and helpful hints to the law enforcement officer in handling this behavior.

Courtesy Paul Neuthaler

Historical Background

Psychopathic behavior was originally described by an English psychiatrist, Pritchard, in the nineteenth century. He called individuals who had an unimpaired intellect but who had lost their power of self-control *morally insane*. After he introduced this concept, it was thought for a while that these individuals might have an organic disease of the central nervous system that caused this morally insane behavior. The term *constitutional psychopathic inferiority* was used to indicate this organic component, which some observers still believe exists.

Studies have shown that there are common characteristics shared by those who manifest different types of psychopathic behavior as well as a developmental history which sets them apart. These will be discussed after the presentation of several case histories. These case histories offer a spectrum of behaviors which are readily recognizable by the police officer since those who manifest these behaviors are commonly encountered during a day's work.

Case Histories

CASE EXAMPLE 1: MICHAEL CRAWFORD

After being persuaded to give up his precarious position on the window ledge of a hotel high above Louisville, Kentucky, Michael Crawford sobbed to sympathetic listeners a tale of woe and despair that readily captured the interest of many who had observed his plight. He was quickly offered a job and shelter as well as companionship by a pretty young woman who had been one of those trying to persuade him to come off the ledge. Newspaper reporters, who had been called to the scene, gave considerable attention to his human interest story.

John Flynn, a local policeman, read the story in his morning newspaper the next day and recalled a similar incident which had taken place in Boston several weeks earlier. Details of the events were so similar that, out of curiosity, he decided to check further. To his surprise, Michael Crawford and the man rescued from the hotel window ledge in Boston were the same person. With his interest heightened, he checked further and discovered that Michael was AWOL from an army hospital where he had been taken after his first "suicide" attempt in Boston.

The Louisville police quickly returned him to military control and he was admitted to a nearby army hospital for evaluation and treatment. After several days on a closed ward, he was transferred to an open ward and allowed to roam throughout the hospital.

He soon found his way to the Red Cross building, where he offered his services to the overworked staff. Very shortly he was their right hand, showing movies, setting up chairs, serving refreshments, and being helpful in every possible way. Volunteers quickly began to comment how charming, earnest, and hard working he was. They began to talk at coffee about the patient, the heroic combat record in Korea which he described (but which was untrue), and his desire to leave the army and return to college (although he had never finished high school). The impression he made was so great that they began to discuss ways in which they might offer some assistance to him toward achieving his goals after discharge.

These early discussions of possibly assisting him became even more positive following a fire in one of the hospital buildings. During the fire, Michael led other patients to safety, helped drag equipment out of the building, and performed other spectacular feats.

However, these extremely impressed and appreciative volunteers lost their enthusiasm several days later when it was discovered that Michael had set the fire. Following his arrest, he was taken to the stockade to await a court-martial. While there, his behavior became so crazy and unmanageable that he had to be sent back to the hospital and admitted to the closed ward. Following his return, he made numerous dramatic suicidal gestures, organized a small patient rebellion, and finally escaped from the facility and was never heard from again.

CASE EXAMPLE 2: BILLY DALTON

There are some citizens in Crescent City who would like to talk to Billy Dalton. There are also some people in Hollywood who would like to talk to him. What they would all like to talk to him about has been described by the Crescent City police as a grand hoax on local businessmen involving the filming of a television show. Described as a small man in his late thirties dressed in Western style clothing, Billy arrived in Crescent City on Sunday and was gone by Tuesday.

In these forty-eight hours, he left a trail of behavior which is still being talked about.

He came to town with a briefcase marked "Paramount" and represented himself as an advance agent for the television series "Mannix." He checked into a local motel and told the manager that he needed accommodations for 210 cast and crew members who would be arriving within several days to film a segment of the show. However, he immediately booked seven rooms for the next night to be used by some production company members who would be arriving early.

He then contacted the new owner of the local theater, Mr. Chapman, and gave him the same story. He obtained the use of the theater as well as a promise to help him put together a Monday night dinner party for the star of the show. He also secured the local fairgrounds building as a mess hall for the arriving cast and crew.

As Mr. Chapman later recalled, "he struck me at precisely the right moment." The prospect of having a well-known actor help publicize his theater interested Mr. Chapman. Consequently, he not only accompanied Billy to a local bakery and ordered refreshments for the party, but also gave him close to $300 to buy the rest of the food for the party.

At 3:30 P.M. on the day of the party, Billy told the hotel manager that he was going to meet the star at the theater. Shortly thereafter, the manager received a call from a man who identified himself as the star. He asked the manager to tell Billy that he would be a little late.

When the dinner began, with no sign of the production company members but with others invited by Mr. Chapman present, Mr. Chapman received a phone call from an unidentified person who told him that the star had been delayed in another city but would arrive later.

He never appeared. Mr. Chapman picked up the entire tab and began to become suspicious. The next day, he called Paramount Studios and was informed that they had never heard of Billy Dalton and that there were certainly no plans to film a "Mannix" segment in Crescent City. At approximately the same time, Billy was leaving the motel, telling the manager that he was going to a local laundromat to wash some clothing. No one in Crescent City has seen Billy Dalton since.

It can be reported that, several months later in another state, Billy Dalton was arrested and charged with obtaining property by false pretenses. His rap sheet showed fifteen arrests since 1968 for writing bogus checks, grand theft, drawing checks on insufficient funds, theft by fraud, and other similar offenses. The presentence evaluation included the following excerpt from the report of the court psychologist.

> Mr. Dalton presents himself as a mousy, insecure, extremely nervous little man who is overwhelmed by society's callous disregard for his obvious virtue. This attitude is difficult to understand in view of his record of collisions with the law. His history illustrates his incapacity to learn from experience and his inevitable failures. He does not appear to be conscience-stricken for any of his acts and avoids accepting blame for them.

CASE EXAMPLE 3: HARRY MORRIS

Harry Morris was first seen by one of the authors just after he had turned eighteen. By that time Harry, who was the adopted son of a senior army colonel, had been in trouble with the Juvenile Court since age ten. He had already been admitted to the closed wards of several military hospitals at posts where his father had been stationed and had been treated by many psychiatrists and psychologists.

As a juvenile, Harry had been arrested for assault after he had threatened his mother with a knife, a table leg, and several other weapons. He had also been arrested for mail fraud when he advertised for sale through a pornographic magazine "two sanitary devices" for only one dollar and then either kept the money or sent out two cheap handkerchiefs.

At the time he came to the author's attention, he had been arrested for shoplifting. His father came seeking help for Harry since the judge had agreed to release Harry if he would appear once a week for treatment.

Initially, everything seemed to go well. Harry obtained a job in a local bowling alley and, because he was well liked by the owner, was soon promoted to night manager. However, this change in hours required Harry to have his own transportation and so he convinced his father to make a down payment on a secondhand car with the understanding that Harry would keep up the payments. Harry came promptly to therapy each week, seemed to be getting along well with his parents, and was making plans to return to school the following semester.

Then, quite suddenly, Harry's therapist was notified that Harry was in trouble again. Apparently, earlier that evening Harry and a friend had been driving to work in Harry's car. They had stopped for a red light and a car had pulled alongside. Because Harry had been engrossed in conversation, he had not immediately noticed when the light changed to green. Consequently, the other car had pulled away first and cut in front of him.

Harry, who took pride in always making the fastest getaway when the lights changed, was insulted. He immediately went after the other car, finally forcing it to the shoulder of the road. He stopped his own car, got out, walked to the other car, and pulled from his pocket a small dime-store badge which read "Deputy Sheriff." He proceeded to give the other driver a piece of his mind, becoming quite profane and hostile and ending with a remark that the other driver was lucky because Harry was in a hurry; otherwise, he would have "thrown his ass in jail."

The other driver listened patiently to this tirade and then calmly told Harry that perhaps they should go to jail together since he had been on his way there when Harry had stopped him. The driver then added, "If you would like to see a real deputy's badge, look at this." As it turned out, Harry had stopped a deputy sheriff on his way to work. Shortly thereafter, Harry was in jail again, accused of impersonating a police officer, using obscene language, and disorderly conduct.

In one impulsive moment, out of anger at being second to pull away from a green light, Harry threw away all that he had gained, all that he claimed to have been working for in the months since he had last been released from jail.

CASE EXAMPLE 4: PROVOST MARSHAL THOMPSON

For years, ranchers had grazed their cattle on the grasslands of a large military reservation without incident. Suddenly, however, cattle began to disappear and the ranchers became convinced that someone was stealing them. They immediately took their complaint to Provost Marshal (Colonel) Russell Thompson. He turned the matter over to some of his assistants for investigation. It came as a complete surprise to the ranchers when the Colonel and his sergeant were arrested as the rustlers.

The Colonel was immediately sent to a nearby hospital for psychiatric evaluation and brought to trial. During the trail, many strange behaviors came to light.

For example, the Colonel used to keep defanged rattlesnakes loose in his home and sometimes even in his office. He would also keep one on the floor of his car and delighted in offering rides to women walking on the post. There had been talk about the Colonel's strange practical joke, but nothing was ever said officially and the females on the post learned to say "no" to his offers.

One of his drivers also testified how, after an officers' function and while returning to his home, the Colonel had ordered him to stop. Apparently, the Colonel had seen an opossum passing in front of the car's headlights. He got out of the car and approached the opossum, which had feigned death in the middle of the road. The Colonel knelt and drew a bowie knife from underneath his jacket (a weapon he always carried). He waited patiently until the animal moved and then quickly slashed him with the knife. This game of cat and mouse continued until the animal was dead. The Colonel then calmly wiped off his knife, got back into his car, and ordered the driver to proceed ahead.

CASE EXAMPLE 5: LARRY LINDGREN

Larry graduated two hundred and twenty-ninth out of 240 students in his high school class and went to work in an auto plant where his father had worked for many years. Although he was soon offered an opportunity to become a sponsored trainee, which would eventually mean a better paying and more responsible position, he decided that this was too dull.

Although he had never been interested in college, he told his father after quitting his job that he was going to a nearby university to look things over. However, he was refused admission because he did not have credits in certain subjects which he had failed in high school. Instead of returning to another regular job, he continued to wander about the campus and to attend classes without formally enrolling. After a while, he became quite comfortable with his masquerade and began to fake report cards to send home to his parents, telling them that he had won a scholarship.

In his biology class, he became interested in the human body. He went out and bought a secondhand stethoscope and a record which played the sounds of normal and abnormal heartbeats. After he had listened diligently to this record and compared the sounds to those of his own heart, he began to walk through the corridors of the university hospital wearing an intern's white coat and carrying the stethoscope protruding conspicuously from the pocket. Because of his large size, he looked older than his age and, consequently, no one questioned his masquerade. He later recounted, "I knew what I was doing; I was the perfect image of the young doctor." Larry spent three years in this environment, observing everything as he walked around the hospital and becoming friendly with the staff, but always being very careful not to overdo it.

He became enamored with this way of life and one day the idea occurred to him that, if he could keep it up, he might eventually be able to become a doctor. And so, for another three years, while holding down a job, he continued to go to the hospital and mingle with the medical students. He became fast friends with many of them, telling them that he worked elsewhere in the hospital.

Finally, he felt ready and "his" class graduated. He even attended graduation, standing in the back as the Dean announced the conferring of the degree of Doctor of Medicine on the students. Shortly after his "graduation," Larry had a fake diploma made and moved to another town where he hung up his shingle and waited for patients to come.

His co-tenant in the building was a dentist who complained to Larry about feeling tired most of the time. From what he had learned and his astute powers of observation, Larry diagnosed his condition as anemia and discovered a bleeding ulcer which he treated. The dentist was very grateful and became one of Larry's strongest boosters. Soon, patients and money began to roll in. As patients later recalled, "He made us feel so cheerful and healthy because he was young. Children loved him."

Within seven months after opening his practice, Larry was seeing an average of two hundred patients a week. His practice grew and, at the time he was exposed, he was netting over sixty thousand dollars a year. He and his wife, whom he had married several years before and who was not aware of his masquerade, enjoyed their new-found affluence by joining a country club, building a new home, and owning two cars.

After several years of "practice," Larry began to notice that he was stumbling, becoming awkward with his instruments, and tiring quickly. Privately, he consulted a doctor in another community without revealing his profession or his identity. The doctor told him that he had multiple sclerosis.

Larry's immediate concern was for his family. Knowing that his disease might eventually be fatal, he asked his local insurance agent to double his policy without revealing that he had multiple sclerosis. This insurance application was his undoing. A routine credit check revealed that no doctor by that name was licensed in the state. At first, he tried to lie his way out of it by claiming that he had been licensed in a different state and simply had not had the time to take out a new license. However, when he was asked to produce evidence, he knew the game was up and he confessed the entire hoax.

Immediately, patients and friends came to his defense. Many wanted to give him money for his defense while others wrote or phoned the prosecutor urging him to drop the charges. At Larry's church, one of the ministers reminded the congregation of the biblical injunction to "judge not, lest ye be judged" and suggested that they pray for the young doctor, their friend, who was "in a little trouble." One member of the congregation even wrote to the President of the United States asking for special dispensation for Larry.

Larry was charged with practicing medicine without a license and illegal possession of barbiturates and narcotics. He was sentenced to one year in prison. At his sentencing, the judge stated: "Maybe you helped people. I am not sure. But it is also possible you might have hurt people." The presentence evaluation of the probation officer stated that Larry had shown no remorse and had freely admitted that "I'd do it all over again."

Characteristics

These five examples illustrate various features of psychopathic behavior with which the police officer should familiarize himself.

Manipulation of People

The psychopath manipulates people like objects to gain his own ends. Recall the case of Billy Dalton who used people to get what he wanted and, when their usefulness was ended, left them stranded. In this way, and through similar behavior, the psychopath not only ends up with no friends, but also does not seem to want any.

He is really a self-centered person who has little or no regard for the welfare of others, even though he is a good con artist and inspires confidence and faith. As Billy Dalton was able to do, he can bring people with whom he comes in contact to do things that they might not do, under normal circumstances, for anyone else. Unfortunately, however, much of the faith and confidence he inspires only ends in grief and misery.

This ability to manipulate people can also lead the psychopath to remarkable success in whatever role he assumes. Larry Lindgren, without a formal education, was able to manipulate people and inspire confidence in himself to the extent that he was remarkably successful in his masquerade as a physician.

Unexplained Failure

Most psychopaths are above average in intelligence. There are periods during their lives in which they are able to succeed at whatever they choose. Larry Lindgren, who was able to function as a physician, is an excellent example.

Sooner or later, however, the psychopath usually fails. Harrington remarks, "We have one near certainty; sooner or later, when the classic psychopath comes on stage, things will go wrong . . . patterns of temporary success or at least stability are followed by strangely brutal and irresponsible behavior with accompanying stupid and unnecessary falls from grace for which there can be no rational explanation" (Harrington 1971).

Recall the case of Colonel Thompson who, despite his high position of Provost Marshal, fell from grace very rapidly when he so naively failed to deflect the investigation which eventually uncovered his rustling activities.

However, single unexplained failures are often not enough to unmask the psychopath. Often, only after many have occurred will people begin to realize that something is indeed wrong. Prior to this, they are more apt to look for shortcomings or mistakes in themselves rather than to see the situation for what it is, a shrewd manipulation on the part of a psychopath.

Absence of Neurotic Anxiety

The psychopath is not plagued by anxieties, phobias, physical symptoms, or other characteristics of a neurotic. Like Larry Lindgren, he is most often at ease and poised in situations where a normal person would be tense and upset. How many normal individuals could successfully carry off a masquerade for close to six years and eventually achieve the success of "graduation" from medical school?

However, it is equally important to recognize that, if the psychopathic personality is deprived of the opportunity to act out his abnormal behavior, *situational anxiety* may occur. Michael Crawford, when taken to the stockade to await a court-martial for setting the fire, went crazy and became so unmanageable that he had to be transferred to a hospital and admitted to a closed ward. Furthermore, after being admitted to the closed ward, where his opportunities to act out were more limited, he made numerous and dramatic suicidal gestures as a further consequence of his situational anxiety. It is also important to note that, in contrast to the neurotic whose anxieties are often unrelenting, the psychopath, when pressure is relieved, loses his anxiety. This is why it is called situational.

Absence of Psychosis

The well-integrated and functioning psychopath is not psychotic. His behavior is not divorced from reality nor does he have delusions or hallucinations. However, like Michael Crawford, he can act crazy in order to escape an unpleasant situation. This ability to act crazy can present a difficult diagnostic problem to anyone who is called upon to evaluate the psychopath. However, like situational anxiety, the seemingly psychotic behavior will tend to disappear when the stress is removed.

Persistence of Self-Defeating Antisocial Behavior

Although a psychopath is capable of plotting and executing very clever crimes to attain a material goal (e.g., money), he may also follow a pattern of criminal activity that is self-defeating to all personal goals which he claims are important. Certainly Harry Morris, in attempting to dupe the deputy sheriff into thinking that he also was a deputy sheriff, was engaging in a pattern of behavior which was self-defeating, especially in view of his more recent history of responsible behavior.

Even after he had the support of the women he had charmed into backing his effort to go to college, Michael Crawford set fire to a portion of the hospital, losing the support that had previously been offered. Finally, Colonel Thompson risked his entire career, honors, and retirement to rustle a few cattle. In each case, we see how self-defeating the antisocial behavior of the psychopath is.

An Inability To Distinguish Truth from Falsehood

Cleckley, in his famous book *The Mask of Sanity*, comments on the psychopath's remarkable capacity for disregarding the truth

(Cleckley 1955). As typified by Larry Lindgren, the psychopath can appear confident and wholly at ease in situations where the average man would feel embarrassed. It is not enough to realize that the psychopath may lie. It is equally important to know that when he lies, his lies are not trivial and he has a remarkable capacity to live with them as if they were true.

An Inability to Accept Blame

Larry Lindgren, while being interviewed during his presentence evaluation, demonstrated no remorse for the activities he had carried out during his masquerade. Billy Dalton, after he was caught, also did not appear conscience stricken to the psychologist who evaluated him prior to sentencing.

Failure to Learn by Experience

By their actions, psychopaths repeatedly bring disaster to themselves, their families, and friends. Harry Morris, who had enlisted the support of many people to help him, tossed it all away in one impulsive moment. This happened despite the fact that all of his previous acts as a juvenile were impulsive and even though his impulsivity had already been pointed out to him by many professionals. To the psychopath, the consequences of his actions are inconsequential.

Incapacity for Love and Closeness

Although the psychopath may possess an astonishing ability to engender and receive devotion from many people, he has no real capacity for love. He is unable to form mature relationships with others and finds it difficult to tolerate any closeness. If a friendship is developing, he will take steps to alienate that person to avoid closeness.

Lack of Insight

Because of his intelligence, it often appears to the casual observer that the psychopath has a remarkable capacity for insight. This is strengthened by the impression he gives that he is always ready to reassess his position, identify his misbehaviors, and present plans for change. However, his subsequent actions clearly show that this is not true insight but, rather, as Cleckley has called it, a "mimicry of

141

insight" (Cleckley 1955). His resolutions to do better, such as those offered by Harry after he was released on probation by the judge, are made without any real understanding of the behavior which led to the situation.

Shallow and Impersonal Responses to Sexual Life

As a corollary to his incapacity for love and closeness, the psychopath is also unable to achieve any deep response in a sexual relationship. This is true despite the notorious promiscuity of many psychopaths of both sexes. On close examination, it is apparent that these sexual activities are shallow, impersonal, and very self-centered.

Callousness and Sadism

Although greater attention will be given to this topic in the chapter on deviant sexual behavior, it is important to note now that callousness and sadism are often important characteristics of psychopathic behavior. Recall the behavior of Colonel Thompson, who tortured the opossum to death. The callousness of this sadistic behavior was illustrated by the manner in which he very calmly wiped the blood off the knife, put it away, climbed back in the car, and asked his driver to take him home.

Suicide Rarely Carried Out

Michael Crawford's suicidal behavior is typical of the psychopath. He frequently will threaten suicide or even make sham suicide attempts with a high degree of dramatic content. These gestures, designed to gain attention, will often be staged with stunning authenticity. On one of the many occasions when Michael attempted suicide, he staggered dramatically down the hospital corridor, dripping blood from the "slashes" in his chest. In reality, these were only superficial cuts which he had made with a small piece of glass or a razor blade. He had very carefully cut nothing other than the small capillaries on the skin's surface. However, before this could be discovered, Michael had created quite a stir by collapsing in a moaning heap at the feet of the nurse whose sympathy he was trying to get.

When the rare suicide occurs in the psychopath, it is commonly noted that he died with a surprised look on his face, probably as a result of the poor judgment he displayed in overstepping the bounds of "safe" suicidal behavior.

Periods of Marked Creativity

We have previously described the psychopath's pattern of self-defeat. Because of a tendency to focus on this impressive record of self-defeat, repeated failures, criminal activity, and even hospitalization, it is easy to overlook periods of extensive creativity, industriousness, and effectiveness. One of the problems in helping the psychopath is how to convert these brief periods of creativity into a stable pattern of behavior not subject to a pattern of self-defeat.

Underlying Factors

The factors underlying psychopathic behavior are not specifically known. However, the characteristics of the psychopath and, in particular, the difficulties he encounters in all forms of interpersonal relationships suggest the importance of carefully examining early childhood development.

O'Neal and her co-workers, in their study in which they obtained data about the families of those who eventually developed psychopathic behavior, determined that parental rejection in early childhood, a high frequency of broken homes, alcoholism, and low socioeconomic status were important underlying factors. They also found that those who developed psychopathic behavior had usually encountered a specific form of parental rejection characterized by either the complete absence of parental discipline or its presence in a very inconsistent or lenient form (O'Neal et al. 1960).

From this, it may be hypothesized that the absence or inconsistency of parental discipline deprives the child of an important mechanism for obtaining feedback about his behavior which might help to develop his own internalized system (the superego) for controlling it during adult life. Furthermore, not having experienced early parental relationships based on positive interactions, he does not develop any capacity for engaging in compatible adult relationships.

In this context, psychopathic behavior may be viewed as an acting out against the society which, in adulthood, is the representation of the early rejecting parents. Furthermore, the absence of anxiety about this acting out behavior, another common characteristic of psychopathic behavior, is another reflection of the absence or inconsistency of parental discipline during childhood. Without it, the child has not been able to assess what behavior or situation should make him anxious.

As mentioned earlier in this chapter, many people have thought that psychopathic behavior may have some underlying organic factors. Many attempts have been made to demonstrate that the psychopath is constitutionally inferior. Recent research has especially looked for evidence of either brain injury or brain damage. However, despite many studies which show high rates of abnormality in the brain wave patterns of adult criminals, there has been no positive proof that this abnormality is a precondition to the development of psychopathic behavior.

Helpful Hints to the Law Enforcement Officer

There are several important signs which will help the police officer recognize the possibility that he is dealing with a psychopath.

1. Review his arrest record. The psychopath's rap sheet will reflect a variety of crimes. Because of his immature need for immediate gratification, his crimes are extremely unpredictable. Unlike other criminals who tend to develop a specialty and stick with it, the psychopath will engage in a variety of crimes that may run the gamut from sodomy to armed robbery and murder one. Further, when engaging in a robbery, rape, or some other crime, he may not hesitate to kill his unresisting victims or witnesses just to experience the sensation of killing.

2. The police officer must develop the ability to recognize the con man's glib style of conversation. When this is coupled with the psychopath's inability to follow through or engage in any behavior that is not self-seeking, it should tip off the officer as to the kind of person with whom he is dealing.

3. If you are interviewing a suspect whom you find yourself liking or hating too much, he might be a psychopath. From training and ex-

perience, most professionals will develop a professional attitude toward those with whom they come in contact. Generally, there are those whom we like, those whom we do not like, and even some whom we are indifferent to. However, the individual who gets us so irritated that we tend to lose our professionalism or who motivates us to want to enter into some type of rescue on his behalf is possibly a psychopath.

4. The police officer should very carefully note as a possible psychopath the criminal who is able to involve many people in his behavior, his crimes, and his rescue. Many of the cases presented in this chapter did not involve the psychopath alone.

5. The well-integrated and functioning psychopath can usually "beat" a lie detector (polygraph) or at least produce an inconclusive result. Since it is an instrument that measures certain psysiological corollates of anxiety and guilt such as skin response, blood pressure, pulse, and respiration, it is an "emotional detective." If the test subject feels guilty or anxious about certain questions, there will be disturbances in the polygraph pattern. However, since the psychopath is immune to feelings of guilt and anxiety unless placed under severe stress, these physiological disturbances are not likely to appear even when he is responding to questions which might make the normal individual feel guilt or anxiety.

6. It has been said that speech is given to man to conceal his thoughts. This is certainly true of the psychopath. He is completely capable of responding to vague questions with vague answers and to concrete questions with concrete answers. In this way, he is often able to persuade himself that he is telling the truth (MacDonald 1966). For example, if you are questioning a suspect who is a psychopath and you ask a vague question such as "What did you do after leaving Los Angeles?" he may reply that he took a plane to Denver. He conveniently leaves out that he stopped over in Las Vegas where he participated in three armed robberies or in Tucson where he committed two rapes.

As another example, if you ask him if he has ever been in jail before, he may answer "No!" since he can assume that you are talking about this particular jail. He may, however, have been in several others or in a state penitentiary. Unless specifically asked, he will conclude, with proper justification to himself, that he has not lied in response to the question.

Consequently, it is easy to become discouraged when interviewing a psychopath. It may often be necessary to repeat the question several times and to formulate it in different ways. Only persistent and careful questioning will bring out the necessary information. However, if this procedure is done with hostility, the psychopath is likely to clam up and not respond to further questioning.

7. It is important not to bluff a psychopath. He is a master of this and certainly better than you are. The best way to interview him is to prepare yourself by knowing every detail of the case.

8. It is important to be firm and clear with the person who is suspected of being a psychopath. Saying exactly what you mean and setting appropriate limits upon which you are prepared to act are critical to handling him appropriately. Although a psychopath can be very charming, he can also make you very angry and may maneuver you into a situation in which you violate his rights. This is obviously to be avoided.

Differences Between the Lawbreaker and the Psychopath

While it is true that many criminals show some evidence of psychopathic behavior, there are important differences between the ordinary lawbreaker and the true psychopath.

The ordinary lawbreaker is most often motivated by what his crime will net him, whether it is twenty-five thousand from a bank robbery or another profitable venture. The psychopath, on the other hand, often steals things for which he has no particular use or will forge a check for a small amount when he has more than that in his own pocket.

The ordinary lawbreaker will seek to avoid detection and apprehension. The psychopath will do likewise for a period of time, but if he goes undetected for too long, he commits foolish crimes or leaves telltale clues behind which tend to insure his apprehension.

The ordinary lawbreaker will avoid the police and not volunteer to help them solve crimes. The psychopath, on the other hand, often sees his criminal activities as a game between himself and the police and is often detected in this way.

The ordinary lawbreaker generally maintains some creed of loyalty to friends, his family, or even to his opposition to society. The psychopath, however, is the uncommitted individual with loyalty to no one and no sincerely held attitudes for or against anything.

146

Summary

The psychopath, because of his persistent involvement in antisocial behavior, is very likely to come in contact with law enforcement officers. Because of the features he presents, he can also create specific problems in detection, handling, and subsequent care following arrest. Finally, he is potentially a very dangerous person because he doesn't need a reason to kill anyone, including a police officer.

REFERENCES AND ADDITIONAL BIBLIOGRAPHY

Cleckley, H. M. 1955. *The Mask of Sanity.* St. Louis: Mosby.

Dallas Police Department. 1973. *The Dallas Repeat Offender Study.*

Franks, D. M. 1956. "Recidivism, Psychopath and Personality." *British Journal of Delinquency* 6:192–201.

Halleck, S. L. 1972. *Psychiatry and the Dilemmas of Crime.* New York: Harper & Row.

Harrington, A. (December 1971). "Coming of Age of the Psychopath." *Playboy,* pp. 201–203.

————. 1972. *Psychopaths.* New York: Simon & Schuster.

MacDonald, J. M. 1966. "The Prompt Diagnosis of Psychopathic Personality." *American Journal of Psychiatry* 122:45.

Mannheim, H. 1965. *Comparative Criminology.* Boston: Houghton Mifflin.

O'Neal P.; Bergman, J.; Schafer, J.; and Robins, L. 1960. "The Relation of Childhood Behavior Problems to Adult Psychiatric Status." In *Scientific Papers and Discussions,* ed. J. Gottlieb and G. Tourney. Washington, D.C.: American Psychiatric Association.

Petersen, D. M. 1972. "Police Disposition of the Petty Offender." *Sociology & Social Research* 56:320–330.

Chapter 11

Deviant Sexual Behavior

DEVIANT sexual behavior represents an important category of abnormal behavior with which the police officer frequently comes in contact. When encountering sex crimes, such as rape, child molesting, and exhibitionism or crimes which often have an underlying sexual component, such as arson, shoplifting, and homicide, the officer will be able to carry out his work more effectively if he has a basic understanding of the associated psychological concepts.

Furthermore, the community, because of the threats to its welfare posed by sexual deviants, often places great pressure on law enforcement, challenging its competency if apprehension of the criminal is delayed. The public often does not realize the many obstacles which frequently impede investigation of sexual crimes, such as scanty evidence, lack of witnesses, and the reluctance of victims to file complaints.

The sexual deviant may also create problems for the officer by offending the officer's personal values, morals, and sense of decency. Sexually deviant behavior arouses feelings of disgust and indignation in the average person and the police officer is no exception. This personal reaction may decrease the effectiveness of the officer in the

Bob Fitch / Black Star

performance of his duties. A better psychological understanding of sexually deviant behavior may help the officer handle his personal reactions more effectively, thereby allowing him to deal with deviant sexual behavior from a broader and more professional frame of reference.

General Definitions and Concepts

Prior to a discussion of specific types of sexually deviant behavior, it is important to understand some general concepts relating to normal and abnormal sexual behavior.

Sexuality

Sexuality may be defined as all behavior associated with relations between the sexes and reproductive functions. In the theories of Sigmund Freud, as discussed in Chapter 3, normal sexuality depends on the successful completion of a sequence of early childhood events between birth and age five. During this time, the individual's involvement with and reactions to the various reproductive, receptive, and eliminative organs primarily determine the direction of personality growth. Relations with parents and peers further serve to shape individual identity and personality.

Normal development leads to a mature, adjusted individual who is capable, during adulthood or sooner, of entering into relationships with a member of the opposite sex which are both physically and emotionally stable and satisfying. Adult sexual relations are goal directed and designed to achieve satisfaction without excessive fear or guilt.

Although these relations may not be free from conflict, they will be based on a core of emotional stability which allows for resolution of any conflict which may occur. Consequently, the individual who has attained a normal sexual behavior pattern possesses a personal awareness of his own physical and emotional needs and has the judgment necessary to fulfill these needs in a realistic fashion within his environment.

Deviancy

Just as it is difficult to define *normalcy,* it is equally hard to define *deviancy.* Statistics is a common method used to distinguish between normality and deviancy. In this framework, deviancy is that unusual or rare behavior which is set apart from common behavior by its *infrequency of occurrence.* Therefore, in our society, *sexual deviancy* is interpreted as behavior which seeks stimulation and gratification by means other than heterosexual, genital intercourse, which is considered to be the *statistical norm.*

Designating a form of sexual behavior as deviant by a statistical methodology does not necessarily imply that the person exhibiting this behavior is mentally ill. An example of this type of deviant sexual behavior is the man who engages in homosexual activity for a short period of time and then never again. In this instance, homosexual behavior may result from a momentary urge to experiment rather than from any deep-seated fears of heterosexual relations. On the other hand, continuous homosexual relationships as the primary source of sexual gratification would be considered deviant, since they arise from underlying conflicts which have not been resolved in the course of normal development.

Deviant Sexual Behavior and Criminality

Just as all sexually deviant behavior does not clearly indicate mental illness, all sexually deviant behavior should not be considered criminal. While the mental health professional is interested in sexually deviant behavior to determine if it is a sign of mental illness, the police officer is interested in it to determine its legality or illegality.

Unfortunately, the laws of our society which determine the legality or illegality of behavior are not always clear or based on rational thinking. An example is offered by the crimes of *statutory rape* and *assaultive rape.* In the former, a person is liable for criminal action even though the sexual intercourse took place between a consenting couple and the behavior was not sexually deviant. On the other hand, assaultive rape involves an unwilling victim and is clearly an example of criminally related deviant sexual behavior.

Other sex crimes are also often unclear as to the course of action demanded from the police since they are *victimless crimes,* either because the partners are consenting (e.g., in a homosexual act) or the sexually deviant behavior of the individual is not directed against another person (e.g., transvestitism).

It is not our purpose to resolve these complex legal issues, but simply to point out to the police officer that the confusion surrounding many laws in this area allows him some flexibility of judgment when determining his course of action. Since he has this opportunity for discretion, it becomes even more important to understand psychological principles associated with the varieties of sexually deviant behavior. This will help him to choose a course of action consistent with individual needs and the laws of our society.

The Varieties of Deviant Sexual Behavior

Some forms of deviant sexual behavior are illegal while others are not. However, all have the common characteristic of being statistically less frequent practices than other forms of sexual behavior and also possess as a common psychological base a fear of normal heterosexual relationships.

In describing each, we will focus on their basic characteristics, the underlying factors in their development, and the problems which they present to law enforcement.

Homosexuality

With the recent trends toward liberalization of sexual mores and attitudes, the labeling of homosexuality as a form of deviant sexual behavior has aroused great controversy. Many groups have consistently attacked this labeling of homosexuality, suggesting that the choice of a partner of the same sex is as normal as a choice of a partner of the opposite sex.

Although statistics do not support this claim, the argument is valuable since it helps point out that much homosexual behavior is not criminal. Nevertheless, there is often a criminal element associated with some part of the homosexual community because of the known attraction to the homosexual community of a variety of criminals who prey upon them through entrapment, swindling, robbery, or blackmail and, in the extreme, murder. This contributes to the police problems associated with homosexual behavior.

The occurrence of homosexuality is documented throughout literature. Male homosexuality has been practiced in almost all cultures, both ancient and modern. Female homosexuality also has a long history; for example, *lesbianism* is derived from the name of a Greek island (Lesbos) believed to have been inhabited solely by women.

It has been theorized by many, including Freud, that there are latent homosexual tendencies in everyone, including those who prefer and engage exclusively in heterosexual relationships. Evidence for this is seen in the many varieties of exclusively male or female associations which are considered to be normal, socially acceptable outlets for these latent homosexual tendencies. These include men's clubs, women's clubs, sporting groups, civic organizations, and others.

Although a continued pattern of homosexual behavior is uncommon, the occurrence of occasional overt homosexual activity in the lives of many individuals is more frequent. Many of these can be classified as childhood experimentation or as a one-time experience during early or middle adulthood growing out of a period of pressure or crisis. It is important to recognize that, for these individuals, homosexuality is not the dominant sexual outlet and that they invariably return to a normal heterosexual pattern of behavior. These individuals should not be considered sexually deviant.

However, early homosexual experiences of others tend to be repeated and may become the exclusive form of sexual relations. In these cases, homosexuality should be considered a form of deviant sexual behavior since it is both infrequent in relationship to other forms of sexual behavior engaged in by most individuals and the choice is often based on unresolved psychological conflicts.

The underlying factors for male and female homosexuality may be found in early personality development. As the child passes through the several stages of physical and emotional development from childhood to adolescence (Chapter 3), he faces a variety of stresses. These are often associated with conflicts around various sexually related behaviors such as eating, urinating or defecating, and masturbating.

Psychological problems may arise because of difficulty in successfully completing a specific stage of development. This may lead to an *arrested* development at that stage or a return to it (regression) during periods of extreme stress, often as a result of strong sexual fears. It may become necessary for the child or adult to adopt certain behaviors to deal with the fear (Chapter 4). If the fear has focused around heterosexual relationships, the individual may reduce it by moving away from heterosexual relationships and toward homosexual behavior.

Consequently, homosexual preferences often develop from extreme denial of affection for the parent of the opposite sex. A son may have a great guilt about affectionate feelings toward his mother and they may be increased by a fear of punishment from the father. He may avoid the whole problem by abandoning any conscious effort to relate positively to females and instead associate exclusively with males.

The same process may occur in the female when conflicts arise about positive feelings toward the father. She is unable to handle these feelings of affection toward the father as well as her fears of the mother's reaction. She then turns away from normal heterosexual relationships with males.

In some individuals, a homosexual behavior pattern may emerge in early adolescence and continue unabated into and throughout adulthood. In others, this pattern may first be adopted in later life as the individual encounters some great stress such as marriage and its responsibilities.

Contrary to popular opinion, homosexuality is treatable. The individual who experiences anxiety about his homosexual behavior is often an excellent candidate for treatment since this anxiety is a motivation for a therapeutic relationship. Recovery of a normal heterosexual pattern depends not only on the individual's motivation, but also on the length of time for which the homosexual behavior has been practiced. The homosexual who began this pattern during early adolescence and has continued it exclusively throughout adulthood is more difficult to convert to a heterosexual pattern than the person who began homosexual relations later in life and has practiced them concurrently with heterosexual behavior.

Fetishism

The fetishist achieves sexual excitement and gratification by substituting an inanimate object or a part of the body for the human love object. The range of fetishistic behavior is great and can include many activities, some of which are nearly normal and others which are highly abnormal. For example, nearly everyone is engaging in fetishistic behavior when they preserve mementos from a loved friend or relative. Similarly, it is also a form of fetishistic behavior when individuals choose sexual partners on the basis of their conformity to certain preferences of hair color, body shape, or other physical features.

However, the fetishistic behavior which usually comes to the police's attention is associated with an inability to achieve sexual satisfaction except through contact with the object or the anatomical part. In these individuals, sexual satisfaction can only be achieved in the presence of the fetish.

Fetishism appears to be almost an exclusively male form of sexual deviancy, although some cases in women have been reported. Kinsey theorized that this striking finding is possibly a result of the male's greater susceptibility to the conditioning of early sexual experiences and the objects associated with them, but there is little evidence to support this. However, some elements of early childhood development are significant. The higher prevalence of fetishistic behavior among males does not imply an inborn difference between the sexes.

Fetishistic behavior may appear at any age. For example, it is exemplified during the elementary school years by the six-year-old boy who masturbates with a piece of a favorite blanket and, in adulthood, by the inability of some males to achieve sexual climax without considerable foreplay involving the stroking of a part of the body other than the penis.

Another characteristic of the fetishist is his difficulty in interpersonal relationships. This is understandable when the tendency of the fetishist to find security only with material objects is considered.

The origins of fetishistic behavior begin with the child's relations with inanimate objects. For example, in very early childhood the child derives security and reduces anxiety through oral activities such as sucking, using the thumb, a piece of a blanket, or a pacifier. As the child grows up, the importance of this early object may be transferred to another, perhaps a doll or another toy. Parents often rely upon this object as a way of pacifying the child and this gives greater significance to the object than the child might have given it himself.

This association may continue until the child is no longer able to separate from the object without severe anxiety. This may lead to fetishistic behavior. If the object (such as a toy) is also a means for achieving sexual satisfaction, it is a fetish because its loss is equated with the loss of sexual gratification. The occurrence of events should not be confused with normal situations in which children have favorite toys that acquire special significance. These are not fetishes if these children are able to find satisfaction in relating to other people and develop other outlets for sexual impulses.

Robert Dickes describes the case of an eight-year-old boy whose strange behavior concerned school authorities (Dickes 1970). While in counseling, the boy's mother revealed that she had been giving her foot to him for fondling ever since his first year. This play had continued and become ritualized with the eventual occurrence of accompanying sexual satisfaction and stimulation for the child. Once this behavior was revealed and brought into the boy's treatment, he was able to give up the practice. However, his mother reacted inappropriately and attempted to bribe him into restarting it. When confronted by the therapist with her inappropriateness, she stated that she did not see any harm in this game. This emphasizes how the development of deviant sexual behavior may be related to the interactions between parents and children.

Transvestitism

The transvestite achieves sexual excitement and gratification from, at times, wearing clothes and enacting the role of the opposite sex. (This is in contrast to the transsexual, who has completely assumed the identity of the opposite sex either through his behavior or a sex change operation.)

The homosexual transvestite primarily seeks out someone of his own sex as a partner for the gratification of these sexual desires. To make himself more attractive for this homosexual relationship, he will dress and affect the mannerisms of the opposite sex, becoming either a male or female impersonator. Nonhomosexual transvestites engage in this behavior less frequently and between periods of normal heterosexual activity. In these cases, sexual deviancy is less pronounced.

Since parental attitudes are key factors in the child's development of a proper sexual identity, it is not surprising that confusion of sexual identity in early childhood can be an underlying factor in the later development of transvestite behavior. For example, if the male child does not establish a proper sexual identity by identifying with the father, he may become confused and this may be reflected in later transvestite behavior.

Sadism and Masochism

The sadist obtains sexual gratification by inflicting pain upon others, while the masochist achieves the same level of sexual gratification by enduring pain inflicted upon himself. The sadist may achieve this sexual satisfaction by engaging in serious criminal acts such as torture, rape, and homicide. In other instances, such as arson, the underlying sadistic sexual impulses may not be clearly evident to the police, but the officer who is familiar with the underlying sexual aspect of this behavior can keep this in mind as he conducts his investigation.

While the masochist may not pose as great a danger to the community as the sadist because his impulses lead to activities in which he himself is the victim, it is important to recognize that his behavior may still involve others. For example, in *bondage* the masochist places himself under the power of a person of the opposite sex or, if a homosexual, under a person of the same sex. He then encourages this person to tie, chain, and/or beat him so that he may achieve sexual excitement. Fantasy both during and after the bondage is an important component. These fantasies are used to achieve sexual satisfaction and/or to stimulate continuation of the behavior.

Both sadism and masochism can be partially understood as an acting out of subconscious or unconscious feelings of guilt. Associated with these guilt feelings is a need for punishment which the sadist directs against others and a masochist takes upon himself. This is not surprising when one considers how, for example, religion, law, and sports support the belief that the guilty must pay. This leads to numerous situations in which punishment is expected and encouraged.

Parental strictness can also play an important role in the development of these behaviors. Impossibly high standards of conduct for the child or frequent unrealistic punishments can lead to excessive guilt. Although these feelings may work themselves out as the child grows older and discovers that the behaviors for which he originally felt guilty do not require this feeling, other children may not grow out of this pattern and may adopt sadistic and masochistic behavior patterns to alleviate guilt feelings.

A variation of sadistic behavior is its association with psychopathic behavior (Chapter 10). This may seem paradoxical since the psychopath operates with a lack of guilt while the sadist is usually motivated by excessive guilt. However, it is important to remember that the psychopath's "absence" of guilt is in reality a severe repression of guilt dating back to the developmental years. Sadistic behavior, which directs aggressive feelings toward others, also helps keep guilty feelings repressed.

This combination can lead to highly dangerous behavior and is associated with some of the most severe crimes noted. Homicides associated with extreme sadistic behavior are commonly the work of sexual psychopaths who combine within their personality the extremes of sadistic and psychopathic behavior. The following case examples will help illustrate this.

CASE EXAMPLE 1: NEVILLE G. C. HEATH

One rapist-murderer, Neville G. C. Heath, brutally murdered, raped, and mutilated two women. His history included forgeries, thefts, housebreaking, fraud, impersonating an officer, court-martials, and a dishonorable discharge from the armed forces.

The acts of murder were very sadistic. Each of the two women was tortured and killed by Heath within a three-week period. One woman had a nipple bitten off and this had almost been accomplished on the other woman. Autopsy revealed that some instrument, possibly a poker, had been thrust with great force into the vagina, rupturing it and damaging the abdominal viscera. One body had been lashed severely and the abdomen of the other woman had been ripped open. Heath was described as extremely poised and calm after these deeds and entirely free of remorse or guilt.

CASE EXAMPLE 2: THE BOSTON STRANGLER

In the case of the Boston Strangler, the police photographer's description of Mary Sullivan's body indicated the probability that the offender was a psychopath. Mary Sullivan, who was killed shortly after Christmas, was described as a "gay, friendly girl" who worked as a nurse's aid in a Cape Cod Hospital.

She had moved into a third-floor apartment with two women her age. On a Saturday, these two women came home from work, opened the door, and found Mary murdered. To quote directly from the police photographer's report regarding the position of the body:

on the bed in propped position, buttocks on pillow, back against headboard, head on right shoulder, knees up, eyes closed, vitreous liquid, probably semen, dripping from mouth to right breast. Breasts and lower extremities exposed, broomstick handle inserted in the vagina, steak knife on bed, semenal stains on blanket. Knotted about her neck was a charcoal colored stocking, over that a pink silk scarf tied with a huge bow under the chin, and over that, tied loosely, almost rakishly so that one could admit one's hand between it and her neck, a bright, pink and white flowered scarf. A gaily colored New York's card reading "Happy New Year" had been placed against the toes of her left foot (Frank 1971).

Only a psychopath could have been so callously sadistic and still added that last touch of macabre humor.

Exhibitionism

The exhibitionist attains sexual gratification by the impulsive exposure of his own genital organs or his entire body. To the police, this usually harmless form of sexual deviation often presents problems because of the reaction of the community rather than from the reality of any actual threat posed. Exhibitionism is, therefore, a good example of the confused situation which can arise when legal restrictions vary from locality to locality because of the different standards and mores of the community rather than from the behavior itself.

Like fetishism, exhibitionism is almost exclusively a male phenomenon. Exposure of the male genitals has a long history in many cultures, some sanctioning it as an accepted way of accentuating masculinity, strength, or prowess. In our own society, although exhibitionism of the genitals is proscribed by law, many acceptable forms and forums for exhibitionism, particularly for females, have been sanctioned. These include beauty contests, movies, and magazines.

This more liberal sanctioning of exhibitionism by society has helped to overturn one of the more popular myths associated with it, as well as underscoring one of its prominent characteristics. The exhibitionist is not oversexed; the opposite is true. Most exhibitionists lack masculine aggressiveness and self-confidence and feel markedly inferior to other men. Furthermore, the exhibitionist often shows an indifferent attitude toward women.

Another important characteristic of the exhibitionist is that he invariably acts as though he wishes to be caught. He may exhibit several times in relatively safe places and then, inexplicably, near a police officer. The desire to be caught and the setting up of a situation to accomplish this helps alleviate anxiety and guilt.

The exhibitionistic act is carried out many times on an impulse and many exhibitionists may be unaware of what they are doing at the time. Although a few men may unexpectedly begin to demonstrate exhibitionistic behavior in adulthood, it more commonly begins in early life and continues episodically throughout.

Underlying factors include early experiences which reinforce a belief that the male is inferior to the female. The future exhibitionist, therefore, does not develop characteristic male aggressiveness or self-confidence. Normal self-assertive behavior is feared by exhibitionists because they view it as a threat to possible loss of maternal and feminine affection. The onset of exhibitionism often occurs after stress situations in which self-confidence is being threatened or questioned. The behavior can be viewed as an attempt to regain some of this lost self-confidence.

Voyeurism

The voyeur achieves sexual gratification by watching a nude woman or man in some form of the sexual act. The peeping Tom, as he is popularly known, is usually, but not always, harmless and more of a nuisance than a serious threat to others or the community. However, in contrast to exhibitionism, which usually occurs in the absence of other forms of sexual deviancy, voyeurism may be associated with a wide range of deviant sexual behavior. While some may only look, others may employ voyeurism as a prelude to further sexual activity which may be aggressive and violent.

The "simple" voyeur is engaging in immature sexual behavior, more appropriate to a very early stage of development. Normally, this curiosity about anatomical differences and the manner in which sexual organs function reaches a peak between ages three and five. During this time there is considerable peeping and displaying behavior by the child. Parents often make many demands in their attempts to divert this curiosity into more acceptable forms of behavior while, at the same time, allowing the child to satisfy his or her desire to know more about sex.

A prudish attitude may instill in the child a morbid curiosity which will later result in an irresistible desire to peep. Likewise, very strict prohibitions and overly severe punishment may make the child fearful of normal sexual activity.

Incest

Incest is the practice of sexual intercourse between closely related persons of the opposite sex whose marriage is prohibited by law. Prohibition against incestuous relations is practically universal, but the laws against it and the prescribed punishments vary considerably.

It is not a sexual deviation in the same sense as homosexuality, fetishism, and exhibitionism because it does not involve difficulty with normal heterosexual intercourse. However, it is considered a form of sexual deviation because it violates normal societal values.

Consequently, the young son or daughter who is forced or enticed into incest by either mother or father will be thrown into a severe conflict. Resulting guilt and anxiety may lead to profound regression and mental illness.

Sociologically, incest is viewed as a threat to the basic fabric of society and its principal unit, the family. However, this prohibition against incest does not prevent the development of strong erotic interests between family members. Consequently, many family activities are designed to divert these erotic interests into normal and acceptable behavior. Failure in this process may often be an underlying factor in family disputes and should be taken into account by the police officer when he intervenes.

Pedophilia

In pedophilia, like incest, the choice of the love object is inappropriate. The pedophile or child molester, as he is commonly known, may engage only in slight physical contact such as a pat on the head or, in the extreme, he may engage in intercourse or sodomy. Furthermore, child molesters may assume either a passive or aggressive role in their relationships with children.

The passive pedophile is usually inhibited in all social areas and the feelings he displays are mixed with warmth and tenderness. He is more likely to approach the child in the manner of courtship than by force.

However, other pedophiles may demonstrate a marked sadistic attitude and their molestations may include forceful acts of intercourse and, in some instances, torture and mutilation. The aggressive pedophile is more likely to be involved in a sexual crime, including murder.

Although the two types appear to be fairly distinct, there are a few cases in which the passive pedophile may progress to more aggressive acts. The police officer should always be alert to the possibility of the seemingly harmless offender becoming more violent, espe-

161

cially in response to panic at the moment of discovery or in fear of being discovered.

The practice of pedophilia many times begins in early adolescence and continues throughout adult life unless treatment intervenes. More rarely, it begins in later life, brought on by senility, impotence, or some other adult crisis.

Bestiality and Necrophilia

These two deviations occur infrequently. Bestiality is the achievement of sexual gratification from intercourse with a living animal and includes the practice of sodomy. It is not uncommon among people who live in rural areas, particularly farmers and others who have frequent contacts with animals. A milder form of bestiality (zoophilia) is represented by those who keep numerous pets at home and prefer their company to people. Those who suffer from bestiality are unable to function normally in society and also have other serious psychological disturbances.

Necrophilia is the desire to engage in sexual intercourse with a dead body. Its presence is an indication of serious mental illness. It can become a police problem because some necrophiliacs acquire the desired object through the desecration of gravesites or, in rare instances, homicide. A milder form of necrophilia, in which actual physical contact does not take place but there is a frequent and perverse pleasure associated with conditions of death, is harder to detect.

Helpful Hints to the Law Enforcement Officer

Because some sexual deviations are against the law and because crimes are committed in association with or as a result of these deviant sexual motivations, it is important for the law enforcement officer to acquire professionalism in dealing with the sexual offender. If he understands the personality characteristics of the sexual deviate, he may be better able to anticipate this behavior and use his knowledge to facilitate earlier apprehension.

The police officer should also examine his own attitudes toward sexual deviancy and recognize that these offenses result from motives and impulses which are often not understood or controllable rather than from moral perversity. This does not lessen the seriousness of crimes associated with sexual deviancy, but should increase the police officer's ability to act professionally and responsibly.

This professionalism should also carry over into his contacts with the victims. If the victim is not treated respectfully and courteously, he or she may be unwilling to divulge information which could be helpful in identifying and apprehending the offender.

Homosexuality

The officer who encounters homosexual behavior must have an attitude which will allow him to make an objective examination as to whether any realistic criminal element has been associated with it. Failure to do this will not only often result in an inappropriate arrest, but also can be a potential danger should the homosexual react with anger about being picked on unfairly.

Consequently, the officer should approach each incident of homosexual behavior with tact, indicating his respect for the individual's choice of behavior while, at the same time, pursuing his concern that a criminal act may have been committed. The empathetic officer who acts in this manner will avoid placing the homosexual on the defensive and will decrease his anxiety about the situation, thereby possibly preventing an outburst of anger or violence.

On the other hand, the officer should not automatically assume that all homosexual behavior is between consenting adults. The pressure of an active partner in a homosexual relationship can often make the passive partner willing to consent while feeling an underlying resistance to the behavior.

Finally, the officer should also take into consideration the environment in which the homosexual behavior has taken place, since criminal aspects of homosexual behavior may include not only the behavior but also the location in which it is practiced. For example, if it occurs in a public place in association with pick-ups or solicitation it may be criminal, in contrast to its occurrence in the privacy of the home. This criminality will vary, however, in different jurisdictions.

Fetishism

It is rare for fetishistic behavior to come to an officer's attention, because the fetish is usually inanimate or a part of the body. Furthermore, because fetishistic behavior does not usually involve another person, it may not be readily associated with criminal behavior.

However, it is interesting to note that some episodes of shoplifting are associated with fetishistic behavior since the objects sought have significant value through the sexual feelings they arouse. In these cases, shoplifting becomes a fetishistic experience and exemplifies how deviant sexual behavior can indirectly lead to crime and, if not looked for, may be missed as an underlying factor in the crime.

Finally, violent behavior can occasionally be associated with fetishism if the individual is aggressively engaged in the pursuit of a particular part of another's body or an object which someone else has.

Transvestitism

Similarly to fetishism, transvestitism does not usually involve the police, since most transvestites are clever about concealing their true sexual identity and do not call attention to themselves.

However, some are more overt and can present a problem to the officer when their behavior is called to his attention by outraged members of the community. It is important for the officer not to over-react to these pleas, since there is usually little he can accomplish except to encourage the transvestite to be more aware of his impact on others (which he usually already is).

Exhibitionism

The law enforcement officer should not consider the exhibitionist a dangerous criminal in most cases. He usually lacks the ability to demonstrate normal levels of aggression and is more passive than the average citizen. Since he is not seeking sexual intercourse, he is more likely to retreat from fear if a woman should approach him directly or invite him to have sexual contact. Further, exhibitionists do not usually demonstrate a tendency to progress to more serious or violent crimes unless their acts are associated with sadism or masochism.

As exhibitionists grow older, the behavior is more likely to subside or to be transferred in direction more toward children than adult women.

From this discussion, it is apparent that law enforcement officers who encounter the sexual criminal must know enough about sexual deviations to be able to make appropriate judgments about each sexual criminal as an individual. Not every sexual deviation yields only one type of behavior. The importance of this fact is emphasized by studies which indicate that as few as 10 percent of sexual deviants must be considered immediately or potentially dangerous, but that all types of sexual deviations may be associated with dangerous behavior in a specific case.

Common misconceptions about sexual criminals include the beliefs that there is a high correlation between brain damage and sexual deviancy and that sexual offenders are usually suffering from severe mental illness. Furthermore, while "hard" drugs are rarely a factor in sexual crimes, there is strong connection between the use of alcohol and deviant sexual behavior, with excessive alcohol intake leading to the release of inhibitions.

Although overt aggression in association with sexual deviancy is relatively infrequent, sadistic fantasies are more common. For this reason, police officers should *always* be alert to the potential for dangerous behavior. In questioning the sexual deviant, the police officer should go beyond the actual behavior and try to find out more about the individual's fantasies. By doing so, he will get a closer picture of this person's potential for dangerous behavior.

Summary

In this chapter, we have outlined the varieties of deviant sexual behavior. Characteristics have been described and the importance of each behavior to the police officer has been emphasized.

The criminality of deviant sexual behavior can vary considerably. Not all forms of sexually deviant behavior are criminal nor are all sexual deviants criminals. Only by understanding the characteristics of the individual sexual deviant will the officer be able to maintain a professional attitude. This attitude should include a recognition that while the sexual criminal is not necessarily a monster, neither is he simply an unfortunate individual. Whereas he should not be treated inhumanely, he should also not be allowed to involve others in his deviation to the extent that it interferes with the usual conduct of society and its members.

REFERENCES AND ADDITIONAL BIBLIOGRAPHY

Banay, R. S. November 1969. "Unconscious Sexual Motivation of Crime." *Medical Aspects of Human Sexuality.* 3:91–102.

Beiber, I. 1962. *Homosexuality.* New York: Basic Books.

Cohen, M. L. and Boucher, R. J. March 1972. "Misunderstandings about Sexual Criminals." *Sexual Behavior.* 2:56–62.

Dickes, R. January 1970. "Psychodynamics of Fetishism." *Medical Aspects of Human Sexuality.* 4:39–52.

Eysenck, H. J. November 1973. "Personality and Attitudes to Sex in Criminals." *Journal of Sex Research* 9:295–306.

Frank, G. 1971. *The Boston Strangler.* New York: New American Library.

McDonald, J. 1973. *Exhibitionism.* Springfield, Ill.: Charles C. Thomas.

Mathis, J. L. June 1969. "The Exhibitionist." *Medical Aspects of Human Sexuality.* 3:89–101.

Chapter 12

Delinquent Behavior

UP TO THIS POINT in the discussion of assessing and managing abnormal behavior in the field, the focus has been on the adult. However, the abnormal behaviors of those under eighteen (juveniles) pose significant problems for the law enforcement officer.

General Overview

Most police officers usually come in contact with juveniles only when they have indulged or are indulging in antisocial or acting out behavior. Because of his limited range of contacts with juveniles, an officer may perceive most children as either delinquent or potentially delinquent. Although common sense tells us that this is not true, it is sometimes easy for the police officer to develop negative attitudes toward those juveniles with whom he comes in contact.

Furthermore, the line which exists between *delinquent behavior* and *delinquent criminal behavior* is not always clear and can add confusion to the situation. For example, many offenses for which a juvenile may be arrested and, therefore, labeled a criminal are not

Bruce Roberts / Rapho-Photo Researchers, Inc.

offenses for which an adult would be detained. Running away from home, violation of curfew, and possession of alcohol are offenses only for those under the statutory age.

Consequently, although we tend to categorize all juvenile behavior which comes to the attention of law enforcement as *delinquency*, it is important to recognize that some is a violation of the law only because the offender is under eighteen. This is not to suggest that an officer should ignore or condone this behavior, but that a referral to another community agency might be more helpful to the child than a referral to juvenile court.

The officer's flexibility in decision making when dealing with juveniles makes it even more important for him to understand delinquent behavior. The appropriate use of this flexibility may not only prevent a child from acquiring the stigma associated with a juvenile criminal record but also help prevent the progression of delinquent behavior to a point where it becomes a fixed life style continuing into adulthood and leading to an adult criminal record.

Before presenting some helpful hints to the law enforcement officer for handling delinquent behavior, it is important to discuss more specifically some of the underlying factors involved in the onset of antisocial or delinquent behavior.

Underlying Factors

Broken homes, neglect, poverty, low intelligence, brain damage, mental illness, and other factors have been proposed at one time or another as the "cause" of delinquency. However, none, in isolation, has stood the test of time or scientific scrutiny. Rather, juvenile delinquency is a series of complex behaviors involving many factors which have complex relationships with each other.

In today's society, it is often tempting to look for simple answers to complex problems. Oversimplifications such as "delinquency is caused by parents being too damned easy on their kids" or "all delinquents are suffering from emotional confusion and an identity crisis" should be avoided.

The American Psychiatric Association Diagnostic and Statistical Manual (DSM-II) describes two disorders which are particularly relevant to delinquent behavior: *adjustment reactions of childhood* and *adjustment reactions of adolescence.* These are types of stress reactions; the former occurs during childhood (before age twelve) and the latter during adolescence (between twelve and eighteen). Behavioral responses to stress may include actions which are labeled antisocial or delinquent. The child in the midst of stress and an adjustment reaction may lie, steal, commit malicious mischief, or run away from home. The adolescent may drive while intoxicated, shoplift, commit an armed robbery, or physically assault another person.

Consequently, to know more about the factors underlying delinquent behavior, it is important to be aware of important stresses during childhood and adolescence. The stress situations to be presented are not a complete list, but are intended only to give examples of those situations which can lead to delinquent behavior.

Childhood

When a child experiences rejection, it is not unusual for him to disappear. Feeling that no one wants him, he may indicate his anger by running away. Through this retaliation, the child is saying "I don't want you" in response to the rejection. Alternatively, the child may decide to test his parents as a way of finding out if they really care. These tests may include accidental arson in which the child lights a match to see what might happen (for example, a lot of attention).

The death of a loved one, particularly a parent, may also lead to antisocial behavior. Instead of expressing feelings of depression and grief, the child may demonstrate hostility against society for having taken the parent away.

Sometimes a child may be labeled a troublemaker by teachers, playmates, and parents with little basis in fact. However, once labeled, the child may begin to act as others see him. For example, if you are going to be blamed every time something is missing, then you might as well take it and enjoy it or, if you are going to be blamed for starting a fight no matter what happens, then probably the best way to handle things is to hit the other guy first and at least get an advantage.

Antisocial behavior may also result from conflicts with parents. Some parents are overprotective and overindulgent while others are too strict. Some may set standards of conduct and/or achievement which no child can possibly attain, while others do not set any goals for their children. Many parents are so busy trying to maintain their own marginal adjustment that they are unable to help their children handle their problems. These parents, through their behavior, may indirectly encourage the child to act out as a way of placing the blame for their own failures on the child.

Adolescence

Adolescents can be affected by the same stresses of childhood which have been described, but they are also subject to other stresses unique to this period of life. For example, as a child grows older, he may begin to face stresses with regard to a choice of schooling, particularly whether or not to go to college. Difficulties with his parents may increase because, as he grows older, he is able to be more independent, or because he may want to remain a child and not grow up. This difficult choice between independence and dependence may lead to conflict with his parents, who also have mixed feelings about watching him grow up.

As he searches for an identity, he may have trouble with his self-image and worry about his popularity. A girl may have difficulty finding an acceptable moral code; a boy may feel uncertain as he begins to relate to girls socially. Anxiety and other feelings may lead to antisocial behavior as an inadequate way of resolving them.

Finally, if he finds as he grows up that adolescence does not meet his expectations, he may become depressed and isolated. He may conclude that he is a failure because others have goals that they are striving toward, but he does not. Faced with loneliness and isolation, he may engage in acting out behavior to enhance his self-image.

An adolescent's ability to handle these stresses will be dependent on the strengths he has developed while growing up. If his self-image is adequate, he will be better able to withstand these stresses and the likelihood of his resorting to delinquent behavior as a means of dealing with these situations is less.

If he is unable to handle these stresses except by developing a pattern of delinquent behavior, he is likely to come in contact with the police. Through his actions, the officer inadvertently may support the continuation of acting out behavior or he may be able to offer help before more serious trouble occurs. Consequently, it is important for an officer to recognize what he shouldn't do and what he should do when confronted with acting out juveniles.

Helpful Hints to the Law Enforcement Officer

In the opinion of many juveniles, the police officer has two strikes against him even before contact occurs. First, to some he is a symbol of all bad experiences with other authority figures including fathers, mothers, teachers, and older siblings. As a result, the officer may become a victim of displacement, as angry feelings which the juvenile has for other authority figures are put upon the officer.

In addition, the norms of the juvenile's peer group may indicate that the police should be viewed as enemies and that manhood and toughness are demonstrated by "not letting the cops shove you around" or by "clamming up" whenever an officer asks questions. It is, therefore, important for an officer to recognize that any relationship he forms with a juvenile will be dependent upon the manner in which he approaches him, the methods he uses, and his ability to communicate.

Negative Approaches

Regardless of what abusive language may be used by a juvenile, the officer should never respond in kind. He must remain professional at all times and treat the youth with courtesy and respect, at least until the juvenile's conduct clearly shows that he does not merit this treatment.

An officer should never make fun of juveniles or their predicament. A deputy recently stopped two boys riding their motorcycles along the side of a county dirt road. While he was writing out a citation for this illegal activity, another deputy, who had arrived on the scene, sat in his car and smiled. What he was actually smiling about was never determined, but the boys interpreted it as being directed at them. Later, they told others that the sheriff's department "stunk" and that deputies had nothing better to do but drive around and hassle teenagers who were riding bikes too close to the road. This incident certainly did not improve the officers' image.

Police officers should avoid using excessive authority. Although an officer should be firm, he should not be overbearing. Juveniles will not respond to an approach which implies, "I'm a cop and you kids have to do what I say." The officer who is afraid that he will lose control of a situation unless he adopts an overbearing attitude is in trouble from the beginning. Children are very sensitive to the insecurities of adults and the officer who is overbearing will be "tuned out."

While nothing will make the average cop angrier than an awareness that the person to whom he is speaking is not listening, police often do this themselves, especially with juveniles. A local judge reported that this is a frequent complaint of those brought to the Juvenile Court Center. For example, if an officer has found a kid out after curfew, he should listen to him and learn the circumstances. This will let the juvenile see that he is interested in what he is saying, rather than in "turning him off."

Although traffic laws should be enforced, many juveniles complain that the officer doesn't give them a second chance on questionable offenses. Too rigid enforcement of minor traffic laws against juveniles may be related to an officer's unwillingness to listen to the reasons a juvenile gives for his actions. For example, a juvenile may not interpret certain traffic control procedures in the same way as an adult. An adult who gets a speeding ticket is more likely to dismiss it as bad luck and/or concede, after reflection, that he deserved it. However, a juvenile, because he is usually more insecure, is more likely to feel that the officer was unfair because "the kid down the street speeds all over the neighborhood and never gets caught."

In these minor offenses, justice may be better served if an officer is a little lenient. A warning, administered firmly but with respect for the juvenile as a person, may give him a good feeling about his interaction with the officer. Giving a citation, even though it is technically justified, may turn the juvenile off and leave him with the impression that all policemen are "hard asses" whose main goal in life is to harass kids.

Some officers refuse to help juveniles in situations where they would normally offer assistance to adults. When this occurs, the juvenile feels discriminated against.

Officers should not talk about a juvenile or his actions as if he were not present. Reciting his offenses, especially in a way which will cause embarrassment or shame, is not desirable. They should avoid lecturing or sermonizing and confine their communications to either advice or clear admonishment.

Finally, it is important for an officer never to lie to a juvenile. If an officer gives a juvenile the impression that certain actions will or will not be taken and then does not follow through, the juvenile will feel betrayed and angry. Deception and a failure to keep promises are doubtful policies with anyone, but, with juveniles, they are never advisable. If a juvenile develops an early mistrust of law enforcement, it is unlikely that trust will ever be gained.

Positive Approaches

The officer should respect a juvenile as he would an adult. Even if a juvenile is wrong, the officer should be patient. He should remember that children test limits, not only with parents and teachers, but also with policemen.

The officer should be firm, but not grim. Humor and a relaxed manner can reduce tension, dispel hostility, and help ease a situation. This approach will help a juvenile to see that police officers are human and compassionate and that they can understand how he feels.

An officer should explain his actions and answer a juvenile's questions. He should recognize that explanation is different from justification. Justification may not be necessary, but an explanation is always useful.

While it may be appropriate for an officer in some situations to criticize a juvenile's behavior, an officer should never attack his personality or character. In treating a child, a therapist tries to help a child understand that it is certain aspects of his behavior which are unacceptable, rather than his entire personality. This principle also applies to the interactions between police and juveniles. The focus should always be on the offending behavior and should not attack the juvenile's worth as a person (i.e., "that behavior was stupid" rather than "you are stupid").

An officer should become familiar with those agencies in the community concerned with the welfare of children and adolescents. He should be acquainted with their programs as well as their eligibility and referral policies. In larger communities, there is usually a book available listing those resources which offer programs for juveniles. All officers should be familiar with this reference and those assigned to juvenile work should have a copy readily available.

Finally, it is important for law enforcement officers to be involved with the community's youth through activities which may include police department tours, athletic and other school programs, university courses, and visits to juvenile court centers and detention homes.

Summary

In this chapter, we have presented some of the more important issues for law enforcement officers who work with juveniles. The officer should recognize that the juvenile is an individual and that a knowledge and understanding of child and adolescent behavior will enhance his ability to rehabilitate children who stray. The effective officer may also be able to avoid placing many of them in the criminal justice system through the juvenile court.

A definition of delinquency has been presented and the fallacy of trying to find a single cause or cure for this complex behavior has been pointed out. Some of the causes, particularly stress situations in childhood and adolescence, have been described. Finally, we have presented some of those police behaviors which turn kids off and have also suggested more desirable actions which will help improve communication.

By following these prescriptions, the professional officer may not only carry out his law enforcement responsibilities but may also perform a responsible community service through helping to guide and direct the growth of young people.

REFERENCES AND ADDITIONAL BIBLIOGRAPHY

Aichorn, A. 1935. *Wayward Youth*. New York: Viking Press.

Ferdinand, T. N., Luchterhand, E. G. 1970. "Inner-City Youth, the Police, the Juvenile Court and Justice." *Social Problems* 17:510–527.

Ginott, H. 1969. *Between Parent and Teenager*. New York: Avon.

Hagan, J. L. 1972. "The Labelling Perspective, the Delinquent, and the Police: A Review of the Literature." *Canadian Journal of Criminology & Corrections* 14:150–165.

Hardt, R. H. 1968. "Delinquency and Social Class: Bad Kids or Good Cops?" In *Among the People: Encounters with the Poor*, eds. I. Deutscher and E. J. Thompson. New York: Basic Books, pp. 132–145.

McCord, W. 1956. *Psychopathy and Delinquency*. New York: Grune & Stratton.

Pursuit, D. 1972. *Police Programs for Preventing Crime and Delinquency*. Springfield, Ill.: Charles C. Thomas.

Walker, R. N. 1973. *Psychology of the Youthful Offender*, 2d ed. Springfield, Ill.: Charles C. Thomas.

West, D. J. 1967. *The Young Offenders*. New York: International Universities Press.

Chapter 13

Drug Dependent Behavior

DRUG DEPENDENT BEHAVIOR usually occurs in the context of more basic patterns of maladaptive behavior. It is seen not only in individuals with personality disorders but also in those with neuroses and psychoses. Before proceeding to a more detailed discussion of specific forms of drug dependent behavior, its underlying factors and behavioral manifestations, some general considerations will be presented which will assist the law enforcement officer in developing a comprehensive perspective on this critical police problem.

General Considerations

A *drug* may be defined as a chemical substance which, when introduced into the body, produces changes in its functioning. If, for example, a person has a fever, he uses aspirin to lower it.

However, some substances (drugs) also affect psychological func-

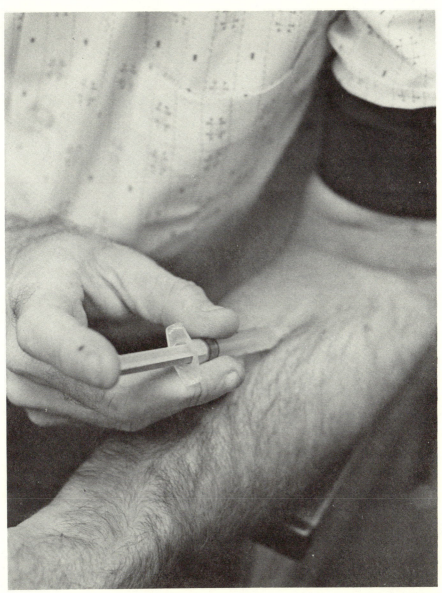

Courtesy Paul Neuthaler

tioning. For example, a small quantity of LSD (lysergic acid diethylamide) will cause a disturbance in psychological balance through hallucinations, both visual and auditory, derived from false perceptions of the environment.

Because of the impact of drugs on their behavior, drug abusers often come to police attention. Approximately half of all incidents which police encounter are related to the use or abuse of alcohol and other drugs. These may include a traffic accident involving a drunken driver, a heroin overdose brought to the emergency room, or a homicide occurring during a drug rip-off.

Because the police officer most frequently sees the most sordid effects of drug abuse, there is a tendency to classify all abusers as "drunks," "junkies," "acid freaks," and "pot heads" with all the moral condemnation that these terms imply. By becoming thoroughly familiar with the behavioral aspects of drug use and abuse, the officer can approach this aspect of his job in a professional and nonjudgmental manner.

The point at which drug use is transformed into abuse is largely determined by the point of view from which it is considered. *Medically,* the doctor considers the use of aspirin to relieve headache and reduce fever as legitimate. However, he would consider it a case of aspirin abuse if his patient had swallowed dozens of aspirin tablets in a suicide attempt, arriving at the hospital unconscious. Likewise, the physician may legitimately prescribe morphine, an opiate, to ease the suffering of a terminal cancer patient. This use of an opiate is appropriate when nothing else will alleviate the severe pain. Consequently, from these examples, it is clear that a physician considers a drug abused if it does not contribute to the individual's ultimate health and well-being.

Drug use and abuse can also be viewed *behaviorally.* An example is LSD, which was originally synthesized to be used under carefully controlled experimental conditions in the treatment of certain personality disorders. However, when abused through indiscriminate use without expert supervision, it produces abnormal behavior which may be dangerous both to the user and to others.

Drug use and abuse can also be defined *legally.* For example, while it is legal to sell and use alcohol, it is illegal to drive an automobile while intoxicated, a condition defined in most states as a blood alcohol concentration of greater than .10. Even though an individual may not have actually reached this level of blood alcohol, he may still be abusing alcohol if he stops at his favorite bar on the way home from work to have several highballs, knowing full well that he must drive after drinking. However, other drugs, regardless of their impact on behavior, are considered as having been abused simply because their possession is illegal.

From these examples, it is apparent that the precise understanding of *drug abuse* depends upon the circumstances of the user and the viewpoint of the observer.

Definitions

To understand behavioral aspects of drug abuse, it is important to be acquainted with the proper definitions of those terms which are used to describe individual reactions to drugs. These terms are used to describe behavioral responses associated with continued use or sudden cessation of drugs and assist in categorizing these drugs according to their impact on the user.

Intoxication

This refers to the state induced through excessive use. Although commonly used in reference to alcohol, it more appropriately describes excessive use of any drug.

In defining intoxication, the critical issue is not how much of the drug has been taken into the body, but rather how much of it is there at any one time and for how long. For example, it is not the quantity of alcohol which a person consumes that governs the impact, but how much is in his bloodstream at a specific time.

However, since most officers do not have immediate access to blood, we generally conclude that a person is *intoxicated* when his behavior changes. Common indices are loud or slurred speech, uncoordinated movements, and/or overaggressive behavior.

Addiction

Similarly, we also encounter inappropriate uses of *addiction* through reference to all states of drug abuse. Technically, however, the addict is a person who cannot abstain from the use of a drug *without suffering severe physical symptoms*. This *withdrawal syn-*

drome is a combination of painful and debilitating physical reactions which occur after an addicting drug is withdrawn.

If the heroin addict appears hurried, preoccupied, and impatient to get his next "fix," it is often to prevent withdrawal symptoms. In fact, many addicts continue taking addicting drugs not to seek a new "high" but to avoid the discomfort of withdrawal.

Tolerance

All drugs which are addicting, that is, capable of producing the withdrawal syndrome, also produce tolerance. This term refers to the inability of the individual to experience the same effects from the same dose of a drug over a period of time. If the effect is to remain the same, the user must constantly increase the dose. It is important to recognize that not all drugs which produce tolerance are addicting, because they do not all produce a withdrawal syndrome.

Habituation

In contrast to addiction and tolerance, which are physiological terms associated with drug abuse, *habituation* refers to the psychological aspects of drug abuse. All drugs which affect behavior are, to some extent, habit forming. The degree to which they are habit forming is a combination of their capacity to produce tolerance, the behavioral changes which they produce, and the personality characteristics of the user.

In addiction, psychological dependence is a factor, but physical dependence is primary. In habituation, it is the psychological dependence which is important because there is no physical dependence.

Drug Dependence

A new term has been used recently to rise above the issue of whether a drug is addictive or habituating. *Drug dependence* has been suggested as a general term to describe the compulsive use of a drug for whatever reason. The specific type of dependence can be noted by applying the name of the drug upon which the person is dependent, for example, *heroin dependence, alcohol dependence,* etc.

Using these terms, all drugs which influence behavior can be categorized.

180

1. *Heroin* produces addiction, tolerance, and habituation.
2. *Alcohol* produces addiction, tolerance, and habituation.
3. *Barbiturates* produce addiction, tolerance, and habituation.
4. *Amphetamines* produce tolerance and habituation but not addiction.
5. *Cocaine* produces extreme habituation, but does not produce addiction or tolerance.
6. *Minor tranquilizers,* such as *Valium* and *Librium,* do not produce addiction but can produce tolerance and habituation.
7. *Marijuana* and *LSD* do not produce addiction or tolerance and in most individuals have only a mild habituating effect.

Although these categorizations describe essential differences in the physical and psychological effects of these commonly abused drugs, it is also important to recognize that the associated behaviors have many features in common. Some of them will be identified in the following discussion of those commonly abused drugs which the police officer is most likely to come in contact with during the performance of his duties.

Alcohol

The frequency with which the police officer encounters behavior influenced by alcohol is indicative of alcohol's role as the most commonly abused substance in the United States. If he makes an arrest, it may be one of the more than 50 percent of arrests related to alcohol. If he is on the road investigating a fatal accident, there is a very good chance the accident involves a drunken driver. It is, therefore, important for him to be aware of alcohol and the behavior which it engenders.

Characteristics of Alcohol Abuse

Many theories have been developed to explain the causes of excessive drinking behavior. Some people believe individuals drink because they are depressed; others point out that excessive alcohol use is often associated with feelings of guilt. Feelings of inadequacy, failure, and low self-esteem as well as poor interpersonal relationships are also factors underlying excessive alcohol intake.

Chafetz describes two types of people who drink to excess, the *reactive* and the *addicted* (Chafetz 1959). The reactive drinker usually demonstrates a reasonable adjustment in family, education, work, and social areas as well as an ability on most occasions to move toward realistic goals. However, he tends to use alcohol to excess when he is *temporarily* overwhelmed by a stress situation and has no other means at his disposal to handle the stress.

The addicted alcoholic's behavior is in contrast. (In using this term, Chafetz is not adhering to the "strict" definition of addiction given previously.) His life style reveals a marked disturbance in adjustments at home, school, and work as well as a behavioral pattern in which no clear point can be defined as initiating excessive drinking. In contrast to the reactive pattern, no marked stress prior to alcohol abuse is noted. Rather, his entire life can be viewed as a single stress and the pattern of excessive drinking is repetitive, contributing to a marked decrease in the effectiveness of his behavior.

Other characteristics of the alcohol abuser which the police officer should be aware of include an extremely low frustration tolerance. He may show a low tolerance toward any wish, request, desire, or demand made of him. If any demands he makes are not granted, he may react with anger or even violence.

Deep depression may also be encountered in the alcohol abuser's personality and, consequently, the police officer should also be alert to the possible presence of depression and suicidal behavior. The loss of self-esteem, which is both an underlying factor in the abuse as well as a consequence of it, is often so intense that it becomes the basis for violent behavior directed against the self. The alcoholic who has recently lost his wife, family, and job may be a high suicidal risk.

Another important characteristic is the almost simultaneous occurrence of feelings of inferiority and an attitude of superiority. After drinking excessively, the alcohol abuser may tell you that he is no good while, at the same time, making demands on others that indicate that he considers himself someone special.

The police officer should also know that most alcoholics are fearful, since this can have important consequences for handling him when he is intoxicated. If he is approached when intoxicated in a way which increases his fears, he may overreact with an attempt at false bravery, thus making it more difficult for the officer to handle him.

Finally, after a binge, he may exhibit a dependent, clinging behavior. This can arouse angry feelings in others (including police officers) and may lead to an inappropriate ignoring of his needs. Such neglect could be dangerous because serious physical problems, which are often masked by alcohol abuse, may be overlooked.

Helpful Hints to the Law Enforcement Officer

The signs of acute alcohol intoxication can include varying degrees of exhilaration and excitement, loss of inhibition and restraint, bizarre behavior, slurred speech, and lack of coordination. When encountering someone who is intoxicated, the officer might remember the last time "he tied one on." Remembering his own feelings, including the sense of power and the glibness of his tongue, will help him to relate better to the "drunk." The officer should be patient, but firm. He should remember that the person involved is "not himself" and probably won't remember how obnoxious he was. If he is belligerent, ignore this as much as possible unless he looks like he is going to hurt himself or others. If you can keep him talking while you are working, your job will be easier.

When alcohol intoxication has been especially severe, drowsiness, stupor, and possibly lack of consciousness may be noted. It is important for the officer to recognize that unconsciousness may mask other physical disorders which have occurred either as a result of the acute alcohol intake or coincidental with it. The former category may include head injuries, pneumonia, fractures, and bleeding from the stomach, while the latter may include such important entities as diabetic coma and the stupor that follows an epileptic seizure.

In a few cases, even small amounts of alcohol can result in markedly abnormal behavior. This is called *pathological intoxication* and refers to cases in which an extremely small amount of alcohol, which in most individuals would have only *minimal* effects, can cause an outburst of markedly irrational, combative, and destructive behavior.

The officer may also encounter the alcoholic at a time when he has stopped drinking, either because of illness or lack of access to alcohol. The alcoholic may then exhibit a number of symptoms of which the officer should be aware so that he can bring the alcoholic to proper medical attention. (These symptoms are not likely to occur in the individual who is a reactive user of alcohol.) They may not occur until after the individual has been arrested and placed in jail, since confinement automatically bars his access to alcohol.

The most common sign of alcohol withdrawal in the chronic (addicted) alcohol abuser is tremulousness ("shakes" or "jitters"). Most often visible in the hand, it is usually associated with irritability, nausea, and vomiting. All of these symptoms will occur relatively quickly and, in jail, they are most notably seen the morning after arrest.

Most chronic abusers, when they stop drinking, will experience nothing more than severe "shakes." Some chronic abusers, however, may proceed to demonstrate more serious conditions such as *alcoholic hallucinosis* or *delirium tremens*. In the former, the subject hears accusatory and threatening voices. These may occur even if he otherwise looks all right and knows where he is and what time it is. The treatment is hospitalization and appropriate medication.

In delirium tremens, seeing and feeling objects which are not present is more prominent than hearing voices (auditory hallucinations). Feelings in this state may include perceptions that bugs are crawling on him or seeing huge insects. In contrast to alcoholic hallucinosis, delirium tremens is associated with a loss of orientation to time and place. Delirium tremens may also be associated with epileptic seizures which can be life threatening. Treatment requires prompt medical attention in a hospital with appropriate medication, adequate diet, and good nursing care.

An important part of the police's past difficulties in handling alcohol abusers has been the neglect these individuals have received from other agencies (hospitals, clinics, etc.). More recently, however, the attitudes of society toward alcohol abusers have been changing. They are exemplified by the nineteen states (as of 1975) which have passed legislation removing public intoxication from the criminal code and defining it as a medicosocial responsibility. Many hospitals are beginning to create comprehensive alcohol treatment programs, and detoxification centers are springing up in many communities.

With the development of these treatment programs, the police officer can now take the acutely intoxicated individual to an appropriate facility rather than ignoring him or placing him in the "drunk tank," as have been the standard practices to date.

The need for the police officer to involve himself in this developing treatment system as both a referral source and as a care giver is emphasized by the following data, which indicate the high costs to the criminal justice system of handling the alcohol abuser without the support of treatment programs. In 1967, the FBI reported that 28 percent of all arrests were for public drunkenness and, when other alcohol-related offenses were included, the total rose to 49 percent. Furthermore, this does not even take into account the informal handling of intoxicated persons by police, such as providing them with a way to get home or giving warnings without arrests. If the cost for handling each case (*including* police time, court time, transportation, booking, etc.) is conservatively estimated at fifty dollars per arrest, the cost of handling the more than two million arrests for public drunkenness alone in the U.S. in 1967 was close to one hundred million dollars (Bacon 1968).

For all of these reasons, it is important for the law enforcement officer as a professional observer of behavior to work closely with other community groups, both medical and nonmedical, in developing programs and methods for getting individuals in need of help to these programs. There is no question that law enforcement's cooperation in this community effort will free the officer to attend to more serious crimes than public intoxication and chronic inebriation.

Other Forms of Drug Abuse

While alcohol is the most commonly abused drug, it is not the only one. There are numerous others to which individuals become addicted, tolerant, or habituated. Since they affect human behavior and since their nonmedical sale or possession in many instances is legally prohibited, they are also of concern to the police officer. Consequently, he should also be familiar with their characteristics and behavioral effects.

In the following discussion, these drugs have been grouped into several general categories. As the officer encounters specific drugs other than those mentioned, he can determine to which category they belong and deduce their general characteristics and effects.

Narcotic Drugs (Opiates)

Narcotics are derivatives of opium and include both natural forms (morphine, heroin, and codeine) as well as synthetics (demerol, methadone, and numorphan). Tolerance and habituation are rapidly produced and abstinence will result in a withdrawal syndrome, leading to their designation as addictive.

They may be taken either intravenously ("mainlining"), by subcutaneous injection ("skin popping") or by nasal inhalation ("snorting"). This last use is only effective with a very high-grade opiate such as was found in Vietnam by our servicemen.

Many conflicting statistics exist regarding the occurrence of opiate addiction in the United States. The most common form, heroin addiction, has had the most attention, but statistics concerning its use are extremely inaccurate and difficult to collect because of the illegal nature of the drug.

In nonaddicted individuals, a single injection will produce a state which has been described as pleasant and euphoric and is often accompanied by a state of semi-sleep known as "going on the nod."

Studies which have attempted to demonstrate personality differences between opiate and alcohol addicts have not yielded conclusive results. The choice of the addicting drug appears to be determined more by social and cultural characteristics. Furthermore, currently many young users are common abusers of both heroin and alcohol, either at the same time or in rapid succession. Additional studies indicate that opiate addicts as well as alcoholics generally possess a maladaptive pattern of behavior prior to the abuse of the drug. Drug use helps them deal with periods of stress for which other behavioral patterns have not been successful.

Hallucinogens

Hallucinogens, otherwise known as *psychedelics*, have been used for many years in their natural state as a part of the religious rites of many "primitive" cultures. They have only recently become substances of abuse in both their natural and synthetic states. Common among the natural hallucinogens is mescaline, derived from the peyote (cactus) plant; common among the synthetics is lysergic acid diethylamide (LSD), first synthesized in 1938.

The acute toxic reactions of hallucinogens include disorganized thinking as well as an altered state of perception of the environment. These reactions are greatly influenced by the social setting and by the individual's expectations prior to taking the drug. These altered perceptions can lead to heightened experiences in any or all of the five senses (auditory, visual, olfactory, tactile, and taste). In contrast

186

to alcohol and the opiates, these hallucinogens are neither addictive nor tolerance producing. In some individuals, depending on personality, they may be habituating.

Marijuana

While classified by some as a psychedelic, marijuana ("pot") is probably best considered by itself not only because of its frequent and widespread use, but also because, in its milder forms, it does not produce hallucinogenic experiences that even approach those associated with psychedelic drugs. In its strongest form (hashish), however, it can produce symptoms similar to those of the psychedelic substances.

Like psychedelics, but unlike alcohol and opiates, marijuana use does not lead to addiction or tolerance. Dependent on the individual's previous psychological state and his underlying pattern of behavior, habituation and dependence can occur in some users. However, many are able to use marijuana without becoming psychologically dependent or habituated.

Cocaine

Cocaine is derived from the leaves of the coca shrub, which is found in portions of South America and Southeast Asia. Like natural psychedelic substances, it also has a long history of use, primarily by the Indians of the Andes. It was first isolated for medicinal purposes in 1855 and can be taken by sniffing or injection.

Because of the intense "high" which its marked exhilarating effect produces, it is often used with other drugs. For example, barbiturate abusers may use it to counteract the "down" of sedatives. Unlike alcohol and opiates, cocaine is not addicting nor tolerance producing. The advantage over amphetamines, which also produce a "high," is its lack of tolerance effects. However, of all those drugs which do not produce tolerance or addiction, cocaine has the highest degree of psychological dependence. Physically, an individual can stop using cocaine rather easily because there is no withdrawal syndrome; however, the psychological effects make stopping difficult.

Amphetamines

In contrast to psychedelics, marijuana, cocaine, and many of the narcotic opiates, amphetamine ("speed") is a drug which physicians have used for a long time, especially to assist patients in weight reduction. Recently, however, the legitimate use of amphetamines is being questioned, primarily because of its high incidence of abuse. Like cocaine, amphetamine abuse is undertaken principally to obtain a "high."

Most abusers take speed in the form of pills ("pep pills" or "goof balls"), but some use it intravenously in a synthetic form (methadrine) to obtain a better "high." This "mainlining" of speed is very dangerous because a severe paranoid psychosis can occur.

In contrast to cocaine, marijuana, and the psychedelics, amphetamines, while not addicting, build up a high level of tolerance and increasing amounts are required to produce the same effect over time. As with other drugs, psychological dependence or habituation occurs.

Barbiturates

Barbiturates, because they are legally available through prescription, are probably the most frequently abused drugs except for alcohol and certain narcotics. Their abuse is particularly dangerous because they produce habituation, tolerance, and addiction. Furthermore, they can increase the effects of other drugs (principally alcohol) when taken with them. This type of combination abuse accounts for a high number of accidental deaths.

Mild Tranquilizers

Mild tranquilizers, such as Valium, Librium, Miltown, and Equanil, have an effect similar to the barbiturates. This is not surprising since many "tranquilizers" are misnamed and are actually more sedating than tranquilizing. Although they do not produce an actual withdrawal syndrome like the barbiturates, withdrawal in the tranquilizer abuser may present similar problems and should be done in a hospital.

Furthermore, because there is a cross-tolerance between many tranquilizers and barbiturates, the abuser may increase the impact of these drugs by taking several kinds.

Helpful Hints to the Law Enforcement Officer

An individual who has overdosed is a medical emergency and the police officer must be able to recognize the symptoms. Acute opiate overdose is characterized by a marked unresponsiveness in the presence of very slow or labored breathing. Needle marks and/or "tracks" will be noted. The pupils are pinpoints and both the pulse and heartbeat are extremely slow. If the overdose has been very severe and the individual is still alive, body temperature will have fallen. When breathing is poor, it is important to immediately create an air passage and to supply artificial respiration while in transit to the hospital emergency room.

In contrast to an acute overdose, chronic intoxication from opiates or withdrawal are not generally medical emergencies. Because of their tolerance producing effects, the addict will require rapidly increasing amounts of the drug to obtain the same effects. However, this process is self-limiting. Once the addict's habit has reached a certain level, his primary motivation for continuing to use the drug is to avoid withdrawal rather than to reach a new "high."

Addicts dread withdrawal because it is extremely uncomfortable. Runny nose, excessive tearing, sweating, as well as severe nausea and vomiting will be noted within eight to sixteen hours after the last dose if no further opiate is taken. Later effects include severe muscle cramps and spasms, marked sleeplessness, and an increase in nausea and vomiting. If untreated, the addict is in a state of "cold turkey" and the withdrawal syndrome will reach its peak within forty-eight to seventy-two hours. Most addicts are not able to go "cold turkey" unless they are in jail, where access to opiates is unavailable. Otherwise, the temptation to relieve the withdrawal symptoms by another fix is too great to resist.

In this connection, Inspector Marion Talbert of the San Antonio Police Department states that heroin addicts who cannot get into a treatment program will sometimes approach a police officer and ask to be booked for some offense which will draw ten days in jail if they are convicted. The addicts plead guilty in order to withdraw "cold turkey" in jail because their tolerance level has reached the point where they can no longer steal enough to support their habit. At this point, they "arrange" to go to jail, not to quit drugs but to lower the amount they need.*

* Inspector Marion Talbert 1974; personal communication.

The difficulties associated with withdrawal and the history of re-addiction in many addicts, even after successful withdrawal, have led to the use of a synthetic opiate, methadone, for both withdrawal and maintenance. Its use in withdrawal is indicated because its administration can be more carefully controlled than heroin since it is long-acting and can be taken orally. Its use in maintenance of chronic heroin addicts, even though it is substituting one addiction for another, is also indicated for the same reasons, since it appears to enable the addict to function more successfully than when on heroin, although in a continuing addicted state.

The criminal aspects of narcotic drug addiction have been well publicized and are related primarily to the addict's need to obtain finances to support the high cost of his addiction. However, some addicts have exhibited criminal behavior before their addiction and it increases their need to engage in it.

These serious problems associated with hallucinogen abuse are secondary not only to the acute psychotic symptoms of a toxic reaction but also to the possible acting out of violent impulses directed either against others or himself. The chronic user may have uncontrollable and overwhelming panic reactions in association with "flashbacks," a state in which the effects of hallucinogens are reproduced although none have been taken. These episodes are extremely frightening and can create a severe panic state which will make the user a potential danger to himself and/or others.

Because of the acute panic often associated with a bad reaction to hallucinogens, emergency measures should include efforts to prevent the user from hurting himself or others. These precautions include a restriction of movement, either through placing him in a closed room or by using restraints. Other efforts to reduce the input of external stimuli coming to him may include placing him in a quiet, nonstimulating environment. Police who come in contact with a person under the effects of a hallucinogen should lower their voices and talk calmly to him (the "talk-down" cure). This also helps to reduce external stimuli.

The acute paranoid psychosis which may result from amphetamines is often difficult to differentiate from the functional paranoid psychosis. However, anyone encountered by the police in an acute paranoid psychosis requires emergency treatment and the officer should get him to a medical facility. In doing so, the individual should be approached with extreme caution since he can be potentially dangerous (Chapter 15). He is frightened and the officer should not do anything which will increase his fear because increased fear is likely to lead to a greater potential for violence.

The police officer can often identify a chronic barbiturate abuser if he notes a degree of mental confusion, some impairment of intellectual ability, and a staggering gait. Individuals suspected of chronic barbiturate intoxication should also be taken to the emergency room for medical evaluation.

In contrast to the narcotic addict, who is likely to overestimate the amount of drug he has been taking, the barbiturate abuser may grossly underestimate the amount he is taking because he is reluctant to reveal the cause of his physical symptoms. This becomes extremely serious because an underestimation can lead the doctor to place the abuser on an inadequate amount of the drug prior to beginning withdrawal.

Summary

In this chapter, we have discussed alcoholism and other forms of drug abuse, including their characteristics, underlying factors, and physical and psychological effects. The abuse of these drugs results in abnormal behavior and, therefore, the police officer frequently becomes involved.

The officer's role in handling problems associated with drug abuse is a difficult one at best but, in dealing with drug abusers, he must maintain a professional attitude toward those against whom most of society prefers to turn its back. He must have sufficient knowledge of the characteristics of commonly abused drugs and their effects so that he can give first aid to individuals who are suffering severe symptoms from their use, insure that they receive necessary emergency medical care, and, if necessary, act as a liaison between them and the appropriate long-term treatment facilities.

REFERENCES AND ADDITIONAL BIBLIOGRAPHY

Bacon, S. D. 1968. "Studies of Driving and Drinking. *Quarterly Journal of Studies on Alcohol.* Supplement no. 4.

Baker, F. and Issacs, C. D. 1973. "Attitudes of Community Caregivers toward Drug Users." *International Journal of the Addictions* 8:243–252.

Chafetz, M. E. 1959. "Practical and Theoretical Considerations in the Psychotherapy of Alcoholism." *Quarterly Journal of Studies on Alcohol* 20:281–294.

Doctor, R. M. and Sieveking, N. A. 1970. "Survey of Attitudes toward Drug Addiction." *Proceedings of the Annual Convention of the American Psychological Association* 5:795–796.

Hyman, M. M.; Helrich, A. R.; and Besson, G. 1972. "Ascertaining Police Bias in Arrests for Drunken Driving." *Quarterly Journal of Studies on Alcohol* 33:148–159.

Louria, D. 1968. *The Drug Scene.* New York: McGraw-Hill.

Mackey, R. A. 1969. "Views of Caregiving and Mental-Health Groups about Alcoholics." *Quarterly Journal of Studies on Alcohol* 30:665–671.

Ward, R. F., and Faillace, L. A. 1970. "The Alcoholic and His Helpers: A Systems View." *Quarterly Journal of Studies on Alcohol* 31:684–691.

Williams, J. D. 1968. *Narcotics and Hallucinogens.* New York: Gwinn.

Chapter 14

Paranoid Behavior

IN Chapters 8 and 10, respectively, the characteristics of the *para-noid personality* and the *paranoid schizophrenic* were described. These two conditions represent opposite ends of the spectrum of paranoid behavior, one of the most difficult and dangerous forms of abnormal behavior which the police officer encounters. The spectrum of paranoid behavior also includes, as another condition along the continuum, the *paranoid state*.

The Spectrum of Paranoid Behavior

These three presentations of paranoid behavior—the paranoid personality, the paranoid state, and the paranoid schizophrenic—may be differentiated in several ways, as the table on page 195 illustrates.

Other characteristics may be found in all three conditions. Paranoid behavior is always associated with a high level of anxiety. Suspiciousness and distrust are the core elements of the paranoid individual's relationships with others and society. He finds it difficult to confide in others and, if he does, he expects to be betrayed. If he has

Courtesy Herb Reich

any close relationships, they are likely to be limited to a very few people and have difficulty surviving any stress. Usually, the paranoid person has a lifelong tendency toward secretiveness, seclusiveness, and solitary rumination, although these may be concealed behind a façade of superficial give and take.

	PARANOID PERSONALITY	PARANOID STATE	PARANOID SCHIZOPHRENIA
Thinking			
Disturbance	No	No	Yes
Delusions	No	Yes	Yes
Regression	No	No	Yes

He perceives the world in which he lives as dangerous and feels that he must always be on guard against the possibility of attack from others. Consequently, he lives with an endless series of tensions arising from many misunderstandings and misinterpretations.

The Progression of Paranoid Behavior

Paranoid behavior becomes more severe when the generalized suspiciousness and distrust begin to merge with the individual's increasing withdrawal. As he isolates himself from others, he becomes more preoccupied with his inner world and experiences strange feelings of alienation from the outside world. The resulting anxiety increases his vigilance and uneasiness. He begins to scrutinize his surroundings with even more suspicion and searches for hidden meanings in all events that go on around him.

While some individuals may remain in this stage throughout their lives, others deteriorate. This hypervigilant individual may begin to watch the little things people do and to note with increasing wariness their posture, gestures, glances, and movements. He demonstrates a readiness to react to any situation as potentially threatening whether or not an actual threat is present. This is the first sign of the defective reality testing of the paranoid person.

In this preoccupied state, he begins to believe that everything is somehow related to him although he may not know why. As this process continues, both his anxiety increases and his defensive use of projection begins. For example, he may feel that his desk has become disarranged. First he may feel only annoyance, but later he may begin to wonder about it. If he cannot find something in his desk drawer or believes that other things have been disturbed, his anxiety increases. He begins to examine other personal possessions and is concerned that these have been disarranged also. In the street, when people jostle him or crowd him, he begins to feel very angry. He hears remarks and immediately assumes they are about him. If there is laughter, he feels it is directed at him (Cameron 1959).

This use of projection is intended to place many of his own unconscious wishes and feelings onto others. For example, he is able to avoid looking at his own hostile feelings by perceiving them instead, through projection, as the hostile attacks of others. He also uses denial to avoid any reality that would argue against his beliefs. Denial protects him from the stresses he would feel if he faced his own weaknesses and failures. Instead of perceiving them as his own shortcomings, they become the fantasied shortcomings, evil intentions, and/or misdeeds of others. The more he can defensively belittle others, the further he avoids looking at his own weaknesses. The more he points out others' mistakes and sins, the less others may pay attention to his.

All of these events increase his anxiety. Consequently, he must reduce it, so he forms endless hypotheses about what is going on. However, since his ability to test reality is defective, these hypotheses are likely to contain distortions of reality.

To this point in the process, his projects have no specific focus. If he has spoken openly of persecution, he has only referred to "they" or "people" who are doing or planning things without being able to specify who "they" are or what the exact plan is. This situation, however, cannot endure, because its vagueness is too anxiety producing.

To reduce his anxiety, he must begin to conceptualize these dangerous "others" into a specific group or the plan into a specific plot of which he is the intended victim. He may conceive of this group as an organized gang of criminals, a group of international spies, a secret police force, or a racial or religious group. Some of their members may be identified as people he knows and to whom he attaches an important role in this organization that is plotting against him. His thinking crystalizes around a specific plot which this group is formulating and of which he is the center. When this focusing of his delusions occurs, his anxiety is reduced.

However, he soon discovers that he has a new problem. He must now defend himself against this attack or plot. As he mobilizes his own aggression to defend himself, his tactics alienate others and may lead to counteraggression against him. Once he has experienced this counteraggression, he can complain that people are really against him and that he is being interfered with, discriminated against, or persecuted. He must determine what course of action he should take against these people who are part of his delusional system.

In chronic cases, this may appear as no more than a nonspecific resentful or aggressively hostile attitude toward the world, behind which his delusions are more or less successfully concealed. In others, these beliefs are not so well hidden; they may show outbursts of hostility toward others or make unfounded accusations against others. This causes people to avoid close contact with them, pushing them further into social isolation.

Some paranoids, the minority, are driven to even more aggressive action. They abandon the role of passive observer and begin to plan actively against their "enemies." These actions may include an attempt to escape by sudden flight, often with elaborate precautions to cover their trail. Others, instead of fleeing, may attack to catch the "enemy" unaware and take revenge for what they have suffered or to forestall what they fear may happen.

The following case illustrates the important characteristics of paranoid behavior which have been discussed.

CASE EXAMPLE 1: JOE DODGE

[This case was adopted and revised from a lengthy case presentation by Cameron (1959).]

Joe Dodge is an unmarried thirty-two-year-old man who was brought to the hospital by police after a suicide attempt. Although he gave the impression of being friendly, polite, and cooperative during their initial interview, it was also apparent that he was very frightened and that, behind his friendly politeness, he was on his guard. Upon further questioning, he told this story without any recognition of its delusional character.

For several years, he had been living alone in a cheap hotel on a modest but steady income from investments. Despite his youth and good health, he lived as though he were an elderly retired businessman. Occasionally, he would look into new business prospects, but he never found anything that attracted him. He preferred to sit around the hotel lobby and think. When asked what he thought about, he would not say. He stated that he conversed with other men, played cards with them, read newspapers, and, following the custom of the hotel, placed a dozen small bets on racehorses with bookies each day.

His first acute paranoid attack came a day after he had been in a violent quarrel with his bookies over a bet. He had placed a number of bets and one of his horses had come in first and paid good odds. He went for his money only to be told that he had not bet on the winning horse in that race. He was enraged, but did not say anything initially and, instead, went to a nearby bar where he had a few drinks. As he thought more about it, he realized that he had been deliberately cheated. His anger increased and he returned to the bookies and demanded his payoff.

When they refused to give it to him, he began to shout insults at them and threatened to call the police. They threw him out. For a while, he paced up and down the sidewalk until he cooled off a little and returned to his hotel. Although still furious, he was able to sit down and think about the situation. It suddenly occurred to him that, since bookies were notorious for having gangster protection, he might be in danger because he had threatened them. The more he thought about it, the more threatened he began to feel. He fantasied about the gangsters who would come and kill him.

The next morning, when he came down to the lobby, he noticed some rough looking strangers hanging around. He thought they were watching him closely and waving signals to each other. At one time during the morning, when an automobile filled with men stopped in front of the hotel entrance, he was immediately convinced that they were gangsters who had come to kidnap and kill him.

Although this did not happen, his vigilance grew and with it so did the "evidence" that he was in deadly peril. He began to see "strangers" everywhere, all of whom seemed to be watching and shadowing him wherever he went and whatever he did. He felt there was no escape and was convinced that he was now marked for execution. After several days, he retreated in near panic to his hotel room, where he barricaded himself against the coming attack. From his room, he telephoned a relative and told him the whole story.

This relative, who was aware of Joe's intelligence and business skills, accepted everything that he was told as truth and agreed that Joe must somehow escape. This relative, who had unwittingly entered into Joe's delusional system, made a plan with him to leave secretly the next day.

During a sleepless night, in anticipation of his escape the next morning, Joe realized that the gangsters had probably tapped the telephone and heard the entire plan. In a panic, he packed his bag, slipped out of the hotel, and drove off alone without daring to notify the relative who was coming to help him in the morning.

In his automobile, he began to head west toward the home of another relative one thousand miles away. As he fled across the country, it became more obvious to him that escape was impossible. When he stopped for gas, casual comments by strangers made him "realize" that he was caught in a great net slowly closing around him. In one city, he came out of a restaurant to find a policeman looking at his auto license. To Joe, this meant without question that the police were in league with the gangsters and keeping them informed of his movements. In another town where he stopped to eat, the counterman eyed him as he worked. He immediately felt panic.

As he became more certain that death was inevitable, he took precautions against having to live through the horrible torture he anticipated they had in store for him. He stopped to purchase razor blades, which he hid in his suit, and to forge a prescription for a lethal dose of a sedative. He carefully removed the sedative from the capsules and placed it in a chewing-gum wrapper. At night, he avoided motels and slept in his locked automobile, hidden under his coat.

Eventually, he reached the home of his relative. However, by this time his anxiety and terror were overwhelming. Consequently, he wrote a suicide note, describing his terror. He then swallowed the sedative from the chewing-gum wrapper and lay down. Fortunately, the suicide note he had left was discovered in time and the police were called. They took him to the hospital where his stomach was pumped out.

This acute paranoid reaction was the first which Joe had experienced. Unfortunately, it was not the last. His delusions continued to persist and eventually he became a chronic paranoid schizophrenic.

Helpful Hints to the Law Enforcement Officer

As indicated previously, basic distrust is the core characteristic of paranoid behavior. Recognition of this is critical to the police officer who must respond to it. Because significant persons in the paranoid's life have always been undependable or rejecting, he is apt to view any authority figure, including an officer, as undependable and hostile. Consequently, the officer should expect that the paranoid will be suspicious of anything he says. Furthermore, the officer should expect that the paranoid will regard him with dislike and resentment when approached. How, then, does the officer counter this basic distrust?

What the paranoid needs most is understanding without condescension. When he is delusional, he requires a willing ear who will listen with courtesy to the delusional material and neither indicate that he believes it (which he certainly does not), argue with him about it, or convey the impression that the person is crazy. The assumption of a friendly but distant neutrality is usually the safest approach to the paranoid individual.

Second, the officer must remember that the paranoid is usually extremely anxious. Consequently, he must approach him in a way that does not further heighten his anxieties. If the paranoid's anxiety increases, his vigilance will also increase, as will the possibility of a violent reaction.

Third, the police officer should remember that paranoids misinterpret reality and, therefore, may misinterpret his intentions. The officer should proceed slowly and with caution, constantly reassuring the paranoid that he is there to assist and/or protect him.

In situations where an officer has continuous contact with a paranoid, it is important to be alert to any changes in the paranoid's thinking which indicate an increasing severity of his condition and a possible eruption. The officer should look for a focusing of delusional content. For example, if a paranoid who regularly makes complaints to the police begins to change his statements from vague "theys" to specific individuals or groups, this is a danger sign because the paranoid may feel forced to take action to protect himself from this specific threat.

If it is necessary to take the paranoid into custody, the officer should not order the paranoid around. Do not frighten him with Mace or other weapons. The paranoid may panic and react violently.

However, while attempting to gain the paranoid's trust, the officer must never let down his guard. He must remain alert while guarding against the communication of his suspiciousness to the paranoid. Remember also that the paranoid can be suicidal as well as homicidal (Chapters 15 and 16).

Summary

In this chapter, several diagnostic classifications which have been discussed previously and which have paranoid behavior as a core element have been reviewed. The spectrum of paranoid behavior and the methods by which the officer can best approach the paranoid individual have been described. In the next chapter, we will discuss violent behavior and the methods by which it can be handled best by the police officer.

REFERENCES AND ADDITIONAL BIBLIOGRAPHY

Cameron, N. 1974. "Paranoid Conditions and Paranoia." In *The American Handbook of Psychiatry*, ed. S. Arieti, 2d ed. Vol. 3. New York: Basic Books, pp. 676–693.
Federn, P. 1952. *Ego Psychology and the Psychoses*. New York: Basic Books.
Noyes, A. P. and Kolb, L. C. 1958. *Modern Clinical Psychiatry*, 5th ed. Philadelphia: Saunders.
Tynhurst, J. S. 1957. "Paranoid Patterns." In *Explorations in Social Psychiatry*, ed. A. H. Leighton; J. A. Clausen; and R. N. Wilson. New York: Basic Books, pp. 31–76.

Chapter 15

Violent Behavior

BECAUSE of the implied and actual danger which violent behavior portends, a thorough understanding of its causes, characteristics, and management is extremely critical to the law enforcement officer.

Definitions and Concepts

Violence is defined in *Webster's New World Dictionary* as "the exertion of physical force so as to injure or abuse" or "intense, furious, often destructive action." This association of destructive action with a mental intent to abuse or injure implies that feelings of aggression or hostility are present at some level in connection with almost all violent acts. However, the opposite is not true, since aggressive and hostile feelings are not necessarily accompanied by violent behavior. Later in this chapter, we shall describe some critial factors which may contribute to the transformation of aggressive behavior into violent behavior.

In 1939, Dollard and his coauthors at Yale University published *Frustration and Aggression* (Dollard et al. 1939). In their analysis of

Courtesy Tucson Daily Citizen

the roots of aggressive behavior, they theorized that aggression is always a result of frustration and that, conversely, frustration will always result in some form of aggression. To illustrate, imagine a young child (Jimmy) who hears the Good Humor truck coming. He runs to his mother and asks for some money. She gives it to him without question and, with the money clutched in his hand, he runs out the door and down to the Good Humor wagon to get his ice cream bar. In this instance, nothing has interfered with Jimmy's attainment of his goal, namely, the ice cream bar. No frustration was present and, consequently, no aggressive behavior occurred. However, suppose that his mother had said "no" when he came to ask for money or, although willing to give him the money, she did not have it. This would have interrupted Jimmy's goal-directed activity and he would not have gotten his ice cream bar.

According to the Dollard hypothesis, the frustration associated with not obtaining the ice cream bar would probably result in some form of aggressive behavior. It might be limited to verbal abuse in which he would yell, scream, or curse at his mother. He might chase after the wagon while screaming insults. He might sit in a corner for hours, pouting and sulking about not getting the ice cream bar. Since the varieties of possible aggressive behavior are numerous, it is important for the police officer to recognize that violent behavior constitutes only one form of aggressive behavior. In this case, it would have been exemplified by Jimmy's physically attacking his mother instead of expressing his aggressive feelings in any of the other ways described above.

This frustration-aggression hypothesis stresses the importance of the individual's early learning experiences. They form the basis of a *frustration-tolerance threshold* which may be defined as each person's readiness to respond with aggressive behavior to a frustrating situation. While some will be quick to hate and require only a small provocation to release hostile or murderous feelings, others will be slow to anger and have a greater tolerance toward frustration.

Other theorists, such as Eibl-Eibesfeldt have stressed the non-learned aspects of aggressive behavior (Eibl-Eibesfeldt 1961). He views aggression as a biologically adapted mechanism by which members of any species become spaced out in the particular area they occupy and the fittest are selected for survival on their basis of an inborn, nonlearned aggressive ability.

For further discussion, violent behavior may be categorized into three broad areas: (1) *individual violent behavior* in which psychological factors predominate; (2) *social violent behavior* in which violence is a direct outgrowth of group behavior and the actions of the society itself; and (3) *"mixed" violent behavior* in which both individual psychological factors and group social factors are operative.

Individual Violence

In this situation, violent behavior evolves principally from psychological forces within each individual. This violent behavior may be normal and socially approved or may be labelled as *abnormal* and socially condemned. There is a certain amount of violent behavior or the potential for it present in all of us. However, as long as it is controlled or expressed in socially approved forms, the individual does not get into trouble. For example, a boxer may inflict mayhem on his opponent and be rewarded by cheers and the victor's share of the purse; the matador will be cheered in the ring as he spears the bull; or soldiers are taught in basic training that the "spirit" of the bayonet is to "kill." In each case, society approves and the individual does not suffer a penalty.

Other types of individual violent behavior are not approved by society and, in most instances, are in fact labelled *criminal*. If the perpetrator is discovered, he must answer to society through its courts and prison system. However, society may make exceptions. For example, if violent behavior is associated with mental illness, the individual may be held responsible to a lesser degree or not at all.

Later in this chapter, we will discuss those attempts which have been made to predict the potential for individual violent behavior based on an understanding of some of those factors which may influence its presence. However, at this time, we should point out other important aspects of individual violent behavior. For example, studies have indicated that the consumption of alcohol increases the proneness to aggressive acts such as rape, homicide, and assault. In a Chicago study, districts with the highest alcoholic consumption produced three and one-half times as many violent crimes as did districts with the lowest consumption rates (Horstman 1973). These studies indicate a degree of relationship between alcohol and violence even though it can be argued that they do not necessarily indicate a direct one-to-one relationship.

We are also beginning to recognize the correlation between self-destructive acts of violence such as suicide (Chapter 16) and destructive acts against others. Both authors have had many experiences with those who were depressed and wanted to kill themselves, but "didn't have the guts" to do it. Unable to carry out these wishes actively, they began to consider acts which might lead to their being killed, including "being shot while holding up a bank" or "killing my wife and then confessing to get the chair." Case histories of mass murderers such as Charles Whitman, Richard Speck, and Albert De Salvo demonstrate the presence of either suicidal ideation or previous suicide attempts prior to the occurrence of their infamous acts of violence.

Recent studies have suggested that some individuals who are violent may have an associated brain disturbance and that this condition may be partially or wholly responsible for their behavior. In a series of experimental animal studies, Harvard researchers have located several brain centers which appear to be associated with rage reactions. The mechanisms for this are unclear but, in rats, the removal of a certain portion of the brain may cause an uncontrollable rage reaction through a type of release of inhibition phenomenon.

In another study of 130 self-referred violent patients to the emergency room of the Massachusetts General Hospital, one-third of those studied had abnormal brain wave patterns, a rate fifty times that of the general population. Other striking nonphysical findings associated with violent thinking or behavior included the facts that: one-half of the population had a history of bed-wetting after the age of seven; one-quarter had set fires as children; one-quarter had a history of cruelty to animals; and more than half admitted that they drove cars dangerously to vent feelings of aggression. Furthermore, nearly 60 percent of them had been arrested at least once for a violent crime (Mark 1970).

Social Violence

Some destructive forms of social or collective violence will be considered in more detail in Chapters 17 and 18 when we talk about disasters and riots. At this time, however, we wish only to point out that, as with individual violence, society does not necessarily disapprove of all social violence. For example, in sports, it is difficult to think of a more violent group activity than hockey or lacrosse. Also, society may not necessarily disapprove of a riot or civil disturbance before it makes the judgment as to which side it ethically or morally disapproves of. Furthermore, a society may split in its approval or condemnation of some type of social violence. For example, in contrast to the feelings of many others, a significant number of Irish-Americans agree with the goals of the IRA and have lent that organization both direct and indirect support.

However, public support may be a double-edged sword. While initially encouraging some to take more aggressive or violent steps, it may also determine the limits within which demonstrators must remain if they are not to alienate themselves completely from the support they have initially received from society. Again, the IRA serves as an example in that later terrorist activities led to the loss of support from many Irish-Americans who earlier approved of their goals.

"Mixed" Violence

This is a category of violent or aggressive behavior in which both individual psychological factors and social factors play a role. Examples include prison riots, civil disturbances by minority groups, or college panty raids. In these situations, a particular population or subgroup, such as the inmates of a jail, combined with a social situation, such as bad food, cramped quarters, or alleged discriminatory practices, may lead to aggressive or violent behavior. However, every person who is a member of the subgroup may not become involved since the individual's psychological predisposition will also be a determining factor.

The Prediction of Dangerousness

Definitions and concepts of violent behavior are limited in value unless they also increase the ability to predict the potential for violent behavior in a specific individual. The history of the past fifteen years is filled with many examples of those who committed infamous violent acts which were not prevented because no one could make an accurate prediction of dangerous behavior even though the person, in many cases, had had contact with a mental health professional prior to the act.

It is unfortunately true that the mental health profession has not yet achieved sufficient understanding of human behavior to allow it to predict with any significant certainty what individual will be dangerous and under what circumstances. As Dr. Jonas R. Rappaport, a professor of psychiatry and law, has stated: "Right now we cannot predict with enough accuracy to suit anyone or ourselves. I don't know if we will ever be able to completely predict human behavior and, at the same time, protect human rights." In this statement, Dr. Rappaport is also pointing out the importance of guarding against the overprediction of dangerousness since this may lead to depriving individuals of their civil rights without sufficient evidence (Rappaport 1967).

Some mental health professionals have approached this problem by describing signs of dangerous behavior taken from case histories. However, upon reviewing them, it is apparent that many nondangerous patients will show many or all of the symptoms which some have referred to as signs of dangerousness. For example, all of the following symptoms and signs have been named by one authority or another as possible precursors of violent behavior: past history of aggressive acts; enforced repression of normal aggression; parental rejection; the need to protest against dependence upon one or both parents; detachment; introversion; sadism toward children or animals; overemphasis on daydreaming or ritualistic behavior; absence of mood changes; and an increased interest in violent acts on the part of others. However, upon reviewing this list, it is clear that many people demonstrate some of these signs, yet do not commit any dangerous acts even when observed over a period of years.

Despite this negative picture, research into the predictability of dangerousness continues. Without judging the validity of its conclusions, a recent study by Kozol and his associates at the Bridgewater State Hospital in Massachusetts is illustrative of some of the more careful research now taking place (Kozol et al. 1972). They describe a ten-year study involving 592 male, convicted defendants, in which they claim that "dangerousness in criminal offenders can be reliably diagnosed and effectively treated." They substantiate this conclusion by reporting that, of the 304 persons who were examined by the staff and were determined to be not dangerous (using their criteria) and then released into the community, only 26 (8.6 percent) subsequently committed serious violent behavior.

On the other hand, of the 226 prisoners who were diagnosed as dangerous and committed to a special treatment inpatient facility for an indeterminate period, 82 were discharged to the community on the recommendation of the staff after an average of 43 months of treatment. Of these only 5 (6.1 percent) committed serious assaultive crimes during the follow-up period. In contrast, 49 of the 226 who were originally committed as dangerous were released by court order against the advice of the staff. In this group, 17 (34.7 percent) subsequently committed a serious violent crime.

In further defining their criteria for prediction of dangerousness, Kozol and his associates state: "We see the dangerous person as one who has actually inflicted or attempted to inflict serious physical injury on another person; harbors anger, hostility, and resentment; enjoys witnessing or inflicting suffering; lacks altruistic and compassionate concern for others; sees himself as a victim rather than an aggressor; resents or rejects authority; is primarily concerned with his own satisfaction; lacks control of his own impulses; has immature attitudes toward social responsibilities; lacks insight into his own psychological structure; and distorts his perceptions of reality in accordance with his own wishes and needs." To the alert reader, this description closely parallels that of the psychopath (Chapter 10). Indeed, Kozol concludes: "Our concept of the dangerous person is nearly identical with the classical stereotype of the criminal antisocial psychopath."

However, it is important to recognize that, in utilizing these criteria, dangerousness is not viewed absolutely but rather on a continuum from "extremely dangerous" at one extreme to "absolutely nondangerous" at the other. Interplay of many factors determines where an individual will be on the continuum at any one time.

Intensive diagnostic procedures were used, including many interviews and psychological tests designed to reconstruct the life history. It is, therefore, obvious that this process cannot be duplicated in a brief period of time by anyone who is called upon to examine a defendant. Consequently, despite this intensive research, professionals will still have problems predicting dangerousness on the basis of brief contact. This difficulty is reflected in recent legislation which requires commitment to mental hospitals for dangerous behavior to be based on the actual commission of a violent act rather than on an implied or threatened act alone.

Predicting Front Page Violence

Another important study of violent behavior reflects on front page violence, a topic of special interest to law enforcement. Hans Toch, the author and a noted criminologist comments as follows.

Among men who engage in violence, there are monsters who fill the public mind with special dread and revulsion. These men stir the imagination, displace headlines, disrupt peace and tranquility, and inspire massive official action. And these men are not those who account for the bulk of violent damage, nor are they those who engage in repeated acts of destruction. They are, rather, the unexpected authors of violence that is irrational and senseless—the progenitors of acts that are blood-curdling and bizarre (Toch 1969).

On this same subject, Megargee points out that some of the chief characteristics of these people include their lack of previous aggression and violence. They are not aggressive in situations where the normal person would experience such feelings. Typically, they are described as "quiet boys, model young men, slow to anger . . . wouldn't hurt a fly . . . sort of a loner . . . didn't really get to know him" (Megargee 1966).

This extreme passivity is abnormal. It suggests that there are underlying currents of anger and hostility so strong that they cannot emerge into consciousness, even for a moment. The major defense mechanism seems to be reaction formation in which these individuals adopt a life style opposite to what they feel. They become gentle, mild, passive creatures who often have a compulsive need to be perfect. They avoid their rage and destructive impulses at all costs. However, eventually the pressure of these feelings becomes unbearable and then they lash out, seemingly at random, even destroying people they don't know. The prediction of this headline-getting behavior is most difficult because of the absence of any previous history of violence. The key to prevention may be, as Toch suggests, in focusing our attention upon those incidents where violence might have been expected but did not appear. Therefore, school counselors, family physicians, clergymen, and parents should be alert for possible danger signs when a child is observed who seems unable to express even normal amounts of hostility and aggression. The child who is silent and unresponsive in situations that would make other children angry should be watched closely. A marked pattern of nonviolent behavior should merit just as much concern and attention from professionals as a pattern of excessive violent behavior.

This discussion has been presented to alert the police officer to the inadequacies of our current tools for predicting dangerousness. This difficulty is, however, only one facet of the police officer's problems in handling aggressive and violent behavior. In many situations, prediction is not an issue since a violent act has recently occurred or is taking place. How the officer reacts will be critical to his effective handling of the individual and to his own safety.

The Police Officer's Perception of Danger

James W. Sterling, Assistant Director of the Professional Standards Division of the International Association of Chiefs of Police, has pointed out the resemblance between police work and military duty. The police officer may be viewed as someone who daily faces the possibility of combat, especially in the inner city with its turmoil and high crime rates. The anxiety and fear which an officer experiences will influence how he carries out his duties.

In his study, Sterling attempts to define more clearly those factors which influence the officer's perception of danger. Using interviews as well as an assessment of reaction to radio calls, Sterling described the following characteristics. Physically, the officer may note an acceleration of his heartbeat and an increase in both the depth and intensity of breathing. Digestive activity is also slowed, with a subsequent release of sugar from the liver providing increased energy.

Perceptually, under stressful conditions lights appear to be brighter and sounds louder. Because threatening objects seem larger than they actually are, the officer may see a source of danger nearer at hand than it really is. Inaccuracies in judging time and speed may also occur.

Finally, as Sterling points out, the officer who has gained experience begins to accord more importance to the potential dangerousness of those calls which, as a recruit, he perceived as less dangerous, such as "indecent exposure, family disturbance, or suspicious person." At the same time, calls regarding a "committed murder" or an "assault with a deadly weapon" which, as a recruit, he perceived as highly dangerous are now seen as less dangerous. The officer learns that it is the unknown and the unpredictable which has the greatest potential for danger rather than the known and the predictable (Sterling 1972).

Assaults on Police Officers

Two recent studies have appeared which focus on a problem of immediate concern to everyone who carries a badge and everyone who depends on the officer's help when needed—assaults on police. Police are interested not only because their own safety is involved but also because in every department across the country there are police officers who seem to generate an abnormal number of citizen's complaints in their daily contacts with the public. These officers are an administrative nightmare to the brass, while the officer's facility for collecting complaints threatens his own career and self-image. It seems logical to assume that studies of police officers who are assaulted more frequently than their peers and of those who assault them might yield information which would give some guidance in dealing not only with the problem of assault but also with the corollary problem of police-citizen contacts which end in citizen complaints.

The first study was conducted by Toch and is described in his book *Violent Men* (Toch 1969). In this unique study, violent behavior is conceptualized as a "clue, a symptom, a calling card which, if properly read, could expose the central motives and concerns of violent men." Within this framework, Toch demonstrates that individual patterns of violent behavior are consistent with violent behavior occurring only in a restricted range of life situations. Contrary to the popular belief that most violent behavior is senseless, Toch found that it is usually purposive and that its occurrence is often based on the presence of hidden meanings.

Toch's subjects were 32 Oakland Police Department officers who had been assaulted at least once; 19 men who had assaulted police officers (in many instances the officers they had assaulted were part of the officer study group); 44 inmates in the California Medical Facility at Vacaville; 29 prisoners at San Quentin; and 33 parolees with violent behavior records. To test the validity of their findings, the researchers also secured permission to analyze 344 incidents of assaultive behavior on San Francisco police officers.

From their data, Toch and his colleagues classified the following motives for police assaults. They found that the two motives most frequently encountered were (1) reactions against perceived tampering with the person, either verbally or physically, by the officer and (2) the desire to rescue or defend a person who is receiving an officer's attention. In over half the sample, the sequence of events leading to the assault on an officer starts with an individual's negative reaction to an officer's verbal approach. Typically, the officer approaches a civilian with a request, a question, or an order. No serious crime has been committed and the contact could be generally classified as *preventive police work* or *coping with a nuisance*. Violence may occur immediately, but most often does not happen until after the civilian has first expressed his displeasure at the officer's action. The civilian attacks after the officer has made additional moves.

An illustration may be helpful. Two detectives from Burglary were patrolling late one night in an unmarked car when they encountered, in an isolated, poorly lit shopping center, one white male, about age forty, standing beside a pay phone booth (darkened) and a white-paneled pickup truck. Since the shopping center had recently been hit by a number of burglaries, the detectives left their car, showed their badges, and asked the man for identification. He refused to give any identification, stating that "anyone could buy a badge in a dime store, anyone could carry a gun, and besides, other people than policemen have police radios in their car."

Even at this early point, the situation had the potential for escalating into violence. However, the next action of the officers successfully defused the situation. Rather than engaging in further confrontation, they chose another approach. They asked him if he would show identification to a marked patrol unit and he replied that he would do so. Within five minutes a marked unit arrived, identification was made, and the citizen, who turned out to be a reputable telephone company employee, wrote a letter to the police department complimenting the detectives for treating him "like a man" rather than trying to "strong-arm" him.

In contrast to this situation, Toch discovered others in which, through "one-step games," the policeman has little chance of avoiding violence. In these cases, the suspect often has been drinking and the mere approach of an officer is sufficient to trigger violence. This emphasizes the high association of alcoholic intake with assaults on police officers.

Toch also reports another group of sequences which frequently leads to assaults. In these situations, violence exists prior to the officer's arrival. Family disturbances are typical examples and the officer's intervention is seen as a source of annoyance or frustration; a possible ally of the opposition; an intrusion; or simply a new problem to be dealt with. The violence, as a coping device for frustration, is already in play when the officer arrives and simply continues with an additional participant, the officer, being assigned one of the above roles.

Toch also offers a useful classification of those roles and approaches of a violence-prone person (citizen or officer) that tend to promote the occurrence of violent behavior.

1. *Rep-Defending.* A category comprising persons who are allocated by public recognition a role that includes the exercise of aggressive behavior. (The "Godfather" would be an example of this type of person.)
2. *Norm enforcing.* A self-assigned mission involving the use of violence on behalf of norms that a violent person sees as desirable and universal rules of conduct. In some officers, this role emerges in the form of "Super Cop." This officer sees himself as the only individual standing between a helpless society and the criminal element of the population. He may often violate legal and department regulations in his zeal to stamp out "evils" such as drug addiction, prostitution, and other "low" forms of crime.
3. *Self-Image Compensating.* This involves the relationship between low self-esteem and violence. Violence becomes a form of retribution against people who the individual feels have cast aspersions on his self-image. The violence becomes a demonstration of self-worth by those whose self-image places an emphasis on their toughness.
4. *Self-Defending.* A tendency to perceive other persons as sources of physical danger requiring immediate neutralization as compensation for feelings of low self-esteem.
5. *Pressure-Removing.* A predisposition to explode in situations that one is unable to handle.

Toch also describes characteristics such as bullying, exploitation, self-indulgence, and catharting, which an officer may observe early in his interactions with a violence-prone person. In *bullying,* the officer observes pleasure being obtained from the exercise of violence and terror against susceptible individuals. *Exploitation* involves a persistent effort by the violence-prone person to manipulate others into becoming unwilling tools for his pleasure and convenience. Violent behavior may emerge when these people do not react or respond. When a person is *self-indulging,* he operates under the assumption that others exist to satisfy his needs. Violence is often viewed as the penalty for noncompliance. Finally, in *catharting,* the individual is discharging accumulated internal pressure or feelings through violent behavior.

In another study, Horstman and his associates examined all assaults on police officers in Norman, Oklahoma over a five-year period (Horstman 1973). Factors associated with increased violent behavior directed against police officers included weekends, mild and clear weather, the hours between 9:00 P.M. and 3:00 A.M., location frequency (the retail business area), and the assailants' ages (nineteen to twenty-three). The younger, inexperienced officer was also more prone to involvement in assaultive behavior than was his older, more experienced counterpart.

The assailant is usually employed, commonly in the construction business or another form of heavy labor. Findings of other studies regarding the high correlation between alcohol intake and assaultiveness were confirmed, with 74 percent of the assailants being judged as intoxicated by the involved officer. There was also a high correlation between the presence of emotional problems and assault frequency.

Finally, as Toch pointed out also, the assailant is often loud and belligerent prior to the actual attack. However, Horstman cautions the officer to be alert if the individual suddenly becomes quiet without good reason. In more than one-third of their cases, the subject became quiet immediately before the attack.

Furthermore, arrest is not a guarantee against further violent behavior. Sixty-seven percent of Horstman's cases were physically and verbally under arrest at the time of the assault.

Horstman points out also how the personality and the actions of the officer often contribute to the assaultive act. He describes situations in which the officer apparently goaded the suspect into attacking him through an overbearing attitude. Although unable to identify a single precipitating event for the onset of violent behavior, Horstman did describe a "process of escalation, building on each experience between officer and suspect until the 'hair trigger' is honed and pulled by the execution of a critical event such as grabbing a suspect's arm to consummate an arrest."

Other dangerous situations with a high degree of associated violent behavior include the arrest of someone in a group and conducting a search. The humiliation of these acts, particularly when they take place in front of friends, may lead the violence-prone individual to strike out in frustration. If possible, the officer should get the suspect out of sight of friends and onlookers before "patting him down." These potential dangers associated with the arrest procedure suggest several attitudes and behaviors which the officer should keep in mind when making an arrest.

He should indirectly motivate those whom he is placing under arrest into the wagon or car by talking them in rather than by grabbing their arm and escorting them. He should carry this out with a calm voice and manner. Once a person's last name is known, it should be used together with his or her correct title. Using other forms of address, such as first or last names only or nicknames, should be avoided unless the individual is personally known to the officer and willingly accepts this. The officer should be careful not to convey dislike for the individual he is arresting and should not treat the arrest as a personal matter.

When he encounters an arrestee who refuses to comply with his directions, he should clearly indicate that he is acting only as required by law. He might further mention that resistance to arrest only makes the situation more difficult and may result in additional charges. Finally, he may point out that the question of guilt or innocence is up to the court.

In arresting an intoxicated person, it is important for the officer to remember that this individual may not fully comprehend the situation. Influenced by alcohol and in an unclear state of mind, he is more likely to resist the arrest. Therefore, it becomes even more important for the officer to avoid provocative and antagonizing comments and actions.

When the officer confronts an extremely excited individual, he should realize that many people require an opportunity to yell, scream, or threaten for a period of time before quieting down. The officer who employs discretionary patience will find that the individual will often calm down rapidly without the risk of physical injury to both the arrestee and the officer.

Horstman describes an interesting complication of the old "Mutt and Jeff" routine. In this, one cop plays "Mr. Good Guy" and his partner, "Mr. Bastard." The bad cop gives the suspect a rough time and then is interrupted by the good cop, who openly disagrees with the techniques and philosophy of his partner and attempts to convince the subject that he (the good cop) will protect him and help him if only he will trust him and tell him the truth. Horstman found a high incidence of "Mutt and Jeff" routines in assault cases where the bad cop carried his actions too far and violence resulted. Supervisors should watch for this so that men who need additional training in how to handle people can obtain it.

Helpful Hints to the Law Enforcement Officer

Observations such as those described above show how (and why) new officers may pick up violent methods from old-timers. The new officer, just out of the academy and new to the streets, is faced with problems of human behavior that defy solution, make him anxious, frightened, and sometimes in fear of his life. Under such conditions, violence-prone solutions given with confidence ("That's how it really is out here on the streets, kid") by the seasoned officer are often listened to by the young trooper. Whether he becomes involved in violence will depend on his own personality, his own sense of right and wrong, and his own violence or nonviolence proneness. It will also depend upon the officer's knowledge and understanding of violent behavior. The principles which have been described regarding his ability to enter interpersonal situations from a nonthreatening position will increase his ability to act effectively. These may be summarized in the following code of behavior.

1. When you approach a situation, try to analyze what is going on. Before you enter the situation, a few seconds of reflection will enable you to size up the situation more adequately and to reduce the possibility of precipitating violence.
2. Do not play games with a violence-prone individual. Because of his experience, he will be a better game player and the result of game playing is more likely to be the onset rather than the prevention of violent behavior.
3. The officer must learn to listen, not only to what the individual is saying but also to the feelings with which he is expressing himself.
4. A display of personal involvement by the officer will escalate a situation and increase the potential for violent behavior.
5. The excited person should be given time to cool down. Many loud-mouthed individuals will calm down after a while, especially if they are not given any further reason by the officer to put on a show.
6. Remember that the person who resorts to violent behavior is often suffering from either a long-term or short-term loss of self-esteem. Officers should, therefore, do everything possible to preserve the self-esteem of the individual and avoid any actions which contribute to its further lowering. Leave him a way out so his self-esteem is not destroyed further.
7. The officer should never threaten. Any proposed action which he verbalizes should be carried out. If the officer verbalizes something he is not prepared to carry out, he may talk himself into a corner and end up taking an action which he did not really intend.
8. Treat each individual whom you encounter with respect, patience, and tact unless the immediate dangerousness of the situation merits other action.
9. Although the officer should not become personally involved, he should not act like an automaton. He should relax, use humor, if appropriate, and recognize that his authority will not vanish if he smiles.
10. If the officer is not sure of department policies, such as those regarding the use of reasonable force, he should ask his supervisor. He should not rely on his peers because their policy interpretations may have been wrong for years.

Summary

In this chapter, we have discussed a subject of great importance to the law enforcement officer—violent behavior and the handling of the violent person. Definitions, concepts, and characteristics of violent behavior have been presented. While the ability to predict the general dangerousness of an individual is at best variable, there are many immediate behavioral clues which will enable an officer to heighten his perception of the dangerousness of an individual in a specific situation. Emphasis has been given in this context to officer-citizen interactions and how they can lead to an escalation process in which violent behavior is the result. Finally, we have described a behavioral code for the law enforcement officer which will help to reduce the possibility of friction and subsequent violent behavior in his contacts with criminals and citizens.

REFERENCES AND ADDITIONAL BIBLIOGRAPHY

Barocas, H. A. 1972. "Police Crisis Intervention and Prevention of Violence." *American Journal of Psychoanalysis* 32:211–215.

Blumenthal, M. D. 1972. "Predicting Attitudes toward Violence." *Science* 76:1296–1303.

Dollard, J. et al. 1939. *Frustration and Aggression.* New Haven: Yale University Press.

Eibl-Eibesfeldt, I. December 1961. "The Fighting Behavior of Animals." *Scientific American.* 112–122.

Horstman, P. L. December 1973. "Assaults on Police Officers." *The Police Chief.*

Kahan, F. J. 1973. "Schizophrenia, Mass Murder, and the Law." *Orthomolecular Psychiatry* 2:127–146.

Kozol, H. L.; Boucher, R. S.; and Garofalo, R. F. October 1972. "The Diagnosis and Treatment of Dangerousness." *Journal of Crime and Delinquency* 18:373–392.

Mark, V. H. 1970. *Violence in the Brain.* New York: Harper & Row.

Megargee, C. I. 1966. *Undercontrolled and Overcontrolled Personality Types in Extreme Anti-Social Aggression.* Psychological Monographs, 80. Washington, D.C.: American Psychological Association.

Rappaport, J. 1967. *The Clinical Evaluation of the Dangerousness of the Mentally Ill.* Springfield, Ill.: Charles C. Thomas.

Sterling, J. W. 1972. *Changes in Role Concepts of Police Officers.* Gaithersburg, Md.: International Association of Chiefs of Police.

Toch, H. 1969. *Violent Man.* Chicago: Aldine.

Wilds, C. E. 1973. "Evaluation of a Method of Predicting Violence in Offenders." *Criminology* 11:427–435.

Chapter 16

Suicidal Behavior

CONTACT with suicidal behavior is a common occurrence in the work of a police officer. Not only will he be called after there is a successful suicide, but he may also be the first to discover the body while on patrol. If suicide is threatened, he is often asked to "come to the rescue."

In recent years, suicidal behavior has become recognized as a major public health and mental health problem. At least twenty-five thousand successful suicides take place in the United States each year and the number of attempts is much higher. Estimates in various studies range from eight to fifty unsuccessful attempts for every successful one.

If one also considers that an officer may encounter many suicide attempts disguised as homicidal behavior (Chapter 15) or hidden in auto accidents, it becomes clear why it is important for the officer to know more about and to understand suicidal behavior. In this chapter, after reviewing the historical background of this "new" field of suicidology, we will examine the suicidal person, the clues about the suicidal intentions that he presents, and some helpful hints to the officer for handling suicidal behavior when he encounters it.

United Press International

Historical Background

Although recently attaining more visibility and popularity, the field of suicidology, the study of suicidal or self-destructive behavior, is not a new one. Throughout history, every society and culture has demonstrated concern with death and has devised methods to cope with the fear and trauma associated with it. As early as the Greek ages, philosophers argued whether or not a man had a right to take his own life. At various times since then, societies have either condemned or approved suicidal behavior.

Suicide prevention, an important aspect of suicidology, also has deep roots. In 1692 Robert Burton, in his famous *Anatomy of Melancholy,* spoke of the "prognostics of melancholy or signs of things to come." He described how these prognostic signs (referred to by suicidologists today as *prodromal clues*) typically exist for a few days to a few weeks before the suicide attempt is made. Furthermore, he pointed out that recognition of these signs could save lives.

In 1897, the famous sociologist Émile Durkheim, in his treatise *Le Suicide,* advanced the theory of social causation as an important factor in determining suicidal behavior. He believed that man's responses to his environment, including suicidal behavior, were more explainable in terms of social forces than psychological factors.

However, early attention to suicidal behavior was not limited to theorists such as Durkheim. In the early 1900s, for example, the Vienna (Austria) Police Department established a "welfare" division which handled all suicides and suicide attempts. Following an attempt, a summons was served on the attempter. If it was ignored, a second summons was issued. If it also went unanswered, a social worker was sent to investigate and to prepare an evaluation. In 1928, 2,373 cases were handled by this division. Over 1,000 were hospitalized for treatment and an additional 544 were seen as outpatients. Considered a public service function, the program also provided employment, housing, and financial counseling—problem areas closely associated with suicidal behavior.

Other historical perspectives included those of the ancient Greeks. While most Greeks believed that taking one's life was improper, some felt it could be justified in certain circumstances. For example, the Epicureans, a philosophical group in early Greek culture, believed that life was to be enjoyed, but recognized that, when it became impossible to achieve this goal, suicide was an appropriate way to hasten the inevitable. Similarly, in early Roman times suicide was considered an offense only if one took his life to avoid trial or, by his death, caused another party to suffer a loss.

However, with the advent of Christianity, viewpoints toward suicidal behavior began to change. In 693 A.D., the Council of Toledo imposed excommunication upon suicidists and denied them a Christian burial. By the eleventh century, suicide had become a recognized public problem and laws were passed to control it. Guided by Christian values, the courts regarded suicide as "murder of oneself" and, therefore, viewed suicide or a suicide attempt as a criminal act for which not only the suicidist, but also his entire family, could be punished.

These views have continued to exist in one form or another into modern times. For example, laws against suicidal behavior existed in England until 1961. Between 1946 and 1955, nearly six thousand suicide attempters were arrested and over five thousand were found guilty and sentenced to either jail or prison. The United States also had laws against suicide and suicide attempts until the 1960s. As late as 1964, nine states still declared attempted suicide a crime and eighteen others had laws against aiding and abetting a suicide attempter.

Not only did these laws label suicidal behavior as criminal, but, more importantly, they also prevented the achievement of accurate statistics. In most jurisdictions where suicide was regarded as criminal behavior, the admissibility of evidence at a coroner's inquest followed the rules of criminal evidence (i.e., prohibition against hearsay), and this prevented an accurate accounting of suicide attempts.

In the past, financial penalties have been associated with suicide. For many years, insurance companies included suicide clauses in their policies which called for the return of premiums paid rather than the payment of the face value of the policy as in other deaths. Current policies, however, specify full payment but only if the insurance has been in force for a sufficient time.

Another reason for the stigma associated with suicidal behavior is the common myth that suicide is a psychotic act. Therefore, many families prefer to cover up anything which might point to suicide, saying that "we have to admit that he is dead, but we don't have to admit that he was crazy."

Until recently, these legal, financial, and moral prohibitions greatly retarded a realistic study of suicidal behavior. In the United States, two psychologists, Norman Farberow and Edwin Schneidman, became interested in suicide notes found on file in the Los Angeles County Coroner's office. Their study of these notes and the circumstances surrounding the deaths of those who had written them convinced them that suicide was a major public health and mental health problem deserving of further study. They became convinced also that suicide was an individual matter which could be prevented in most cases if warning clues had been recognized (Schneidman, Farberow, and Litman 1970).

As a result of their efforts, the first suicide prevention center was opened on the grounds of Los Angeles County Hospital in 1960. Gradually, awareness of its existence spread and referrals of persons who were giving either verbal or behavioral clues of suicidal intent began coming in. The telephone, as a means of contact, became popular and by 1970 over 99 percent of first contacts were by telephone.

By the mid-sixties, the concept of the suicide prevention center had gained in popularity. Funding was made available from many sources, including the National Institute of Mental Health, to establish more suicide prevention centers in other cities. More recently, many of these centers have discovered that their phones are utilized for all crises and, consequently, they have broadened their services to *crisis intervention.*

The Suicide Attempter

Schneidman has divided those who attempt suicide into four groups based on the manner in which they approach the attempt.

Those in the first group do not intend to die. Their gestures are often dramatic and persistent, with the principal aim of conveying a message to someone that they do not like what is happening and that they want something done about it immediately. This person may take a quantity of aspirin and then immediately tell someone so he can be rushed to a hospital; or he may climb to the top of a high water tower and threaten to jump unless some clearly stated condition is met.

Because these kinds of attempts are often attention getting, there is a danger that those who deal with them may ignore their seriousness or even make fun of them. For example, emergency room personnel often regard those who make this type of suicide attempt as intruding into their busy and "real" life-saving activities. However, if this type of suicidal behavior is not taken seriously, the individual may be goaded into a more serious attempt to convince others that he is not kidding.

Another reason for taking these attempts seriously is that these are the individuals who, if they die, often have a surprised look on their faces. The prisoner who ties a sheet around his neck and jumps from his cell bunk when he hears the jailer approaching may underestimate the time required for the jailer to reach him. The recruit maneuvering on the water tower may misjudge the tower's slipperiness and fall to his death. Although the officer may judge the potential lethality of the act as low, it is important for him to refer these people to mental health professionals so that intervention in any persistent pattern of this suicidal behavior can begin.

The second group is the "gamblers." These people have reached the point at which they are willing to let fate or some other person determine whether they live or die. Examples include the man who plays Russian roulette. Although these people may have given up some control to outside persons or situations, they remain uncertain as to whether they wish to live or die and often wish to do both at the same time.

In these cases, suicide prevention depends on recognizing the coexistence of the wishes to live and die and throwing support to the side of life. It is important to help this troubled individual realize that there are more satisfying alternatives to suicide and that, even though he may feel intolerably miserable at this time, things will change and, with help, he will be able to overcome these feelings. One technique which the authors have found useful in these situations is confronting the attempter with what his contemplated suicide may mean to those he loves, especially any children he may have. Sometimes he will claim that "the kids will be better off without me." He should then be told emphatically that the children will not be better off, that they need him, and that children of a parent who commits suicide are often left with deep psychological scars. It is also helpful to point out the underlying anger by asking, "Do you really hate them that much?" This approach firmly closes the door on the use of rationalizations by the attempter and gives him time to see other ways of handling his problems.

The third group includes those who seriously intend to die but do not die because unforeseen factors intervene and save their lives. One of the authors recalls a retired sergeant who became very depressed and decided to commit suicide. When his wife and son left one morning, he connected a hose to the car exhaust, closed the garage door, and started the car. However, his son had used the car the night before and it soon ran out of gas. He then went back in the house to look for his son's rifle but, upon locating it, discovered that there was no ammunition. He then proceeded to the kitchen where he found some poisonous liquid under the sink. When he tried to drink it, he became sick and vomited.

At this point, his married daughter arrived at the house. Knowing that she usually left the keys in her car, he hid while she entered the front door and then sneaked out the back, started the car, and sped away. Down the road, he ran the auto into a concrete abutment at a speed estimated at ninety miles per hour. The car was a total wreck, but he had only a broken leg. There is no question that this man was trying very hard to die, but that fate had intervened. Despite the seriousness of their attempts, these people often welcome rescue and are later grateful that they were saved.

The fourth group consists of the successful attempters. However, they also might have been saved if someone had been alert enough to detect some of their early clues to this contemplated behavior. Recently, a young professor at a local university bought a gun, went into the desert, and shot himself. From later talks with his graduate students and fellow faculty members, it became apparent that he had given many clues to his intentions.

Yet, as Schneidman has pointed out, we are often loath to suspect suicidal intentions in those with whom we are close or who possess some type of status. For example, Farberow has pointed out that many physicians who commit suicide could be saved if they were treated like ordinary citizens in distress and hospitalized or referred to other appropriate treatment resources. The same situation exists in suicides among police officers. Fellow officers are often reluctant to admit the possibility of suicidal behavior and are even more hesitant to broach the matter to the officer himself (Schneidman, Farberow, and Litman 1970).

Each of these groups of suicide attempters presents clues prior to the attempt. Whether or not the suicide is successful, later investigation will usually reveal that these clues were present.

Clues to Suicidal Behavior

Schneidman has classified the clues to contemplated suicidal behavior into four broad categories—verbal, behavioral, situational, and syndromatic (Schneidman, Farberow, and Litman 1970).

Verbal Clues

Verbal clues can be direct or indirect. For example, a direct verbal clue is a statement like, "I'm going to kill myself" or "I'm going to take my car up the mountain and run it and me off the cliff." Less clear than these are indirect verbal clues or "coded" messages. In our clinic, a depressed young man appeared one day and asked, "How does one leave his body to the medical school?" Other examples include: "Well, I'll never have to worry about that anymore" or "You won't have to put up with my complaining much longer." Vague statements by a person that he might "do something" or expressions of "getting out of control" can be suggestive of suicidal intent.

When a person gives verbal clues, the officer should not be afraid to bring the question of suicide into the open. Some may hesitate because they are afraid that their questions might suggest this act to someone who has not really considered it. However, this is unlikely and, if suicide hasn't been on his mind, inquiring about it is not going to trigger it. Posing a question regarding suicidal thoughts directly will often help the formation of a trusting relationship because the person who has been contemplating suicide will be relieved to find that others are able to understand what he has been thinking.

Behavioral Clues

Behavioral clues also may be direct or indirect. Direct clues include a history of a prior attempt. The officer should be especially alert if the prior attempt was almost lethal or if there has been more than one attempt. However, any history of past attempts, regardless of their potential lethality, should call attention to a suicidal risk.

Behavioral clues may be indirect. The sudden making of a will, the giving away of prized possessions, the sending home of clothing and things needed for daily living may be indirect behavioral clues to suicidal intent. A few years ago, a skeleton of a young man was found by road crews working on an army base. Investigation revealed that the skeleton was that of a young lieutenant who had vanished from the base fifteen years earlier and had been listed as a deserter. Investigators managed to reconstruct the last few days of his life even though many years had passed.

Two or three days prior to his disappearance, he had withdrawn all of his money from a local bank. Some he had lent, without security, to a friend who wanted to purchase a new car. He had sent the rest home to his father along with a footlocker containing his best clothes and prized possessions. He had then bought a revolver from a pawn shop, gone out in the desert, and shot himself. The rusted gun was found with his skeleton.

Although he had no history of depression or suicidal behavior and had given no direct verbal clues, these behaviors were warning signs which might have led to the saving of his life if they had been noted.

Situational Communications

In addition to verbal and behavioral clues, situational communications often indicate contemplated suicidal behavior. Some situations are so stressful that they may lead to desperate attempts to escape them through suicidal behavior. For example, although most prisoners manage to do "time" without cracking up, others find it intolerable and will try to get out of jail or prison through suicide attempts. Although most of these attempts are clearly manipulative and of low lethality, they should not be ignored.

In a recent study of suicidal behavior in jails, the authors found that six out of eight prisoners transferred from the county jail to the psychiatric service of the county hospital because of suicidal behavior admitted that the motivation for their behavior had been to get out of jail and into the hospital. While all six stated that they did not intend to kill themselves, they all emphatically threatened to "do a better job next time" if forced to return to jail. After being returned to jail, four of the six made additional suicide attempts (Beigel and Russell 1972).

Other situations which may constitute serious *emotional emergencies* leading to suicide attempts include hospitalization, the possibility of major surgery, the discovery of a malignancy or terminal illness, and the loss of a job or loved one.

Syndromatic Communications

Finally, Schneidman describes a fourth category of clues known as syndromatic communications. These are a group of symptoms which, if they appeared singly, would not lead to concern. However, as the number seen in a single individual increases, the concern for possible suicidal behavior should increase as well.

SLEEP DIFFICULTY

In nearly every study of suicidal patients, this symptom is mentioned prominently. It may be difficulty in falling asleep or, if the person falls asleep readily, he may awake in the middle of the night and be unable to go back to sleep. He may experience frequent and horrible nightmares as he sleeps fitfully and awakens at the slightest sound.

LOSS OF WEIGHT

Any appreciable loss of weight over a short period of time in the absence of a known physical cause, such as dieting or severe illness.

FEARFULNESS

The person who is contemplating suicide may express vague fears of losing control. If he had a previous depression which included a suicide attempt, he may say, "I don't want to end up that way again."

FATIGUE

Complaints of always being tired may be accompanied by posture and movements which communicate a feeling of great effort.

LOSS OF INTERESTS

These may include loss of interest in hobbies, work, social contacts, and/or sex. The more general the loss of interest, the more serious the depression and the more likely a possible suicide attempt.

IRRITABILITY

Continuing irritability, particularly in the absence of provocation and directed toward those whom an individual ostensibly loves.

FEELINGS OF SELF-DEPRECATION

The person who begins to describe himself as "worthless, bad, evil, and a failure" and who resists attempts to convince him that the opposite is true.

FEELINGS OF HOPELESSNESS

When an individual regards his situation and perhaps even himself as hopeless, it is likely that he is not far away from seeing that there is no way out other than through his own death.

CHANGES IN DRINKING PATTERNS

When drinking patterns begin to change either through increased drinking, drinking alone, or drinking at odd times, an acute state of depression may be present. "Accidental" suicides are often associated with changes in drinking patterns since increased alcohol use combined with taking pills can be a lethal combination even though he or she did not "intend" to die.

Helpful Hints to the Law Enforcement Officer

Establishing a relationship with the proposed suicide attempter, identification and clarification of his or her focal problem, evaluation of his or her suicide potential, assessment of the strengths and resources available to the individual, implementation of rescue operations, if necessary, and referral to appropriate agencies are the critical aspects of suicide prevention which may occur in sequence or at the same time. The law enforcement officer who comes in contact with a potential suicide attempter should have a basic knowledge of these important aspects of suicide prevention.

The Relationship

When an officer is confronted with suicidal ideation, he should be patient, interested, self-assured, hopeful, and knowledgeable. By assuming this attitude and behavior, he communicates to the potential suicide attempter that he has done the right thing by letting the officer know that he is contemplating suicide. He should be accepted without challenge or criticism and allowed to tell his story in his own way while the officer listens.

Any contact with a proposed attempter initiated through a telephone call also requires certain clear approaches. First, the call should be answered with clear identification of the agency and the officer's name. As soon as it is known that the caller is suicidal, a request for the name and telephone number should be made. When some callers refuse to give their names, the officer should calmly accept this refusal, for the moment, and proceed with the conversation. However, at some later appropriate time, names and phone numbers of interested persons such as family members, physicians, or close friends who might be possible resources should be obtained. Since the immediate goal is to obtain information to be used in the evaluation of suicide potential, getting into a discussion or argument about whether the caller is going to reveal his name will be counterproductive.

Identification and Clarification of the Focal Problem

In conversations with officers, suicide attempters may often display a profound sense of confusion, chaos, and disorganization. Because they are often unclear about their main problems and get lost in details, one of the most important services which the officer can perform is to help them recognize what their central problems are and to place them in proper perspective.

For example, a woman called the police department voicing many complaints including feelings of worthlessness, despair, and inadequacy. She said that she was not a good mother because she could not manage her housework and that her family would be better off without her. Careful initial listening by the officer followed by some specific questioning helped the officer to learn that her main problem was her relationship with her husband. When the officer reflected this back to her with authority, she was able to organize herself better and to address this specific problem more effectively.

Evaluation of Suicide Potential

Suicide potential refers to the probability that an individual may kill himself in the immediate or relatively near future. It is important that the officer, as soon as he begins to talk with someone who is contemplating suicide, also starts to evaluate the suicide potential in order to make an accurate assessment of the immediate lethal risk. This is extremely important because the officer's plan of action will depend upon this evaluation.

Statistics indicate that the suicide rate rises with increasing age and that men are more likely to kill themselves than women. A communication from an older male, therefore, tends to be more dangerous than one from a young female. However, young people do kill themselves, although their original aim may have been to manipulate others rather than to die. Therefore, age and sex offer only a general framework for evaluating suicide potential. Each case must receive further appraisal according to other criteria.

One of these criteria is the suicide plan. Three main elements should be considered in appraising the plan. These are: (1) the lethality of the proposed method; (2) the availability of the means; and (3) the specificity of the plan's details. Methods involving a gun, jumping, or hanging are usually more lethal than pills or wrist cutting. Furthermore, if the gun is at hand, the threat must be taken more seriously than when a person talks about shooting himself but does not have a gun. If an individual describes specific details, such as indicating that he has spent time making preparations such as changing a will, writing suicide notes, collecting pills, buying a gun, and setting a time, the seriousness increases markedly. In addition, if the plan is bizarre and the details are apparently irrational, it is quite possible that the officer is dealing with a psychotic person and this fact increases potential lethality.

Information about the precipitating stress is also useful in evaluating potential. Typical precipitating stresses include losses such as the loss of a loved one by death, divorce, or separation; the loss of job, money, prestige, or status; the loss of health through sickness, surgery, or an accident; or the threat of prosecution for criminal involvement or exposure for some reported misdeed. Occasionally, increased anxiety and tension may be associated with success, such as a job promotion with increased responsibilities.

The officer must evaluate the stress from the caller's point of view and not from his own or society's. What an officer might consider a minimal stress may be felt as especially severe by the caller.

The specific clues to suicidal behavior described in the previous section serve also as criteria for evaluating suicidal potential. The officer should keep in mind how these symptoms compare to the stress he has found out about. For example, if the symptoms are great, but the stress precipitating them appears to be minor, then either the story may be incomplete or the individual may be chronically unstable with a history of prior crises similar to this one.

The stress and symptoms must also be evaluated in relation to the individual's life style. For example, the officer should evaluate whether the suicidal behavior is acute or chronic. If the officer discovers that serious attempts have been made in the past, the current situation must be rated as potentially more dangerous. However, a "stable" person with no prior history who is undergoing a severe stress may also be a high risk.

In forming a plan of action, the officer should assess the available relationships of the potential suicide attempter. If he discovers that the suicidal person has severed all communications with others, then the potential danger is increased.

Finally, it is also useful for the officer to inquire tactfully into the medical status of the potential suicide attempter. For example, if the individual is suffering from a chronic illness which has changed his self-image, suicide potential may be greater.

In summary, no single criterion need be alarming by itself with the possible exception of the individual who has a very lethal and specific plan for suicide. Rather, the evaluation of suicide potential will be based on the general pattern which develops after an examination of all criteria in the context of a specific individual. For example, feelings of exhaustion and loss of resources will have different implications in two persons of different ages. A twenty-five-year-old married man stated that he was tired, depressed, and was having vague ideas about committing suicide by driving into a freeway abutment. There was no history of prior suicidal behavior. He reported difficulty in his marriage and talk of separation, but was still in contact with his wife and working at the job he had had for many years. This case was considered a low suicide risk.

In contrast, a high risk was a sixty-four-year-old man with a history of alcoholism who reported that he had made a serious suicide attempt one year ago and was saved when someone unexpectedly walked in and found him unconscious. He had a history of three failures in marriage and many job changes. He said further that his physical health had been failing, that he had no family left, and that he was thinking of killing himself with the gun he had in the house.

Assessment of Resources

In handling the individual who is contemplating suicide, it is as important to assess the resources in the environment within which he lives as it is to evaluate the specific aspects of his thinking and be-havior. For example, although an individual may present many nega-tive feelings and behaviors indicative of suicidal intent, it may be lessened by positive factors such as a continued relationship with a loved one or even a positive reaction to the initial interview with the officer.

The discovery that an individual is already in contact with a treat-ment agency or therapist may also lessen concerns about suicide po-tential. Finally, the presence of loved ones, particularly family and relatives, and their willingness to remain with an individual will also decrease suicide potential.

Rescue Operations and Referral Procedures

The officer's response to a specific situation will be determined by his evaluation of the suicide risk and the information which he has obtained about available resources. In general, those situations which the officer rates as having high suicide potential in the pres-ence of few resources will require immediate intervention. If the person is on the telephone, the officer should attempt to keep him on the line until a police unit arrives at the scene. This person should be immediately taken to a hospital for a professional evaluation unless family or close friends are present who will help bring the sit-uation under control. In either case, the people in control should be instructed not to leave the person alone.

However, most situations encountered by the police are of low or medium risk and, initially, can be handled very satisfactorily by a sympathetic and understanding listener who provides telephone counseling. However, an attempt should be made to refer this indi-vidual to an appropriate agency such as a suicide prevention center or a mental health clinic for continuing care. Consequently, the officer should be familiar with agencies in the community and know their hours of operation and telephone numbers. He should offer to make an appointment and should follow up by informing the person of it, if possible, while he or she is still on the line. Although the call may not be judged serious in terms of immediate suicide potential, the caller still has serious life problems for which he needs help. A failure to respond may eventually lead to a more serious "cry for help."

In the rare situation in which someone calls in the midst of a suicide attempt, only as much information as is necessary to identify the caller should be obtained and a police unit should be sent to the scene immediately. If an individual is calling about another person, the informant should be instructed either to take the suicide attempter to a nearby emergency room or to call an ambulance.

The following are suggestions about general and community resources usually available during these situations. One or more of these resources should be considered by the officer.

The family is often a neglected resource during this crisis. The attempter should be encouraged to discuss his problems with his family. If it is important that someone be with him during the crisis, family members should be called and told of the situation even though the attempter may express reluctance to do so. However, he should be informed that his family will be called.

Close friends may be used in the same way as families. For example, the caller or the attempter can be encouraged to have a friend stay with him during a difficult period. The friend may also be helpful in talking things out and giving him support.

People often turn to their *family doctors* for help because physicians are seen as supportive authority figures. If the potential suicide attempter has a good relationship with his physician, he should be encouraged to discuss his problems with him. Physicians can also be helpful when medication or hospitalization is required. If the potential attempter is religious, the involvement of a *clergyman* may be helpful.

In addition to individuals, the resources of *the community and its agencies* may be utilized. The hospital emergency room, the suicide prevention center, the community mental health center, a social work agency, a private therapist, and/or a psychiatric hospital are appropriate helping resources. When the officer considers utilizing one of them, he should recognize that his responsibility does not end until he has made certain that the attempter has been turned over to their care.

The following examples of typical calls handled by a police station are cases in which suicidal behavior or suicidal ideation was prominent. Following a description of the telephone call, suggestions will be made for handling the problem presented. It should be remembered that these examples have been chosen for teaching purposes and that not all calls will fall within these rather well-defined areas.

Case Example 1

A woman between thirty and forty years old called one night saying that she didn't understand why she felt so depressed. She said she was alone, complained of not being able to sleep, and of having troubled thoughts and feelings. She mentioned that she had thought about killing herself, but that she didn't really want to even though she had been having these thoughts for years. On the telephone, she sounded agitated, depressed, and somewhat hysterical. She was demanding and asked what could be done for her right now because she felt that she would not be able to get through the night. Upon further questioning, the officer was able to determine that many of these episodes had occurred before.

In these situations, it is best for the officer to listen patiently and to wait for an opportunity to point out that things often look worse at night, but that it is not the best time to get help. She should be advised to call her doctor, a social service agency, or a mental health clinic in the morning to make an appointment. The officer should take her number and call her back the next morning to reinforce his suggestion. At the same time, he can suggest that she call a close friend or relative to come over and spend the night with her.

Case Example 2

A woman who sounds between twenty and thirty-five calls the police station but will not identify herself. She asks the officer what can anyone do for a person who doesn't want to live anymore. Although she sounds in control, she alludes vaguely to a long-standing problem. She demands that the officer do something about her problem.

The officer should point out to her that she has a responsibility to cooperate if she really wants help. The officer should tell her that it is important for him to know more about her situation and who she is before he can help her. If she mentions that she has a therapist and who he is, she should be referred back to him. The officer can also tell her that he will call the therapist and notify him that she has called. Although she may initially express resistance to this, it is likely that she will accept the officer's direction.

Case Example 3

A woman who sounds like she is in her early fifties calls one evening to complain that she is very depressed and feels that no one is interested in her. During the phone call, she talks about her many physical problems and complains that her doctor is not helping her enough and that her husband is not giving her enough attention. She states that she feels her life is over and that there is no point in continuing to live.

She should be encouraged to talk with her husband and to tell him how she is feeling. If this is not feasible, either because he is not at home or because she is unwilling, she should be encouraged to call her family physician and talk to him. The officer may offer to call her physician. If none of these resources is immediately available, she should be referred to a suicide prevention center or an appropriate mental health facility.

CASE EXAMPLE 4

A young man who sounds in his early twenties calls the police station. He is evasive and reluctant to give his name. He talks about a problem which he does not identify, but states that he is calling for help because he has reached the point where the only solution to his problem is to kill himself. He describes impulsive suicide plans such as smashing his car on the freeway or cutting himself with a razor blade.

In these situations, it is important for the officer to be supportive. He may commend him for having done the right thing in calling as a beginning effort to get help. He should be given a list of helping resources. In this discussion, it is important to talk with him about which resource he might feel most comfortable contacting. Any assistance the officer can give him in making this contact will be helpful.

CASE EXAMPLE 5

A young man in his early thirties calls one evening to complain that his life is a mess because of his bungling. He talks about having gotten himself in such a jam, financially and with his family, that he now feels the only way out is to kill himself.

Often, the officer will be able to identify a specific recent setback in this person's life. Once he has uncovered this recent stress, he should tell the caller that he is reacting to this specific stress and that he needs help with this particular problem. The caller should be reminded that he was able to function well prior to this setback and that he is probably suffering from a temporary depression for which he needs professional help.

CASE EXAMPLE 6

A man, age fifty, calls one evening and sounds very depressed and discouraged. He is apologetic about calling and troubling the officer. He complains about a physical problem which has prevented him from working and states that he now feels that this problem is beyond help. He expresses many sad feelings about being old and a burden upon others. When asked about his suicidal thoughts, he reveals a specific plan for killing himself.

A police unit should be dispatched and contact maintained with the individual until the unit arrives. He should be told that help is available and on the way. After the unit arrives, family, friends, and other resources should be mobilized and involved.

CASE EXAMPLE 7

A family member or friend calls the police one evening about someone who is depressed and withdrawn. Furthermore, the caller is concerned because he has learned of this individual's plan to kill himself and has even discussed its specifics. The caller is asking how serious the situation is and what to do.

This caller should be advised by the officer to contact the person he is calling about and let him know immediately that he is concerned about him and trying to get help. He should be told to encourage the potential suicide attempter to call a suicide prevention center or another appropriate agency. Contact with the initial caller should be maintained and he should be asked to keep the officer informed about what is happening.

CASE EXAMPLE 8

This caller is a neighbor who is concerned about someone, but is reluctant to identify himself or to involve himself by assuming any responsibility. Instead, he requests that the officer do something for the person he is concerned about. Furthermore, the caller is vague about the situation which concerns him.

In these cases, the officer should get as much information as he can and should tell the caller that it is important for him to take some steps such as contacting the person he is concerned about and letting him know of his concern.

It should also be pointed out to the caller that it is unrealistic for the officer to contact the person about whom the caller is concerned unless he is able to tell that person the name of the person who notified him. If the caller is still reluctant to identify himself, then it is even more important for the officer to emphasize that it is the caller's responsibility to become involved.

CASE EXAMPLE 9

In this situation, a physician, minister, or mental health professional in a position of responsibility calls about someone who needs immediate rescue to prevent a suicide. The officer should get only as much information as he needs to dispatch a unit quickly. He should ask the professional what he feels should be done after the potential suicide attempter is taken into protective custody.

CASE EXAMPLE 10

In this situation a caller informs the police that a neighbor or family member is being physically restrained from attempting suicide at that very moment and cannot be left unattended.

This caller should be advised to immediately take the individual to the nearest hospital. If the caller cannot manage by himself, a unit should be dispatched. In the meantime, the officer should emphasize that any harmful drugs or objects should be removed and that someone should always remain with the potential suicide attempter.

In each of these examples, the officer has a responsibility to obtain as much information as possible and to maintain contact with the situation until it has been resolved. He must avoid empty reassurances and superficial platitudes which will only convey to the individual that he does not understand the problem and that he does not have any real empathy. If the officer conveys this impression, it is likely that the individual who is contemplating suicide will not be able to form a trusting relationship with the officer and possibly will break off communication and make a suicide attempt.

Summary

Suicidal behavior is a public health and mental health problem of major dimensions. It occurs among the rich, the poor, the young, and the old; among members of all races and religious backgrounds; and within all professions and occupations—even policemen. At the same time, it is an individual matter and can be prevented if one is trained to recognize the clues to suicidal behavior which most potential attempters display before making an attempt or successfully completing the act.

Police responsibility involves understanding the personalities of those who are most likely to attempt suicide, knowledge of the various clues to contemplated suicidal behavior, and awareness of those principles of suicide prevention that will allow an officer to respond appropriately to both telephone calls and emergency situations.

REFERENCES AND ADDITIONAL BIBLIOGRAPHY

Beigel, A. and Russell, H. E. 1972. "Suicide Attempts in Jail." *Hospital and Community Psychiatry* 23:361–363.

Berman, A. L. 1972. "Crisis Interventionists and Death Awareness: An Exercise for Training in Suicide Prevention." *Crisis Intervention* 4:47–52.

Farberow, N. L. and Schneidman, E. S. 1961. *The Cry For Help.* New York: McGraw-Hill.

Hendin, H. 1963. "The Psychodynamics of Suicide." *Journal of Nervous and Mental Disease* 136:236–244.

Murphy, G. E.; Clendenin, W. W.; and Darvish, H. S. 1972. "The Role of the Police in Suicide Prevention." *Life-Threatening Behavior* 1:96–105.

Schneidman, E. S. 1967. *Essay in Self-Destruction.* New York: Science House.

Schneidman, E. S.; Farberow, N. L.; and Litman, R. E. 1970. *The Psychology of Suicide.* New York: Science House.

Chapter 17

Behavioral Aspects
of Disaster

IN THE VARIETY of behaviors described in the past seven chapters, the focus has been on a small number of people who demonstrate them, often in association with a mental illness. It is also important for the police officer to recognize that even healthy or normal
individuals can demonstrate abnormal behavior as an acute reaction
to overwhelming environmental stress (remember situational reactions described in Chapter 6).

In police work, the most common events associated with overwhelming environmental stress occur in disaster situations. Fires,
floods, tornadoes, earthquakes, and auto accidents are examples of
this type of acute stress situation which can lead to nonfunctional behavior in an individual who is otherwise healthy.

The ability of the officer to deal effectively with the behavioral
aspects of these disaster situations will depend on his understanding
of the types of reactions which may occur, the factors which lead to
the behaviors associated with them, and the specific intervention
tools which he has available.

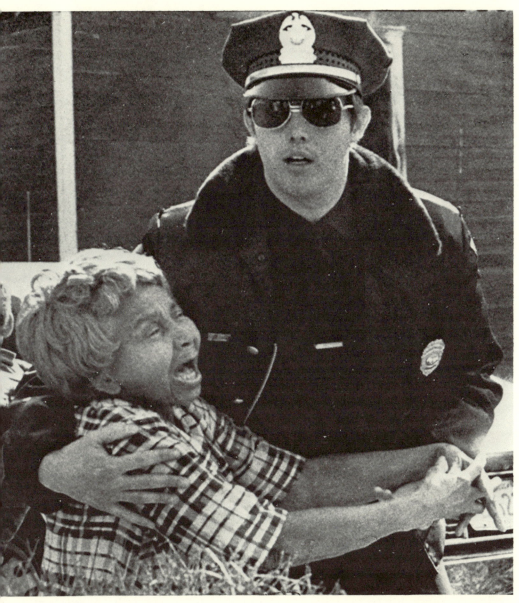

Historical Background

Much of our knowledge about stress and its effects, particularly during disasters, has come from military experiences. During the Civil War, medical personnel first observed and recorded the principle that environmental stresses may produce symptoms of abnormal behavior in soldiers. Surgeons of both the North and the South described a condition (*nostalgia*) which seemed responsible for considerable ineffectiveness. Soldiers afflicted with this disorder showed many symptoms of emotional instability including nervousness, anxiety, discontent, and passive-aggressive behavior. In this group, there was a higher degree of AWOLs and other disciplinary problems. These medical personnel realized that these symptoms were a result of a pathological interaction between the soldier and his environment. They made note of this in their journals, but the war soon ended and the lesson they had learned was soon forgotten.

When World War I began, the military again discovered soldiers with similar symptoms, especially in the combat area. This time the diagnosis offered was *shell shock*, a term coined by Lieutenant Colonel Mott, a British medical officer. He believed that these observed symptoms were a result of a brain concussion of varying severity secondary to the effects of exploding shells. However, later observers noted that not all soldiers exposed to combat developed these symptoms and that, furthermore, some of those with shell shock had not had any exposure to combat and had not been anywhere near an exploding shell. Consequently, the strictly physical explanation for their ineffectiveness was discarded and these individuals were considered emotional casualties of the war.

The British and the French noticed that, when these casualties were evacuated to rear-echelon medical installations, only a few could ever return to combat duty. However, if they were treated "up front," a majority could be returned to full combat duty within twenty-four to forty-eight hours. The treatment was relatively simple and emphasized food, rest, and emotional support along with a firm expectation from the treating officer, repeatedly conveyed to the soldier, that the soldier would be okay in a few hours and able to return to his group.

These well-documented experiences during World War I were quickly forgotten and, at the start of World War II, the military was again found lacking in both knowledge about the effects of battle stress and personnel experienced in combat. When the first full-scale battles in which Americans participated resulted in a large number of unanticipated psychological casualties, these casualties were evacuated to rear-line medical installations contrary to what experience had taught during the latter stages of World War I. Many of the soldiers thus "evacuated" did not recover and ended up with medical discharges and diagnoses of "psychoneurosis" or "psychosis."

However, as the war continued, American psychiatrists became more skilled in treating war neuroses, using techniques of hypnosis and drug-induced interviews to relieve anxiety and restore health. The value of treatment on the front lines was rediscovered and psychiatrists were again assigned to combat positions. Then the high level of psychological casualties decreased (Glass 1953).

From these wartime experiences, two basic principles emerged: (1) treat victims as far forward as possible; and (2) return them to duty as soon as possible. These principles have direct application to civilian disaster situations including floods, tornadoes, fires, industrial accidents, and auto accidents.

The Four Phases of Disaster Reactions

Studies of disasters have led to a description of four distinct phases which can be anticipated in any reaction to a major stress situation. These are: (1) period of warning; (2) impact; (3) immediate reaction; and (4) delayed response (APA 1964). An understanding of these four phases will enable the police officer to apply those effective principles and techniques of psychological first aid that will be described later.

The Warning Period

Warning of an impending disaster is desirable. However, it must also be recognized that this might have a destructive and/or disorganizing effect on individual behavior. While some individuals function at a high level of effectiveness in the face of danger, others may respond to a warning signal as if a disaster had already occurred and become completely helpless.

This latter group usually consists of two types of individuals—those who have experienced a previous and/or similar disaster in which they were helpless and for whom the warning signal rekindles those earlier feelings and those who will always be helpless in the face of any danger or threat. These people are susceptible to panic and must not be left to their own devices or they will communicate their panic to others.

The Impact Period

When disaster strikes, people will experience many frightening feelings. Although desirable patterns of behavior have been well established by drills and training, the initial impact will be stunned inactivity. It has generally been shown that for about the first fifteen minutes no one will be able to act effectively. Approximately fifteen minutes after a disaster has occurred, about 25 percent of the people will be able to resume effective behavior and, within one hour, another 60 percent will be capable of effective functioning. The remaining 15 percent will take from several hours to several weeks before they will be able to react effectively. A few of them may never recover.

Immediate Reaction after Impact

The period immediately following a disaster or stress situation is critical because this is when ineffective behavior is most costly. In contrast, effective behavior can save lives, relieve suffering, and decrease confusion.

Period of Delayed Response

When the community or the individual is no longer in immediate danger, the situation can be evaluated and action taken to meet needs. However, although the immediate danger is over, some people may have a delayed reaction. The person who was observed functioning effectively immediately after the disaster may no longer be doing so. Instead, he may now demonstrate signs of emotional disturbance including anxiety or depression. It should, therefore, be recognized that some people may require continued observation to insure that they do not have a delayed reaction to a disaster.

Normal and Abnormal Behavioral Reactions

The police officer may often have to set priorities as to whom he gives psychological first aid most immediately. It is, therefore, important for him to distinguish between normal behavioral reactions to stress or disasters and abnormal reactions.

He should recognize first that the presence of fear, anxiety, indecisiveness, confusion, and even temporary disorientation can be normal reactions. Their presence does not necessarily mean that an abnormal reaction is occurring. However, abnormal reactions are more complex and can be divided into four general categories.

First, there is the individual who is in a complete *panic*. In addition to the symptoms and signs listed above, judgment and reasoning have completely disappeared. The person who simply tries to escape a dangerous situation is not necessarily in a state of panic. The panicked individual, when he attempts to leave, will do so in an unreasonable manner and without any judgment. It is important that this panicked individual be identified immediately and isolated from others before they are affected by his reaction.

The second category of abnormal behavioral reactions are the *depressed* group. These people are slowed down, numbed, and dazed. The individual with a depressed reaction may sit in the midst of utter chaos, gazing vacantly into space and unable to respond. This is probably the most frequent abnormal behavioral reaction and people suffering from it usually respond very quickly to psychological first aid.

The third category is the *overactive reaction*. At first, this may look like panic, but the critical difference is that the affected individual does not try to leave the situation but instead begins markedly increased physical activity. He may talk rapidly, joke inappropriately, and/or make endless suggestions of little value. If his hyperactivity can be controlled, he may eventually prove to be very helpful in dealing with the disaster. Consequently, anything he is given to do that will work off the excess activity will be helpful. After he has settled down, he can be assigned to constructive tasks.

Finally, the last category of abnormal behavioral reactions to stress or disaster situations are the *abnormal body reactions*. In these cases the physical reactions to stress are severely incapacitating and may include severe nausea and vomiting which will not stop and/or hysterical blindness or paralysis.

Long-Term Psychological Effects

Long-term disabilities arising from disaster situations occur infrequently. Studies which have been completed on the survivors of the nuclear bomb attack on Hiroshima and of the concentration camps of World War II indicate that many of them demonstrated a profound loss of initiative and drive, difficulty with memory and concentration, feelings of apathy, and terrifying nightmares and guilt (Hocking 1970). More recently, experience with our returning Vietnam POWs clearly supports the need for continued counseling to those who may suffer long-term effects from severe stress situations. These effects may not be noted until much later and hospitalization may be required then.

Those who have long-term reactions to disaster situations are more likely to have had acute reactions to other disasters in the past. Consequently, it is important for a police officer to find out, if possible, whether an individual with an acute reaction during a current disaster has been involved in another situation in the past and to learn more about his reaction at that time and what was done about it.

Helpful Hints to the Law Enforcement Officer

Similar to the physical first aid which an officer gives to someone who has been injured in an auto accident, he can also apply psychological first aid to those whom he encounters with acute emotional reactions to disaster situations. His principal goal is to return the greatest number of people to effective functioning in the shortest time. In responding to stress or disaster situations, the officer should keep in mind the following principles.

1. He should respect every individual's right to his own feelings. Just because the officer has responded appropriately, he should not expect that everyone else will. He should realize that there will be as many different reactions as there are different people because each person is unique. A psychological casualty is not an inferior or cowardly person.

2. The officer should remember that emotional disability secondary to a disaster situation is as real as physical disability. No one would expect a soldier who has had both of his legs shot off to "buck up" and go back into the fray. Similarly, the police officer should not expect people who have had a severe emotional reaction to "pull themselves together" and carry on.

246

3. The officer should remember that every physically injured person will have some emotional reaction to his injury. Furthermore, some people may have severe emotional reactions to minor injuries because of their personal significance. For example, the artist who has cut his finger may have a more severe reaction than a housewife with the same injury. Occasionally, the major reason for a severe reaction is not as obvious and may be related to a symbolic event or an unconscious fear. Because of this fear, the victim may distort the seriousness of the injury, consequently increasing his emotional reaction. Finally, it is important for the police officer to recognize that there is often more strength in people than may appear initially. Although this may seem contradictory to the first principle, which states that a person's feelings should be recognized and accepted, it is not. Rather, it encourages the officer to direct his support to the individual's strength. If he can mobilize this strength, he can significantly reduce the emotional reaction to a disaster.

4. In the handling of a disaster situation, the officer must remain calm if he is to be effective. He must keep his wits about him so that he does not inadvertently compound the disaster situation and the emotional reactions of others to it.

Consequently, he should also remember *not* to do the following when encountering those with acute emotional reactions to stress situations. He should not strike, slap, or hit anyone. He should remember that it will not do any good to tell someone to "snap out of it," "use their willpower," or "buck up." Statements such as these will only increase feelings of inadequacy with which the person may be already overwhelmed. Finally, he must not overwhelm anyone with pity, blame, or ridicule since these will also increase feelings of inadequacy.

5. The police officer should establish, as soon as possible, some form of communication, either verbal or nonverbal, with the individual. In this regard, it is helpful to remember what a mother does with a hurt child when he comes in from the playground crying. The good mother will take the child onto her lap, comfort him, and ask him what happened. As he sobs out his story, she may put ice or some medicine on his bruise and get him a bandaid while continually reassuring him that everything will be all right. This is a good example because, in disaster situations, many people regress to childlike behavior.

While the officer may not take a person onto his lap, he certainly can put his arm around him, ask him what happened, and help him ventilate his feelings about the situation. In doing so, the officer is not interested in the truth or falsehood of any statements but, rather, in trying to get a person to talk about his feelings.

6. After establishing communication, the next important thing a police officer can do is to get the person to engage in constructive activity. This will reduce physical tension and divert him from thinking about his own problems. By enabling him to serve others, it will also help to restore his feelings of adequacy. After this physical release has been achieved, he should be encouraged to rest and pay attention to his own needs such as hot food or dry clothing. Throughout your handling of this individual, convey to him firmly the expectation that he will be okay shortly.

7. Remember that to suffer together is to suffer less. Try and get the person back to his family and friends as soon as possible. If there has been a tornado, for example, and people have been rushed to hospitals, try and maintain a list of who went where so that you can assist survivors to find their loved ones.

8. Finally, the officer should always be aware of his own feelings. It is natural to have feelings of resentment, anger, and hostility toward those who do not seem to be physically injured and who contribute nothing to help the situation. The officer must not allow these feelings to interfere with his ability to help others during a disaster.

Summary

In this chapter, reactions to acute stress and disaster situations have been described. Emotional casualties are often more frequent than physical disabilities. By recognizing this, the officer can have an important influence on reducing the abnormal behavior reactions to disaster situations. Not only can he save lives and relieve suffering, but, perhaps more importantly, he can also help people get back on their feet as quickly as possible so that they can assist him in the many tasks demanded by the disaster situation.

REFERENCES AND ADDITIONAL BIBLIOGRAPHY

American Psychiatric Association. 1964. *First Aid for Psychological Disasters*. Washington, D.C.

Baker, G. W. 1962. *Man and Society in Disaster*. New York: Basic Books.

Garb, S. and Eng, E. 1969. *Disaster Handbook*. New York: Springer.

Glass, A. J. 1953. "Psychotherapy in the Combat Zone." In *Proceedings of Symposium on Stress*. Washington, D.C.: Army Medical Graduate School, Walter Reed Medical Center, pp. 284–294.

Hocking, F. 1970. "Extreme Environmental Stress and Its Significance for Psychopathology." *American Journal of Psychotherapy* 24:4–26.

Moore, H. E. 1958. "Some Emotional Concomitants of Disaster." *Mental Hygiene* 42:45–50.

Chapter 18

Behavioral Aspects of Riots and Riot Control

DURING HIS WORK, the police officer must often handle large crowds, some of which are peaceful while others are not. Both disasters, as described in the previous chapter, and civil unrest can lead to behavioral changes in individuals and/or large crowds which will present problems to the officer.

Without knowledge of those psychological principles associated with riot behavior and riot control, it will be difficult for the officer to handle crowd behavior effectively. With knowledge, however, he will be able to plot a course of action that will have the best chance of preventing violence or panic or of controlling such an outbreak if it has already begun.

In this chapter, we will discuss characteristics of crowds and mobs; underlying factors that influence their behavior and countermeasures which the police officer can take to control it; techniques employed by mobs in mob action; types of panic-producing situations that

Much of the material in this chapter is taken from the author's (Russell) notes obtained at the civil disturbance orientation course conducted at the Military Police School of Ft. Gordon, Georgia in 1968.

David Krasnor / Photo Researchers, Inc.

might occur and the actions which can be taken to prevent them; and the type of mental preparation required of officers prior to undertaking civil disturbance duty. Finally, we shall also present a code of conduct for the police officer which can serve as a guide to his behavior during civil disturbances.

Characteristics of Crowds and Mobs

It is important to distinguish between a crowd and a mob since the majority of gatherings do not present any special problems to the police. A crowd is defined as a large number of people temporarily congregated without organization, who think and act as individuals. A crowd may be a *physical crowd* or a *psychological crowd*. An example of the former would be people in a shopping center who have gathered together accidentally without a specific organization or purpose, other than shopping. In contrast, the psychological crowd exists when there is a common interest. This type of crowd can be further described as either *casual* or *intentional*. An example of the former is a gathering at an accident or a fire. In contrast, the intentional psychological crowd might be found at a sporting event, a political rally, or a funeral. It is the intentional psychological crowd which is most susceptible to transformation into a mob.

A mob is defined as a crowd whose members, influenced by stimuli of intense excitement or agitation, lose their sense of reason and respect for law and follow leaders into lawless acts of violence and destruction. It is helpful to classify mobs according to the behavior and motivation of its members.

The *aggressive mob* riots and terrorizes (for example, race riots, lynchings, and prison uprisings). The *escape mob* is in a state of panic or blind flight. Members of an escape mob lose their power of reasoning and may cause their own destruction (for example, fleeing from a disaster). An *acquisitive mob* is motivated by a desire to acquire something (for example, looters following in the wake of an aggressive mob). Finally, a *dispersed mob* may quickly join together, accomplish an act, and then disperse again. Their objective is to create simultaneous disturbances as diversions from the actions of a principal mob (for example, setting fires to incite additional violence).

The Riot Process

Having defined the types of crowds which exist, having character-ized how a crowd may turn into a mob, and having described the types of mobs, it is important to turn now to the riot process and to describe it in detail.

Precipitating Incident

Almost anything can serve as the precipitating incident to a riot. It might be a forceful apprehension by an officer or something as rou-tine as a traffic stop. It may not be an act, but only a rumor which leads people to pour into the streets in a state of agitated anger.

It may not be a single event, but a series of previous incidents and/or rumors that have occurred to set the stage for the final in-cident which triggers the riot's start. For example, in 1971 students at the University of Arizona engaged in three days of civil disturbances. The precipitating incident occurred when some street people were ordered off campus by the University police. They had been drink-ing wine by a campus fountain in violation of University rules. The police found it necessary to physically remove them. When several students intervened, the situation escalated into a riot.

Although this was the immediate precipitating incident, the roots of this riot actually had involved a series of relatively minor happen-ings which had predisposed the campus to be *riot-prone*. One event, several weeks earlier, was the publication by the University of a student code of conduct which many students found objectionable. Another incident, also several weeks earlier, had involved some clashes between street people and local police. The police had been called by local merchants after the street people had begun to block entrances and exits to their stores, interfering with customers. Dur-ing this earlier confrontation, a local druggist had reportedly threat-ened to shoot some of these youths if they continued to harass him. Finally, shortly before the fountain incident which precipitated the riot, a young man was killed in the University area during a narcotics rip-off. Rumors circulated that the police had been in some way responsible for his death. All of these events, prior to the precipitat-ing incident, created an emotional climate that was conducive to the spontaneous eruption of violence after an incident which would nor-mally not have created any special difficulty.

253

Studies have shown that, in many cases, the riot process can be stopped at this point if the mayor or another important official immediately visits the area, talks to the people, and promises to listen to and redress their grievances. An example of this occurred when John Lindsay, then Mayor of New York City, walked the streets of Harlem in 1968, speaking with people and thereby carrying out an important part of riot prevention.

Confrontation

During the second phase, the police must avoid either overreaction or underreaction. Many confrontations exhaust the energy of the riot participants and nothing further happens. However, in some situations, a *keynoting process* may begin. This occurs when the angriest members of a crowd, or perhaps a single more militant individual, urge more violent action.

To counter this, moderate community leaders may try to persuade the crowd to disband, promising that a committee will be formed to channel the protest to city hall. If these leaders win out, the crowd will disband and the riot will be over; but, if the militants or the hostile keynoters win, the riot will escalate to the next stage.

"Roman Holiday"

The "Roman Holiday" phase usually involves young people who are angry, hostile, and impulsive. Although their actions may have been planned in advance, a spontaneous reaction is more likely. They may begin to break windows, overturn cars or set them afire, and engage in other destructive events.

During this stage, it is again important for the police not to over- or underreact. If they respond with excessive force, tales by the victims to the news media will reach dissident communities and lead to further escalation. On the other hand, a permissive attitude may be considered as a go-ahead signal and the result is the same. When this phase is not handled properly, more people, both adults and children, begin to take part in looting and stealing. Firebombs and guns are brought into play and the riot may escalate into open conflict.

Open Conflict

This phase becomes combat in the city as exemplified by the 1968 riots in Washington, D.C. The police must now use force to contain the riot and restore order. Moderate to intense sniper fire occurs. Firebombing increases and becomes used as a selective weapon by the rioters.

The police respond by using automatic weapons and the National Guard is often called in. A dissident community, especially if agitated by militants, may arm itself and assemble its own firepower. Eventually, the establishment usually wins, since the odds are always in its favor because of its greater resources.

The Individual Rioter

Although rioting is mob action, the individual is still the basic unit of the mob. These questions must, therefore, be asked: Why do individuals participate in mob action? What is it about the mob that leads people to lose control and commit acts which they would not do under other circumstances? To help answer these questions several underlying factors that affect individual behavior in a mob must be reviewed.

The first is *anonymity*. A person tends to lose his identity in the mob since he feels that he will not be blamed for his actions. Furthermore, because he sees the things he does as only a small part of a larger picture of violence and destruction, his sense of anonymity is increased.

A second factor is the *impersonality of group behavior*. This may be understood better by recalling the football player who bears no personal grudges against his rival but will do or die for Old Notre Dame, or the soldier who bears no personal animosity against the enemy soldier he may shoot.

The impersonality of mob behavior is demonstrated also when one member of a race or group is not seen as an individual but as a stereotype. The sniper who puts the figure of a police officer in the crosshairs of his high-powered rifle scope may hate, but he hates the police symbol, not the individual officer he is about to try to kill. It does not matter to this sniper that the officer in his sight may have a wife and children or that he may be one of the fairest officers on the force. Neither would it matter if he was one of the most hated officers. The sniper stereotypes him as a "pig" and kills him with an impersonal attitude.

Because of the intense emotions present during a riot, members of the mob tend to suspend their own normally critical judgment and to react impulsively to the suggestions of a dominant member. Police officers can counter this kind of negative *suggestibility* by presenting an alternate course of action to the mob. For example, during the 1967 march on Washington, when agitators were trying to incite tired mob members to continue the disturbances at the Pentagon, undercover police officers infiltrated the crowd and encouraged people to take advantage of waiting buses to rest their tired feet. The mob responded positively to this countermeasure and left the area.

Closely allied to suggestibility is *contagion*. The reader is probably more familiar with contagion when used in a medical sense, such as a contagious disease resulting from the transmission of a virus from the sick to the healthy. Similarly, ideas and feelings can be contagious. People become emotionally stimulated by the feelings and ideas of others although they have not shared the experiences from which they originate.

Imitation is another factor. The urge to do what others are doing is very strong when large numbers of people are gathered together. Group identity grows and draws people closer psychologically. Contrary to popular belief, hostility is not eliminated or reduced by having a good fight or by letting off steam through violent acts. This behavior merely solidifies hostile feelings and develops increased hatred within the mob. As open violence increases, more destruction is likely to follow.

Novelty may also encourage individual participation in a mob. Many who lead dull and uninteresting lives may view a riot as a break in their daily routine and react with enthusiasm. The riot gives these people an opportunity to do things they have always wanted to do but didn't dare. In less harmful circumstances, this is seen in college panty raids when many students join in a novel activity to relieve the boredom of studying.

The Riot-Prone Personality

Recalling the personality disorders discussed in Chapter 7, it is evident that some people might be more apt to become involved in a riot. The passive-aggressive personality, for example, with his underlying feelings of hostility and aggression, may need only a small provocation to release these feelings against others. The paranoid personality, chronically angry, hostile, and suspicious, will take advantage of an opportunity to act out in this way. The psychopathic personality is not only riot-prone but is often an instigator and leader of riots, especially in jails and prisons. On the street, he may engage in riot behavior as a mask for criminal activity or for the attention he receives as a militant leader. Finally, the emotionally immature individual may engage in riots because of his tendency toward immature and acting out behavior. He is suggestible and will be a follow-the-leader type, welcoming the opportunity to release hostility through destructive action. In the mob, he gains courage to do things that he would not do alone.

Techniques of Agitators

To counter the behavior of agitators, it is important for the police officer to understand the principal techniques they use in starting and/or continuing to incite mob action.

The Emotion-Producing Rumor

Police engaged in civil disturbance duty should have an intelligence unit aimed at picking up and controlling rumors, since the adept agitator will use rumors to increase the tempo of a disorder or to change an orderly demonstration into a violent one. Police must be aware of these rumors and put out factual information to defuse them.

Propaganda

Newspaper, radio, television, and magazine propaganda are used by agitators to aggravate existing prejudices and grievances. In this way, they can bring a crowd together at a particular location and/or time and incite emotions by using propaganda to intensify real or imagined inequities. Played upon in this way, the crowd is ripe for transformation into a violent mob.

The police can effectively counter this propaganda through up-to-date, factual information, especially about their own actions or those of other controlling forces such as the National Guard. The mayor of a community may help by publishing proclamations that give the public concise information and instructions.

Forceful Harangue

As a well-trained speaker, the experienced agitator uses emotionally loaded words and phrases to appeal to local needs, fears, and prejudices. Accompanied by emphatic movements such as waving of the arms, he influences individuals to abandon their critical reasoning and to engage in actions which they would rebel against or condemn under normal circumstances.

The police may act by apprehending the speaker (which has the risk of making him a martyr) or dispersing the crowd (which is sometimes quite difficult). The mayor of one large American city undermined the planned actions of an agitator by meeting him at the airport with a courtesy car and appearing on the platform to introduce him. This implied association with the establishment created distrust among those who were prepared to hear and follow the militant.

The Appearance of an Irritating Person or Symbolic Object

A crowd may be brought to a fever pitch by the appearance of an object, such as a flag, or a particular person for whom the crowd has antipathy. This is sometimes difficult to combat since it often occurs accidentally. If this happens, the person or object should be removed as quickly as possible, especially if it can be done without further exciting the crowd. When there is information ahead of time that the appearance of a particular individual might trigger a disturbance, it should be cancelled. In 1960, President Eisenhower's trip to Japan was cancelled because of the danger of civil unrest which, it was felt, his presence in Japan at that time might trigger because of existing anti-American feeling.

Acts of Violence

Acts of violence, when they occur, can be successfully played upon by agitators to begin a chain reaction leading to further violence. Although we have been discussing techniques by which trained agitators can incite crowds, many disturbances are triggered by amateur agitators who seize a spur-of-the-moment opportunity. The following example, taken from the pages of the *Arizona Daily Star* of July 30, 1973, is illustrative.

Dallas, Texas: Quiet returned to downtown Dallas Sunday after a protest march led to a night of rock throwing, burning, and looting.

Police said forty-eight businesses were damaged in the melee which erupted during a march to protest the fatal shooting of a twelve-year-old Mexican-American boy by a policeman.

A large force of city and state policemen and sheriff's deputies quelled the violence after about three hours. At least five policemen were injured, none seriously.

The Dallas City Council met in emergency session after the incident and issued a statement both supporting the police and saying it joins with all Dallas citizens in understanding the outrage and sorrow of the Mexican-American community.

A police spokesman said there will be some inciting to riot charges filed today.

The march to the City Hall had been peaceful, according to a police spokesman Sunday, until a black woman grabbed a microphone in an unmarked police car and began shouting, "Kill the Pigs!" (Italics added.)

The woman was one of thirty-nine arrested. In all, forty-eight businesses sustained damage from glass breakage or looting. Police said estimates of total damage are expected to be high.

Panic may also occur when police begin to move in. The police must be prepared to size up these panic-producing situations and to take active steps to prevent a panic or to control the mob's actions when panic starts. Panic has been described as *blind flight*. It develops when a threat to survival is perceived by the mob and spreads rapidly. This perceived threat may be physical and/or psychological, real or imagined. It is usually regarded as so imminent that flight is viewed by the mob as the only possible means of escape.

In a riot, the presence or threat of riot-control agents, such as tear gas, may be enough to spark a panic reaction. The mob becomes irrational and fearful, seeking only to get away from the danger. Escape routes become clogged and the physical pressure of those in the back causes those in front to be crushed, smothered, or trampled. More panic is then produced and a vicious cycle begins.

Police personnel may counter panic reactions by the following techniques: (1) get up-to-date, factual information to the people and keep it coming; (2) provide escape routes and inform the crowd or mob where these routes are; and (3) keep these routes open and make sure that front-to-rear communication is maintained.

Sufficient communications equipment must be provided and alternate means for backup should be at hand in case the main communications equipment and/or personnel are ineffective. As difficult as it might be, police must be alert to prevent these incidents.

Helpful Hints to the Law Enforcement Officer

Having described the types of behaviors and techniques, both group and individual, associated with riot behavior, it is important to turn to those techniques which law enforcement must employ if it is to successfully contain and control this behavior. Similar to the individual and group activities which are a part of riot behavior, riot control involves actions of the individual police officer and the police as a whole.

Self-Control

The individual police officer and the police as a group must not lose self-control when dealing with riots. A professional, business-like detachment accompanied by impartiality and the sharp execution of orders will enhance the police image and contribute to orderly restoration of law and order. Only force necessary to control a situation should be used, since excessive force in a sensitive situation will destroy what has been previously accomplished and seriously affect future accomplishments.

Alertness

Policemen, especially those in command positions, must be alert so that they can detect rapid changes in the course of a disturbance. Just as soldiers prepare for the sounds and sights of battle through desensitizing techniques such as infiltration courses and mock enemy villages, police personnel should be prepared for the sounds and sights of riots and other civil disturbances.

At the Southern Arizona Law Enforcement Institute, two techniques have been useful in training officers and recruits to maintain their alertness. During a two-hour class on maintaining your cool, the emotionality of certain words and their ability to provoke highly charged emotional reactions are presented. Recruits are told to look at the man on their right and think of the most insulting thing to call or say to him. Then both men are asked to stand and the first recruit is asked to say it to the other man's face using the nastiest tone possible. Then the second man is asked to make the nastiest response he can think of to what he has been called. This exercise dramatically points out the emotional power of words and makes the recruits more alert to their own reactions to name calling and verbal baiting. Developing an alertness to their own reactions will help them maintain their cool during riots when they are called names or are insulted.

The second technique is an attempt to simulate the sights and sounds of battle. During this exercise, one-half of the recruit class is required to handle a disturbance staged by the other half. Depending on the actions of the "police," the disturbance becomes either aggravated or quieted down. After the exercise, a critique is held to discuss the actions of the "crowd" and "police" to determine which actions led to what results. A valuable part of the exercise is that recruits can see how both sides tend to get carried away. Alerting officers to this "being carried away" aspect of riot behavior is important in increasing riot control effectiveness.

Community Support

Acquiring and maintaining community support is an important factor in riot control. To maintain community support, the police must act in a competent and professional manner. As Craig has pointed out: "the key to the real support of the police is to be found in the development of enhanced competence among police officers. The competent police officer performs effectively under any and all conditions. Competency is more important than philosophy in police-community relations" (Craig 1969).

Furthermore, competency is colorblind. For example, in the black ghetto of an eastern city which experienced serious rioting in 1967, there was a "ten most-wanted list" of unpopular police officers. Although only five of the eighty-two officers on the police force were black, two of the ten most hated were black. The two most respected officers were white and had been judged among the most competent by their supervisors and fellow officers.

Another example of how competence can promote community support and help in riot control is illustrated by this example. In one large eastern city, a police officer who was at the top of a promotion list and due to be promoted to supervision was not noted for his liberalism. However, since no disciplinary action had ever been entered in his record, there was no reason to deny his promotion. Consequently, with considerable doubt, he was promoted and assigned to the ghetto. To everyone's surprise he did his job effectively and became one of the ghetto's favorite cops, an officer whom they could rely on for firm and impartial law enforcement. He gave the black citizens protection, respected them as individuals, and responded to their needs. That is really all these residents wanted, just like other residents of the city.

As competency promotes and maintains community support, police incompetency destroys community support. The report of the National Advisory Commission on Civil Disorders gives many examples of how the incompetency of a police officer can aggravate an already tense situation and, in some cases, spark further disturbances. These include the officer who allowed a black teenage prisoner to be handcuffed and, while lying on the ground, to be kicked in the face by a white man. No arrest was made.

In another example, the police in an eastern city were expecting a riot and were testing their tear gas guns on a firing range situated in the middle of a black residential area. When the wind blew the gas into their homes, the residents were understandably enraged. Even if such incidents are excusable because of pressure existing at the time, they cannot be tolerated if the police are to maintain the support of the community.

The Use of Humor

The value of humor is often overlooked as an effective police tactic in crowd control. It can be used in the control of sit-ins, marches, and other mobile demonstrations; in handling confrontations between mobs and control forces which have not yet reached a stage of violence; in dispersing groups to minimize animosity; in reducing hostility when it is necessary to make selected or mass arrests at a demonstration; or in the general prevention of hostility secondary to an issue which has led to a demonstration (Coates 1972).

Where possible, the police should direct the humor against themselves to reduce some of the hostility harbored by the demonstrators toward them. The humor should be verbal rather than something that has to be seen so that it can be fully enjoyed by everyone. If the humor is effective, it tends to be contagious with one laugh facilitating the next. Although initial attempts to use a light touch on a crowd may not be well received, repeated attempts may have a cumulative effect. However, heavy-handed humor should be avoided and, in most situations, ethnic humor is definitely out of place.

These positive benefits of humor in riot control suggest that police departments might identify officers for such duty who demonstrate an ability to handle crowds with wit and humor.

Police Policy

Most law enforcement authorities have policies that are the basis for their handling of crowds or mobs. They should be reexamined frequently to evaluate their effectiveness. For example, a common police practice during riots is to order all men on twenty-four-hour alert and to increase the on-duty time to twelve hours or longer. However, the efficacy of this practice is questionable. A tired policeman is a poor policeman, especially when faced with the stress of a civil disorder. How long can a police officer stay on the street, facing a hostile and potentially violent crowd, without losing his control? A police sergeant commented: "When my men are fresh, they toss off the insults and jeering with good humor. After an hour or two, their patience begins to wear thin. Give them another couple of hours and they're probably ready to bust heads."

Other common practices seem equally ill-advised. For example, in anticipation of trouble with student demonstrators, twenty or more deputies were brought to the scene in a school bus. They were confined in the bus in the hot sun for three to four hours, awaiting a possible call to action. Fortunately, the call never came and the deputies were driven back to the sheriff's office. One can speculate what frame of mind these men were in after about an hour on the hot bus. Had the call to action come, they might have used more force than necessary to control the demonstration.

Since a sense of group identity supports effective action, it is advisable for law enforcement authorities to arrange for officers who are coming off street duty during civil disturbances to spend time with other officers. This will enable them to share experiences, fostering an esprit de corps.

Law enforcement authorities should also plan policies that will reduce the physical and emotional stress of riot duty. A place for the officer to rest in comfort while on call should be set up immediately with drinks and sandwiches available. If possible, this should be provided by a local civic organization, since this will indicate to the officer that he has community support.

Since most officers are trained to work as individuals, more training must be provided to help them work as a team during civil disorders. The attainment of this goal requires constant practice. The police should plan regular team meetings, even if a riot is not looming on the horizon.

The Police Officer's Code of Conduct

As a summary, a suggested code of conduct for the police officer during civil disturbances and riots is presented. Hopefully, it will be a guide to professional behavior not only during these conflicts but also in other stressful situations.

1. Remember you are a professional law enforcement officer. Take pride in your ability to act professionally under any and all conditions.
2. Remember that your most powerful weapons are psychological ones—patience, tolerance, good humor, tact, and the ability to set an example by your own conduct.
3. Remember it is your uniform and your position, as symbols of the establishment, which some people react to negatively. Do not take threats, insults, or abuses personally.
4. Do not look upon all situations as a challenge to your ability as a police officer. No one expects you to take unnecessary chances or to prove anything.
5. Try to learn all you can about how an individual functions in a group, especially under conditions of stress. The more you know about this type of behavior, the better you will be able to predict, control, and alter it.
6. Don't overestimate your endurance threshold. A tired policeman is a poor policeman, especially during civil disturbance duty.
7. Have faith in others. You are not alone. There is a whole system behind you with local officials and other responsible citizens working to restore order.
8. Remember that all riots must end sometime and that the task of restoring affected areas must begin. Therefore, do not do anything during the stress of the disturbance that would jeopardize either your or the department's position in carrying out this task.

Summary

In this chapter, we have presented many of the principles that influence the behavior of crowds and mobs. The underlying factors that influence individuals to participate and the characteristics of those who emerge as leaders have also been discussed. Finally, techniques for law enforcement to use in controlling mobs have been presented along with a suggested code of conduct for the police officer.

REFERENCES AND ADDITIONAL BIBLIOGRAPHY

Coates, J. F. 1972. "Wit and Humor: A Neglected Aid in Crowd and Mob Control." *International Journal of Offender Therapy and Comparative Criminology* 16:184–191.

Craig, D. 1969. "The Police in the Middle of the Conflict." *Journal of Crime and Delinquency* 15:387–392.

Federal Bureau of Investigation. 1967. *Prevention and Control of Mobs and Riots.* Washington, D.C.: U.S. Government Printing Office.

Greenbaugh, C. W. and Zemach, M. 1972. "Role-Playing and Change of Attitude toward Police after a Campus Riot: Effects of Situational Demand and Justification." *Human Relations* 25:87–99.

Hopkins, P. and Feierabend, R. L. 1971. "Correlates of United States Riots, 1965–1967: A Cross-City Comparison." *Proceedings of the Annual Convention of the American Psychological Association* 6:311–312.

Kreps, G. A. 1973. "Change in Crisis-Relevant Organizations: Police Departments and Civil Disturbances." *American Behavioral Scientist* 16:356–367.

Report of the National Advisory Commission on Civil Disorders. 1970. Washington, D.C.: U.S. Government Printing Office.

Spiegel, J. 1968. *Toward a Theory of Collective Violence.* Waltham, Mass.: Brandeis University Press.

Wenger, D. 1973. "The Reluctant Army: The Functioning of Police Departments during Civil Disturbances." *American Behavioral Scientist* 16:326–342.

Chapter 19

Legal Aspects
of Abnormal Behavior

BOTH THE LAW (police officers, the courts, judges, lawyers, and penal institutions) and mental health have a common interest in the person whose behavior deviates from the accepted, explicit codes of society. However, this interest takes a different form for each. The law is concerned with the identification, apprehension, conviction, and punishment of the criminal. Mental health is concerned with identifying the reasons for the individual's abnormal behavior and with restoring him to normal functioning in society. The methods of the law are directed toward ascertaining facts and allocating blame for criminal acts. Mental health uses methods which also include the gathering of pertinent data; but, in contrast, these data are used to intervene in the ongoing process of an individual's functioning and to alter or redirect certain aspects of his behavior.

Mental health and the law often come together in the courtroom during a trial. Courtroom procedure, especially in Anglo-Saxon countries such as the United States, is characterized by the use of the *adversary* process. In it, the two sides of a question are argued by a different representative, the prosecuting attorney and the defense

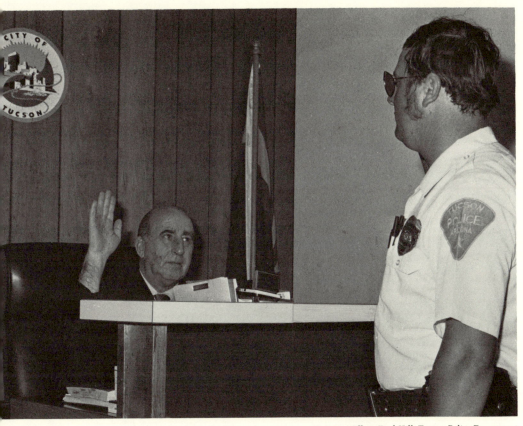

Courtesy Officer Fred Hill, Tucson Police Department

attorney. Mental health professionals are often called upon to testify on behalf of both the prosecution and defense, a practice which has led some people to believe that a mental health professional can be found to testify on any side of a question, and others to feel that it is a practice which recognizes honest professional differences. These differences in philosophies and roles have led to what Karl Menninger, a noted American psychiatrist, has termed "the cold war between lawyers and psychiatrists" (Menninger 1968).

However, this "cold war" has not resulted from malicious intent on the part of either profession, but rather from putting lawyers and mental health professionals together under the intense pressure of arriving at decisions on culpability and responsibility without adequate groundwork for this kind of cooperation. In subsequent sections of this chapter, some of the major points at which representatives of the law and mental health must work together in dealing with abnormal behavior will be discussed.

Criminal Responsibility

The court is interested in determining who is responsible for a criminal act. This legal question is decided on the basis of testimony from witnesses and on relevant points of law. One of these critical points relates to the responsibility of the accused person for his act. The court assumes, unless shown otherwise, that the accused is a responsible person in the legal sense. However, if the question of responsibility is raised, it is considered a question to which the science of human behavior may reply.

One of the earliest attempts to deal with this problem was the McNaughten Rule. In 1843, Robert McNaughten shot and killed Edward Drummond, secretary to the English Prime Minister, Sir Robert Peel. He was found to be "insane" by nine physicians and the jury found him not guilty by reason of insanity. The McNaughten Rule states that, to establish a defense on the grounds of insanity, it must be proven that at the time of committing the act the accused party was laboring under such a defect of reason from a disease of the mind as not to know the nature and quality of the act or, if he did know it, that he did not know that what he was doing was wrong. Although still in use in half of the states in this country, as well as in Great Britain, it rests on assumptions about human behavior which most mental health professionals believe are too narrow. Their objections center around their belief in the important role played by subconscious psychological processes in determining behavior. They find it difficult to coordinate their view of "degrees of mental health and illness" with the kind of "black-or-white," "insane-or-not" evaluation required by the McNaughten Rule.

This dissatisfaction with the McNaughten Rule has led to other more recent rulings on the relationship of abnormal behavior and mental illness to criminal responsibility. The Durham decision of 1954 stated that a person *suffering* from a mental disease or defect is not to be held criminally responsible for his act. Rather than equating sanity with knowledge of right and wrong and the ability to act accordingly, as the McNaughten Rule does, the Durham decision allows for relating specific acts to different kinds and degrees of mental illness.

Other alternatives to the McNaughten Rule have been proposed in the Currens decision and a rule formulated by the American Law Institute. The essence of these formulations is that a person cannot be held criminally responsible for an act if, at the time it was committed, he lacked a *substantial capacity* to resist what he was doing because of a mental disease or defect. This concept of *diminished responsibility* is presently in use in several states.

The major problem at present regarding the determination of criminal responsibility is not a lack of alternative approaches to the issue but the absence of a standardized practice in this country so that all courts can operate equitably in this area. The McNaughten Rule is still the most widely used, with the more recent rules usually limited in application to those jurisdictions in which the decisions were originally made. However, the present confusion is increased because these more recent decisions allow for the input of current psychological theory while the McNaughten Rule sets a legal precedent without the benefit of this knowledge.

The courts will continue to resolve questions of criminal responsibility. Mental health professionals can contribute to this process from their specialized knowledge about human behavior. However, because their knowledge is specialized, their role in the courtroom should be limited. They cannot be expected to decide *legal* questions of responsibility. They can, however, offer professional opinions as to the mental condition of persons before the court and testify as to the probable relation between their mental conditions and those specific acts which they allegedly committed.

Competency to Stand Trial

The mental health professional may also be called to assist the court in deciding whether or not an accused person is competent to stand trial. This is a legal criterion designed to safeguard the right of an individual to a fair trial. To insure a fair trial, it is believed that the accused must be able to understand the nature of the charges against him and to assist his counsel in the preparation of a defense. It is believed that the ability to carry these out is based upon the presence of a certain mental clarity.

An examination by a mental health professional may be ordered by the court to determine the competency of the individual about to be tried. This mental health professional is capable of offering an expert opinion as to an individual's state of mental health and the expectations for his behavior based on that state. He can say whether an offender is depressed, deluded, hallucinating, or normal. While these opinions should be used by the court to make the ultimate determination of competency, since competency to stand trial is a legal decision, the situation in many courts today is that it is actually the mental health professional who makes this determination without use of the adversary process.

What frequently occurs is that a mental health professional *pronounces* a person incompetent to stand trial and then the accused is immediately admitted to a mental health facility to be detained until he is restored to competency. In some jurisdictions, this procedure may deprive the accused of his right to be brought to trial quickly. Furthermore, detention may be prolonged since a return to competency offers the individual only the prospect of a criminal proceeding. All of this suggests strongly that changes may be needed in competency rules and proceedings to further clarify and delineate the role of the mental health professional and the adversary process while protecting the rights of the accused.

Confidentiality

Conflict abounds between mental health and the law over the issues of confidentiality and privileged communication. In the case of mental health professionals, this means holding in confidence whatever the client has communicated because the essence of the treatment process is the open exchange of information between therapist and client. If treatment is to be beneficial to the client, he must develop and maintain a strong sense of trust in the therapist. This trust is dependent on the complete privacy of the interview.

While mental health professionals consider the confidentiality of the therapist-client relationship of major importance, law enforcement officers and lawyers are more concerned with the discovery of all evidence relevant to a particular case. They often feel that the confidentiality of the therapist-client relationship is an obstacle to the satisfactory performance of their duties.

The states of Georgia and Connecticut have existing legislation granting privileged status to the psychiatrist-patient relationship and six other states protect by law the communication between psychologists and their clients. In all situations where this issue arises, the client has the right to waive confidentiality and, in many cases, his counsel and psychiatrist may urge him to do so for his own benefit. Other instances may occur wherein his right is waived for him, such as when he introduced testimony concerning his mental state in his own defense or when an institution offers information about a patient committed to its care.

Mental health and the law often find it difficult to work together on this issue since standardized or unequivocal rulings and procedures do not exist.

Credibility of Witnesses

Establishing the veracity of the testimony of a witness or trying to help a suspect or witness to recall certain crucial events relating to an investigation may involve a mental health professional. Many police officers have erroneous ideas about the appropriate use of what has been called "truth serum."

Actually, there is no drug available today which, when administered, will make anyone tell the truth about anything he consciously wishes to conceal.

"Truth serum" is actually a sedative which is administered to the subject to lower his defenses, thereby allowing repressed and denied material to emerge into consciousness. This medication was widely used during World War II to treat *battlefield neuroses.* In this condition, the soldier who had repressed frightening battlefield experiences was given an appropriate sedative. Using this, the doctor was able to take the soldier back to the traumatic events and allow him to recall the true story of what happened to him. By reliving it, he was able to work out his feelings.

This technique has since been used in civilian psychiatry. Occasionally, it has been useful to investigative officers when they have a cooperative subject who may have repressed and denied certain facts and events for psychological reasons. For example, a witness of an armed robbery may have seen the license number of the getaway car but repressed details of the event because the experience was so frightening. Under sedation, he may recall the license number clearly.

What an individual discloses under the influence of the serum depends to a large extent upon his mental state at the time of the interview, his unconscious drives, and his residual ability to resist probing of this kind. Considering these limitations, the "truth serum" method is far from infallible and results from it must be weighed carefully.

Expert Testimony

The court must rely at times on the testimony of experts to clarify or establish technical points relating to a particular case. Mental health professionals may be called as experts in human behavior for this purpose, just as testimony may be requested from ballistics or fingerprint experts.

The major problem facing a mental health professional in this situation is that he must offer his opinions in an adversary setting on behalf of the prosecution or the defense. The kind of testimony he is trained and prepared to offer is often not suited for the adversary conditions in which he finds himself. There is no dispassionate search for truth, but instead the conflict of two sides arguing for an advantage. If both sides present their own expert witnesses, differences of professional opinion may develop and be exploited. The mental health professional may find himself subject to the criticism that he knows little about human behavior or that what little he does know is useless since there is no agreement. The mental health professional may also experience difficulty in communicating effectively in these situations. He may use technical language that makes his testimony not understandable to others in the courtroom. Terms like *psychosis* and *paranoid schizophrenia* may be clear to him but confusing to others, and he may have difficulty in translating these terms to a lay audience.

Similarly, some words and phrases may be used by both mental health and legal professionals, but be understood differently. *Commitment,* for example, may mean to the law enforcement officer the removal of a potentially dangerous individual from society, while, to the mental health professional, it may mean the beginning of a helpful process designed to return an individual to a socially useful role. *Insanity* may denote to a lawyer the inability to distinguish right from wrong, but, to the mental health professional, it may have a variety of meanings including the presence of a mental illness which decreases the individual's ability to function. These discrepancies are natural and unavoidable, but they can be worked around if mental health professionals, law enforcement officers, and others attempt to make clear their understanding of these phrases when they are used.

Commitment and Hospitalization

Often a police officer will pick up an individual whom he feels is obviously suffering from some kind of mental illness—a person who is acting "crazy." With the best of intentions, the officer will bring this person to a local hospital expecting mental health personnel to take him off his hands. Many times the hospital will refuse admission, leaving the officer with the feeling that he has been betrayed by those who have publicly stated that mental cases do not belong in jail.

Or, perhaps, the person is admitted only to be released within the next few hours or days to repeat the behavior. What the police officer must realize is that people cannot be admitted to hospitals involuntarily except under strict legal conditions—just as he cannot stop, search, or arrest an individual unless certain legal criteria are met.

Usually the legal conditions which mental health professionals must meet require that the person be suffering from a mental illness and, *as a result of that illness,* be dangerous to himself or others. There are also criteria for dangerousness that usually involve the likelihood of imminent bodily harm to himself or others.

Thus, the mental health professional, like the police officer, is often frustrated in that he cannot hold and treat someone he believes to be in need of help unless the person is imminently dangerous to himself or others. Because of these problems, there is a need for law enforcement officers to be aware of local commitment procedures and regulations so that their actions in handling "crazy" people in the community, who will not voluntarily seek help and who have not committed a crime, will be consistent with the law.

Summary

In this chapter, several outstanding issues that affect both the law enforcement and mental health professions have been discussed. These legal aspects of abnormal behavior have been presented to facilitate communication between the professions. It is unfortunate that more has not been done to resolve these issues. Only enlightened and sincere contributions from all professionals involved with human behavior will resolve these vital questions.

REFERENCES AND ADDITIONAL BIBLIOGRAPHY

Commonwealth v. *McCusker:* 1973. "The Use of Psychiatric Testimony in Pennsylvania Homicide Trials." *Temple Law Quarterly.* 47:156–171.
Halleck, S. 1968. *Psychiatry and the Dilemmas of Crime.* New York: Harper & Row.
Menninger, K. 1968. *The Crime of Punishment.* New York: Viking Press.
Steadman, H. J. and Cocozza, J. J. 1973. "The Criminally Insane Patient: Who Gets Out?" *Social Psychiatry* 8:230.

PART V

Conclusion

Chapter 20

The Police Officer
as a Person

IN Chapter 1, the changing role of the police officer during the past one hundred years was discussed. Emphasis was given to the increasing recognition of the officer's role as a student of normal and abnormal behavior. The next eighteen chapters focused on the characteristics and causes of a variety of normal and abnormal behaviors with which the police officer is liable to come in contact. Emphasis has been given to those strategies which will assist him in handling, assessing, and managing abnormal behavior more effectively.

In this final chapter, we will give closer attention to the police officer himself. Contrary to what many choose to believe, the police officer, like those with whom he must deal, is a human being. Similarly, the majority of policemen, like the majority of citizens, are conscientious, hard-working individuals who try to do their best in their personal lives, their jobs, and their community. Being human, they may sometimes behave brilliantly and, on other occasions, stupidly. With the training they receive, it is hoped that officers can increase the former and reduce the latter.

Like all people, the officer has emotions, including fear and anger.

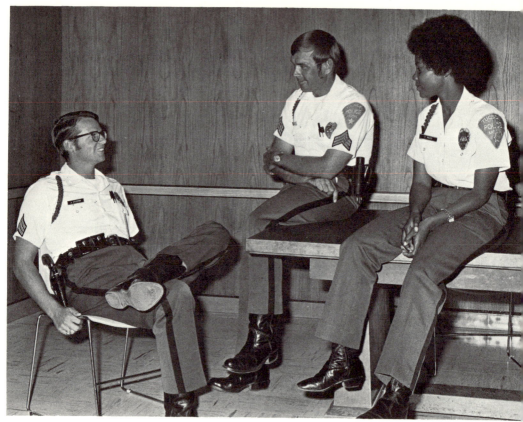

Courtesy Officer Fred Hill, Tucson Police Department

Furthermore, he also has his share of problems. As Douglas Grant has commented in his book *Agents of Change: A Study in Police Reform:*

The officer must perform with a style of temperament, emotional expression, and communication which extends into his private life and reflects him as a human being. He must act as a product of police training and influence, filtered through preexisting conceptions and expectations. He works within an organization that faces him with pressure and demands, whose perception is reflected (positively or negatively) in his encounters. He relates to his partner, assesses his opponent, and may be angry or upset because he missed his lunch, resents his wife, suspects his mistress, and worries about his preschool child. And he faces a suspect who represents a civilian counterpart of equivalent determinants in a game which has a life of its own (Grant 1974).

With this description in mind, let us examine specifically some of the salient characteristics of those who enter police work; the influence of police work on the individual who chooses this career; the environment within which the police officer works; and the stresses, professional and personal, associated with that environment.

Who Enters Police Work?

James W. Sterling has studied recruits in four different cities (Baltimore, Cincinnati, Columbus, and Indianapolis). His data revealed that police officers are likely to be "locals" rather than coming from outside the city or state in which they work. Furthermore, those who choose police work have a high residential stability. Sterling concludes: "Just as the farmer is tied physically and psychologically to his land, the police recruit is tied psychologically to his city. These men have observed their city grow and change in terms of its population and its physical characteristics. They can view things in retrospect and feel nostalgia" (Sterling 1972, p. 31).

In this study, the mean age of recruits in each of the four cities ranged from 23.8 to 25.3 years. The majority were white and, at the time of the study's completion in 1971, all departments were having difficulty in recruiting nonwhites. The majority were married (63 percent), with 6 percent of the remainder being either divorced or separated. Over 60 percent of new recruits had been in the military and this seemed to have been an important influence on their decision to become a police officer.

Contrary to a common belief that policemen tend to come from lower-class backgrounds and that certain undesirable police behavior is a result of this origin, Sterling found that most recruits in these four cities had come from predominantly middle-class families with fathers who were described as "upward-striving" (Sterling 1972, p. 40). All were high school graduates and one-third had attended college. For the majority, their new job as a police officer represented a rise in income. This was also a significant factor in determining their career choice.

Surprisingly, the most frequently held previous jobs of these new recruits were *not* people oriented. Rather, their old jobs had dealt primarily with data and objects. Most had had little occupational experience in dealing with people, nor had they expressed much interest in that type of work. The single most significant factor in determining their career choice was that they had friends or relatives who were policemen.

How Does Police Work Change the Police Officer?

Police work, like other occupations such as medicine and the law, seems to affect the individual totally—his attitudes, his beliefs, and his choice of friends. However, those specific experiences which have an impact on the officer as a person are less clear.

Recalling Sterling's observation that recruits tend to come from jobs which are more oriented to data and objects rather than to people and that they originally had little interest in people-related jobs, his findings concerning personality changes in the officers during the first eighteen months of their on-the-job experience are noteworthy. He found a shift toward a "more active, assertive, and self-directing orientation" with a concomitant further decrease in the need to help others and to treat them with sympathy (Sterling 1972, p. 280). These data suggest a general attitude at the end of eighteen months which could engender an even greater potential for role conflict in the officer than was already present when he started training.

As Sterling points out:

If one considers the proportion of total time a patrolman spends on service activities and the nature of changes in personality needs which occurs as a consequence of taking on the patrolman's role, one is led to an impression of incompatability. Police experience appears to modify a man's personality so as to make him less able to perform the major part of his job, service to people, without abrasiveness and conflict (Sterling 1972, p. 281).

One way in which police officers handle the conflict inherent in this incompatability is to continue to focus primarily on the criminal part of their work, even though the majority of their time is spent in service-giving functions. However, since the majority of an officer's time is devoted to service functions, the reality is that he spends most of his time, from his point of view, rehearsing for the real thing. Therefore, as Sterling comments:

The client of the police may also have to put up with a degree of aggressiveness and bluntness knowing that these characteristics are necessary for the effective performance of the police role in controlling crime. Perhaps that is the price that must be paid to keep a man at the ready in a violent society (Sterling 1972, p. 281).

The Police Officer's Environment

The older, experienced police officer has a tremendous influence on the young officer, sometimes to the detriment of the latter. It is not uncommon for a recruit who has just graduated to be told by an older and more streetwise officer, "Look kid, the first thing you do is forget all that s--t they taught you at the academy." Since a rookie is eager to be accepted by the "in group," it is often easy to adopt the attitudes, policies, and procedures of the experienced officer without realizing that his experience may guarantee nothing, except perhaps more and more experience in doing the wrong thing.

This common attitude of older officers gives an important clue to the *organizational climate* within which the new recruit functions. The expectations of these established group members are felt by every new officer who enters police work. Regardless of department directives and policies or what he is taught at the academy, his eventual performance as an officer cannot differ too markedly from that of other officers without running the risk of peer disfavor and isolation. In his study, Grant found that the prevailing values and beliefs of established department members are so influential that even men who, by their personalities and training, are oriented to a different set of values and beliefs upon entering police work very quickly begin to adopt other, originally unacceptable, values and beliefs (Grant 1974).

A senior officer of the Tucson Police Department recalled an incident that happened when he was a young and inexperienced patrolman. While driving one night so that his partner—an old-timer—could get some sleep, he received a call about a fight in a bar. He promptly swung his squad car around and headed for the scene with what he considered appropriate speed. The older officer woke up and told him to slow down to about 20 miles per hour saying that, if they went slowly, the contestants would be all worn out and the place quieted down by the time they got there. As he explained it, they could then walk in, decide who was wrong, and haul them away without difficulty. As he told about the event, he remembered the conflict he felt between accepting the established procedure which the older officer had followed for years and his own concern that, by slowing down, he was ignoring the possibility that a citizen "could have his head bashed in" while he took time getting there.

Another important aspect of the environment within which the police officer works is the court system. Cynicism develops easily when the police officer sees the man whom he has arrested the night before on the streets the following day or when he goes into court and is made to feel that he is the one on trial, rather than the person he has arrested. This cynicism is picked up quickly by the young officer and, when measured against his idealism after he graduated from the academy, increases his conflict.

This is why many students of police training methods believe that changes in attitudes will be effective only if they are built into the organizational structure by the department's leaders. These changes cannot be imposed from outside the department by people who are not policemen, no matter how professional or well-intentioned they are. The police officer himself must be the agent for change and he can function effectively in this role only if he understands the problem and participates in its solution.

The Stresses of Police Work

In addition to stresses which the officer as an individual feels, there are other stresses inherent in the job itself.

Publicity

The police officer is always in the public eye, especially when he is in uniform. While most officers eventually accept this spotlight or at least learn to tolerate it, always being visible may create feelings of depression, anxiety, and occasionally anger. As one officer complained, "I hate being under observation all the time. Whenever I'm in that damn car, people are looking at me. When I go in to eat or to get a cup of coffee, everyone's got to turn around to see the damn cop."

Danger

We have already discussed (Chapter 15) how the officer perceives danger and how this part of his job may have a profound effect on his performance, especially when he is in contact with the public. In addition to the general dangerousness of police work, there are certain assignments, such as narcotics, in which the element of danger is particularly acute.

As one officer described his exposure to danger:

It used to be that on a buy, we'd never get any action. But now there are so many damn rip-offs that you can expect a shoot-out in three out of every four cases. That makes the men uptight; they are a lot more nervous than they used to be and that can mean trouble. Some guy, maybe even another cop, is going to get dusted because everybody's on edge.

Operating under this continuous tension, it is, therefore, not surprising that police officers, like soldiers, may occasionally suffer from combat exhaustion (Chapter 17). This will influence their effectiveness and decrease their capacity to make accurate judgments. Supervisors should always be alert for symptoms of combat exhaustion so that an officer may be relieved of his duties through transfer or leave. If this is not done, it may lead to violent behavior on the part of the police officer himself.

Tunnel Vision

As stated earlier, police officers, because of the environment within which they must work, are likely to grow more cynical and callous as their years of service increase. Rather than being able to accurately evaluate people, they develop stereotypes. The citizen is no longer perceived as an individual, but falls into the general category called *assholes.*

This emphasis on stereotypes is another form of combat exhaustion. In this situation, partial prevention lies in a system of rotation which will ensure that the officer is exposed to a variety of duties and citizens. Under a systematized rotation policy, stereotyping is less likely to occur.

Difficulties with the Bureaucracy

Bureaucracy is defined in *Webster's Seventh New Collegiate Dictionary* as the "administration of government through departments or subdivisions managed by sets of rules and regulations and inflexible routine." Police departments have a bureaucratic structure and working within this structure may occasionally present problems to the officer. For example, he may experience difficulty adjusting to a particular supervisor because, like the military man, he may be limited in his ability to react to what he sees as discrimination, inefficiency, or stupidity on the part of his supervisors. The police officer must learn to take orders and to treat his superiors with a certain deference. He must be able to "ride out" undesirable assignments if he is to advance.

Occasionally, difficulty with a supervisor may create sufficient stress to interfere with the officer's job proficiency, leading to psychological or physical symptoms. In these situations, the police officer should not hesitate to seek help from either the staff psychologist, if the department has one, or a professional at a community agency or in private practice. Having the need to seek help because of psychological and/or physical symptoms does not mean that the officer is "crazy." Rather, help at the time of emotional crisis may not only prevent more serious difficulty but also lead to a better understanding of himself and his behavior. By taking this action, the officer will promote rather than harm his career. If he does not seek help, it is possible that his symptoms will increase until his efficiency is reduced to the point where he loses his health and/or his job.

Another unfortunate characteristic of a bureaucratic organization is the split that frequently develops between the "brass" (administrators) and the "troops" in the field. Unless there is effective communication both down and up the ladder, directives from headquarters will be seen as "red tape" obstacles, or the "troops" may feel

284

that the "brass" doesn't understand the circumstances under which they have to work. Comments such as, "Yeah, I know the Chief came up through the ranks, but things have changed a lot since he was on the streets," reflect this feeling of isolation. The officer must realize that, in most cases, there are reasons for a rule or regulation and that the "view from the top" is often different not only in terms of the action required but also the responsibility assumed.

While most officers will intellectually acknowledge the necessity of investigation by Internal Affairs of citizens' complaints, emotionally they may feel anger and resentment. The officer may feel that the "hoods" he arrests have more rights than he does when he is under investigation. This feeling is realistic. For example, his right to remain silent may be negated by a department directive forcing him to answer questions. He may even be required to take a polygraph examination to establish his veracity. Even though the results may not be admitted in court, they are admitted as evidence in various board proceedings and may be instrumental in the officer's suspension or dismissal. Officers forced to undergo such investigative procedures must learn to deal with their natural feelings of anger, resentment, and frustration by realizing that these procedures are necessary to insure an honest department. Officers must also look closely at their own behavior to ascertain if there are any remedial measures which they can undertake to insure that they will not be again the subject of complaints and/or investigations.

The Dishonest Cop

The police officer shares with the military man another unfortunate burden; namely, if a man in uniform misbehaves, he becomes a discredit to all other men who wear the same uniform. Newspapers tend to ignore the daily, efficient, and often heroic performances of most police officers while giving headlines to cases involving dishonesty or brutality. Therefore, dishonesty, either alleged or actual, has a demoralizing effect on all policemen, especially if the alleged offender has a position of high rank or status. For example, several years ago, when the Pima County Sheriff's Department was under investigation for the alleged actions of its sheriff and several high-ranking deputies, deputies in the field were often subject to verbal taunts and abuse which increased the stress on them and, at times, affected their individual performance.

Scapegoating

Unfortunately, the average citizen often tends to project many of the negative feelings about authority, society, racism, and other problems onto the police officer whose uniform and badge becomes a symbol for all he may hate or fear. For example, while police do not create the conditions under which residents of the ghetto are forced to live, they are often seen as the oppressing force which keeps ghetto residents from improving their lot. If, during a civil disturbance, many police officers are sent in, they are often seen as having caused the riot by overreacting. On the other hand, if they are not sent in, they are likewise seen as having caused the riot, this time by underreacting.

Unfortunately, no guidelines exist to help police administrators determine just how many officers are needed under such conditions. Yet the absence of these guidelines does not prevent the accusations that officers may receive as a result.

Policewomen

Throughout this entire book, we have been addressing the *policeman*. Two reasons exist for this admitted bias. The overwhelming majority of police officers are men and it is awkward to use the term *police person*. All that we have written in this book pertains to officers of both sexes.

However, in discussing the "police officer as a person," it is appropriate to address those special stresses that are experienced by female officers. Women are not "new" to police work. At the turn of the century, New York City hired its first policewomen and Washington, D.C. followed in 1917. However, until recently, women were hired for limited duties such as those of guarding and handling women prisoners and juveniles, investigating destitution, insuring the protection of young girls, and returning runaways. "Responsible" police officials did not believe that women could perform all the duties demanded of law enforcement officers, including patrol.

As late as 1972 a study conducted for the Police Foundation by Catherine Milton found that the quota for policewomen in the average police department was less than 2 percent (Milton 1972). Although most policewomen were college graduates, had been trained as police officers, and were given the same pay, many served only as secretaries or in specialized areas such as those mentioned above. Promotion opportunities and career growth were limited.

Milton also found that many policemen held views of women which were insulting, debilitating, and degrading. Furthermore, many policemen believed that women were not equipped, emotionally or physically, to do police work.

Even in those departments where women have had some patrol experience, male prejudice is hard to overcome. Only one in fifteen men would rather have a female than a male partner. Policemen also had a general tendency to protect policewomen, thereby limiting their opportunities to act on their own.

Contrast these findings with another study at the Urban Institute in Washington, D.C. It showed that "new women officers" handled all aspects of patrol, including the handling of angry, drunk, and violent citizens, as effectively as a comparison group of "new male officers" (Bloch and Anderson 1974).

It is apparent that, with the ending of sex discrimination, more and more women will have the opportunity to enter all phases of police work. Although new laws and court decisions require equal treatment, there is little doubt that female officers will still encounter prejudice and differential treatment under certain circumstances from some male officers and police officials. They will also encounter hostility from female old-timers who have been in the department for years and resent the intrusion of these younger "female tigers" who are ready to do all sorts of new things. Consequently, the female officer may find herself subjected to job stresses that are difficult to deal with because they emanate from the inner prejudices of her fellow officers. The policewoman must depersonalize these situations, realizing that it is her sex and not her personality that is being discriminated against. She must realize that, as the advertisement says, "You've come a long way, baby, but you still got a long way to go!"

Stresses on the Individual Officer

Other stresses of police work are related more to the police officer as a person.

Fear

Because of the dangers inherent in police work, every officer experiences fear. As we have emphasized several times, it is important for the officer to recognize that it is not his fear that is important, since it is normal, but how he handles it. The subject of fear should, therefore, be discussed during recruit training and opportunities afforded for trainees to come to grips with those situations that are more likely to engender this feeling. *Role playing* will enable an officer to begin to gain a better understanding of his own *fear reaction*. This will, hopefully, assist him in handling his fear better when it occurs in the field.

A female officer may often have more difficulty with fear than her male counterpart because of her felt need to prove herself over and above the call of duty. This pressure starts from her first day in the academy when she may feel it necessary to excel in all aspects of her study, especially in self-defense, aggressive tactics, pistol, and baton. As one policewoman said: "You want to excel in these kinds of things because you don't want the guys to get the idea you can't handle your end or back 'em up in case of trouble." Several female officers have confessed that they dread the day when a female officer on patrol pulls a "boner" (i.e., losing a prisoner or failing to secure a crime scene, which are mistakes which might happen to any police officer), feeling that this incident may cause their male companions to say, "See, I told you so . . . they really can't be trusted."

Other females have said that "sometimes the guys are too protective . . . they don't give me a chance to handle it." This male protectiveness will probably disappear as more women begin patrol work. This probability is viewed with ambivalence by some female officers. As one stated: "I sort of hate to see all these new girls coming on patrol . . . I won't be special anymore . . . the guys won't be so protective." She admitted, with a wry smile, that these traces of male chauvinism weren't all bad.

Unrealistic Role Expectations

Unfortunately, because of their own personalities, some officers may see themselves as "super-cop." Their fantasies are often reinforced by the propaganda that movies and television perpetrate, as exemplified by "Dirty Harry" or "James Bond." For example, some uniformed officers are prone to picture themselves as "super-stud."

Certain females are attracted by the uniform or turned on by the idea of going out with a cop. "Super-stud," however, mistakenly attributes his popularity with these women to his own charm, grace, and machismo.

Other officers who are prone to these fantasies may see themselves as the only person standing between an unsuspecting community and a vicious, predatory, criminal horde. Vice cops have a tendency to conclude that all women are tramps. They are constantly involved with females that society regards as "real trash" and, eventually, they begin to think of all women in these terms.

As a natural consequence of their fantasies, these officers begin to see themselves as the saviors of the community's honest citizens and may take upon themselves the role not only of apprehender of criminals but also of judge and jury. When an officer's feelings progress to this point, his behavior generally becomes unprofessional and is not consistent with the team concept of operation of today's progressive police agency.

It is interesting to note that the Urban Institute's study indicates that the "new women officers" are less likely to be charged with "serious unbecoming conduct" than male officers, suggesting that the "super-cop" syndrome may be peculiar to males only.

Shift Work

There is no question that shift work, a common requirement for a police officer, poses a hardship for him and his family at certain times. Yet, even if he is prepared for and accepting of this responsibility, it may become a sore point within his family, especially if his wife believes that her husband has requested a particular shift to avoid responsibilities and unpleasantness at home. In many instances wives of policemen are working wives and if their husband is assigned to a certain shift, they may not see much of each other, causing possible stress and strain in the marriage. Furthermore, long and irregular hours in certain types of police work may make the planning of family affairs difficult or, if they are planned, lead to their disruption, adding to the stress because of the attendant disappointment of spouse and children. A similar situation may prevail for the female officer and her family.

Relationship with Spouses

In the military, it has been found that the wife's attitude determines to a large extent the soldier's potential for a successful career. If his wife is happy, then he is more likely to stay in the service and progress through the ranks. On the other hand, if she hates the military way of life, the soldier eventually leaves the military or ends up with many family problems. Therefore, police administrators should pay considerable attention to the wives of their officers since we suspect that the same is true for the law enforcement officer.

For example, it is not uncommon for a jealous wife to get in the family car and follow her husband while he is on patrol. Most wives realize that he has many opportunities because of his job to have an affair. A troubled marriage can present additional problems not only for the officer himself, but also for his superiors. Some wives are forever calling their husbands' superiors to check on their duties and whereabouts or to voice their suspicions. In some situations, motivated by distrust and jealousy, the wife may come down to Internal Affairs and make statements she knows are or could be damaging to her husband's career.

It is assumed that the potential for jealous behavior also exists for the husband of the female officer. It is interesting to note that several female officers of the Tucson Police Department have said that their husbands preferred that they not work with a permanent partner.

Officers' wives who do not work may be inexperienced in money matters. Since it is relatively easy for an officer to obtain credit, wives, occasionally aided and abetted by their husbands, will run up charges beyond their ability to pay. It is not unusual for an officer's superior to be notified by creditors. In other situations, wives may retaliate after an argument by spending money which the family does not have. Therefore, it is important for the police administrator to realize that the department may have to provide certain direct personal services to officers who need them.

Ideally, a police department should have its own psychologist. Since this is not possible except in large departments, it is advisable for a department to seek a reputable therapist or counselor in the community who is willing to act as a chief referral source for officers and/or their spouses who are experiencing personal problems. In this way, familiarity and trust can be built up between the department and the referral source which will lead to the most effective handling of the problem officer. However, when an arrangement like this is made, it is important for the police department to recognize that its primary and only responsibility is the continuing assessment of the effectiveness of the officer. It can do this from its own observations. The treatment relationship between the officer and the counselor to whom he has been referred, like any doctor-patient relationship, requires confidentiality.

In this regard, a program developed by Dr. Martin Reiser, psychologist for the Los Angeles Police Department, to train sergeants to recognize the early warning signs of emotional disturbance and to acquaint them with brief crisis intervention techniques is of interest. This training was not done to make junior psychiatrists or psychologists out of front-line supervisors, but to increase their effectiveness in the performance of one of their major supervisory responsibilities—counseling. The sergeants also received information regarding community referral resources and procedures (Reiser 1971).

The training of police of all ranks in crisis intervention techniques is becoming more common because mental health professionals see police officers as front-line workers with the emotionally disturbed. In preparing the officer for this role, the mental health professional does not try to make the police officer into a proxy psychologist or psychiatrist. Rather, he attempts to help the officer who must deal with someone in an emotional crisis to be more effective *in using his or her own skills and techniques*. The officers are not being asked to use psychological or psychiatric techniques in which they have not been trained.

Relationships with Children

The children of police officers, like those of ministers and doctors, are often in the public eye. It is not unusual for a community to be less tolerant of deviant behavior on the part of police officers' children than it is of similar behavior in other children. This is especially true of delinquent behavior.

Furthermore, the problem will be worse if police-parents do not allow for the normal acting out and exploratory behavior common in adolescents. If they expect their children, particularly their sons, to be "super-straight" because of their own role and responsibilities, without adequately recognizing the peer pressure children exert on each other, there is likely to be trouble.

Retirement

Similar to the military, police work is a way of life and retirement may present special problems. This is especially true because of the excellent retirement and pension plans available to most officers which allow them to retire while still in their forties, after twenty or more years of service. While many officers talk about putting in their "twenty," few make plans for that magic day. The result is that the officer may suddenly pass from an active police role to an inactive, sideline role. While he may wish to continue to see his fellow officers who are still on active duty, contact with them is soon reduced because he is no longer a part of their world. At this point, it is not uncommon for depression to occur; suicidal ideation in the retiring police officer can become a serious problem. Inspector Marion Talbert of the San Antonio Police Department observes: "We have had several suicides of retirees. Some were related to poor health, real or imagined. At least one case was the result of the loss of attention which a popular officer suffered when he retired. People had spoken to him regularly when he was in uniform, but did not recognize him when he was in civvies." *

Consequently, it is important for officers to plan ahead by deciding how long they are going to stay on active duty and what they will do when they retire. If they make plans for a new career, training, if necessary, should begin while the officer is still on active duty. If retirement plans are for further education or travel, it is especially important for the officer to have long-term plans rather than just for the months immediately following retirement.

Summary

In this final chapter, we have pointed out that the police officer, like all other people, is first and last a human being. The police officer is a person with a job to do—a job which most officers carry out with sincerity and dedication. We have described the characteristics of those individuals who enter police work and have taken a look at some of the changes that may occur in their concepts of themselves and their role. The importance of the environment within which the

* Inspector Marion Talbert 1974: personal communication.

officer must work, both within the department and the community, has been stressed. The critical stresses which officers face from their job and those which affect them as individuals have been discussed.

In closing, we would like to emphasize that there are few professions in our society today which are as challenging and important as that of the police officer. The structure of our entire society rests upon the foundation of law; without effective law enforcement, society could not exist. Police work is not just a job; it is a way of life. If the police officer does not like his work, he will not find rewards sufficient to justify his continuing in it. If he likes his work, he will not leave it voluntarily. When the time does come to do so, he will leave it with regrets and much looking backward.

It is our hope that the material in this book will better prepare police officers for their work by increasing understanding of the behavior of individuals with whom they come in contact and of their own behavior. We trust that this book will help professional police officers become more adept at handling those aspects of their work that involve human behavior, thereby improving their effectiveness.

REFERENCES AND ADDITIONAL BIBLIOGRAPHY

Bell, R. L.; Cleveland, S. E.; Hanson, P. G.; and O'Connell, W. E. 1969. "Small Group Dialogue and Discussion: An Approach to Police-Community Relationships." *Journal of Criminal Law, Criminology and Police Science* 60:242–246.

Bittner, E. 1970. *The Functions of the Police in Modern Society.* Washington, D.C.: U.S. Government Printing Office.

Bloch, P. and Anderson, D. 1974. *Policewomen on Patrol: Final Report.* Washington, D.C.: Police Foundation.

Cruse, D. and Rubin, J. 1973. "Police Behavior." *Journal of Psychiatry and Law* 1:167–222.

Fenster, C. A. and Locke, B. 1973. "Neuroticism among Policemen: An Examination of Police Personality." *Journal of Applied Psychology* 57:358–359.

Grant, D. 1974. *Agents of Change: A Study in Police Reform.* Cambridge, Mass.: Schenkman.

Milton, C. 1972. *Women in Policing.* Washington, D.C.: Police Foundation.

Reiser, M. November 1971. "Psychological Research in an Urban Police Department." *Police,* pp. 15–18.

Richard, J. T. 1969. "A Study of the Relationship of Certain Background Factors and the Choice of Police Work as a Career." *Dissertation Abstracts International* 30:1028–1029.

Sterling, J. W. 1972. *Changes in Role Concepts of Police Officers.* Gaithersburg, Md.: International Association of Chiefs of Police.

Symonds, M. 1970. "Emotional Hazards of Police Work." *American Journal of Psychoanalysis* 30:155–160.

Index

Abnormal behavior, 54–78; classification of, 73–78; common misconceptions about, 56–59; defining, 55–65; guidelines for judging, 59–65; historical background to 74–75; how to handle, 66–69; legal aspects of, *see* Legal aspects of abnormal behavior, modern classification of, 75
Abnormal body reactions to disasters, 245
Accomplishment: sense of, defined, 28
Acquisitive mob: defined, 252
Acrophobia: defined, 100
Addicted drinker: defined, 181, 182
Addiction: defined, 179–80; *see also* Drug dependent behavior
Adjustment reactions: of adolescence, delinquent behavior and, 169–70; of childhood, delinquent behavior and, 169–70
Adolescence: adjustment reactions of, delinquent behavior and, 169–70; behavior disorders of, 75; delinquent behavior in, 171; *see also* Delinquent behavior
Adversary process of justice system, 266, 268
Affective disorders, 117–23; helpful hints on, 123–25; historical background on, 118; involutional psychotic depression in, 122–23; manic-depressive reaction in, 119–20; psychotic depressive reaction in, 120–22; underlying factors of, 118–19
Agents of Change: A Study in Police Reform (Grant), 279
Agitators: techniques of, 257–60
Agoraphobia: defined, 100

Aggressive behavior: frustration, conflict and, 38–40; violent behavior compared with, 202, 204; *see also* Passive-aggressive personality disorder
Aggressive mob: defined, 252
Alcohol abuse: classification of, 181; described, 181–83; drinking patterns and suicide, 229; helpful hints on, 183–85; sexual deviancy and, 165; violence and, 205, 215
Alcoholic hallucinosis, 184
Alerting mechanism: defined, 93
Alertness: in riot control, 260–61
Alienating behavior: as abnormal, 56
American Law Institute, 269
American Medical Association, 75
American Medical Psychological Association, 75
American Psychiatric Association, 75, 169
Amphetamines: abuse of, 187–88; classification of, 181; paranoid psychosis from, 188, 190–91
Anatomy of Melancholy (Burton), 221
Anonymity of rioter, 255
Antisocial personality, *see* Psychopathic behavior
Anxiety: absence of neurotic, in psychopath, 139–40; normal and pathological, distinguished, 41; as reaction to frustration and conflict, 41–43
Anxiety neuroses: described, 92–94
Appropriateness of behavior, 60
Arizona, University of, 253
Arizona Daily (newspaper), 259
Assaultive rape: defined, 151
Assaults on police officers, 211–16

Associations: loosening of, defined, 111
Attempter: characteristics of suicide, 223–25; *see also* Suicidal behavior
Auditory hallucinations, 64
Autonomy: sense of, defined, 28

Barbiturates: classification of, 181; dependence on, 188; helpful hints on, 191
Battered child syndrome, 39
Battlefield neurosis, 19, 242–43, 272
Behavioral clues to suicide, 226–27
Benedict, Ruth, 55
Bernheim, 103
Bestiality, 162
Big changes in behavior: abnormal, 62
Black Dahlia murder, 43
Blame: psychopath's inability to accept, 141
Bleuler, Eugene, 113
Blocking of thought, defined, 111
Boston Strangler (case example), 158–59
Bragen, Karen (case example), 121–22
Brain disturbances: violent behavior and, 206
Brewster (case example), 47–48
Bridgewater State Hospital (Mass.), 208
Brown, Floyd (case example), 114–16, 119
Bucko, Sergeant (case example), 47
Bullying: as violent behavior, 214
Bureaucracy: police officer difficulties with, 284–85
Burton, Robert, 221

Cannon, Walter, 31
Casual crowd: defined, 252
Catatonic schizophrenia: described, 117
Catharting: as violent behavior, 214
Chafetz, M. E., 181, 182
Change of life, 122–23
Chapman (case example), 133
Charcot, 103
Child molester, 161–62
Childhood: adjustment reactions of, delinquent behavior and, 169–70; behavior disorders of, 75; delinquency in, 170–71; *see also* Delinquent behavior
Children: police officers' relationship with own, 291
Christianity: suicidal behavior and, 222
Circumstantiality, 111
Cleckley, H. M., 140–42
Click (patrolman; case example), 48–49
Claustrophobia: defined, 100

Cocaine: abuse of, 187; classification of, 181
Code of conduct: for riot control, 264; violent behavior and, 217
Codeine, 185
Collective violence (social violent behavior), 205–7; *see also* Disasters; Riots
Combat exhaustion (battlefield neurosis), 19, 242–43, 272
Commitment and hospitalization, 273–74
Communications: situational, in suicidal behavior, 227; syndromatic, in suicidal behavior, 228–29
Community support: for riot control, 261–62
Compensation: as defense mechanism, 46–47
Compensatory aggression: defined, 38
Competency to stand trial, 270
Compulsive personality disorder, 86–87; obsessive-compulsive distinguished from, 97
Concentration camps: effects of, 246
Conditions without manifest psychiatric disorder and nonspecific conditions, classification of, 75
Confidentiality of therapist-client relationship, 271
Conflict, *see* Defense mechanisms; Frustration and conflict
Confrontation in riot process, 254
Consciousness: defined, 32, 33
Constitutional factors in normal development, 26–27
Constitutional psychopathic inferiority: defined, 131
Contagion: riot, 256
Conversion neuroses (hysterical neuroses; conversion hysteria): described, 103–5
Crawford, Michael (case example), 131–32, 139–40, 142
Creativity: periods of marked, in psychopaths, 143
Credibility: establishing, of witnesses, 271–72
Crimes: victimless, 151–52
Criminal behavior: delinquent, 167–68 (*see also* Delinquent behavior); deviant sexual behavior and, 151–52; psychopathic behavior differentiated from, 146
Criminal responsibility: defined, 268–70
Crisis intervention: defined, 223
Crowds and mobs: characteristics of, 252
Culture in determining what is and is not normal, 55–56
Currens decisions, 269
Cynicism, police work and, 282

Dalton, Billy (case example), 132–34, 139, 141

Danger: as stress in police work, 283

Dangerous (destructive) behavior: as abnormal, 65

Davis, Hilda (case example), 84–85

Defense mechanisms, 36–53; compensation as, 46–47; denial as, 48–49; displacement as, 45; fantasy as, 51; fight and flight as, 44; frustration and conflict in, *see* Frustration and conflict; identification as, 50; internal, 44–52; projection as, 47; rationalization as, 45–46; reaction formation as, 47–48; regression as, 51; repression as, 49; sublimation as, 51–52; substitution as, 50–51

Delayed response reaction to disasters, 244

Delinquent behavior, 167–75; adolescent, 171; in childhood, 170–71; helpful hints on, 172–74; negative approaches to, 172–74; overview of, 167, 169; positive approaches to, 174; underlying factors in, 169–71

Delirium tremens, 184

Delusions: defined, 59; handling, 68; psychotic, 111

Dementia praecox, *see* Schizophrenia

Demerol, 185

Denial: as defense mechanism, 48–49

Depression: abnormal, 65; different types of, 95; involutional psychotic, in affective psychosis, 122–23; manic-depressive reaction in affective psychosis, 119–20; psychotic depressive reaction in affective disorders, 120–22; as reaction to disaster, 245; at retirement, 292

Depressive neuroses: described, 94–97

DeSalvo, Albert (case example), 206

Deviant sexual behavior, 148–66; bestiality and necrophilia as, 162; criminality and, 151–52; deviancy, defined, 151; exhibitionism as, 159–60, 164–65; fetishism as, 154–56, 163–64; general definitions and concepts on, 150–52; helpful hints on, 162–65; homosexuality as, 152–54, 163; incest as, 160–61; normal sexuality, defined, 150; pedophilia as, 161–62; sadism and masochism as, 157–59 (*see also* Sadism); transvestitism as, 156, 164; voyeurism as, 160

Deviancy: sexual, defined, 151

Diagnosis and Prognosis of Dementia Praecox (Kraepelin), 113

Diagnostic and Statistical Manual of Mental Disorder–I (DSM–I), 75

Diagnostic and Statistical Manual of Mental Disorders–II (DSM–II), 75, 92, 169

Dickens, Robert, 156

Dine, Martin (case example), 95–97

Direct aggression: defined, 38; as restricted by society, 39

Disasters, 240–49; delayed response to, 244; four phases of reactions to, 243–44; helpful hints on dealing with reactions to, 246–48; historical background to behavior during, 242–43; immediate reaction after impact of, 244; impact period reaction to, 244; normal and abnormal reactions to, 245–46; warning period reaction to, 243–44

Discrimination (prejudice): adverse effects of, 27

Dishonest police officers, 285

Dispersed mob: defined, 252

Displacement: as defense mechanism, 45

Dissociative neuroses: described, 105–6

Dodge, Joe (case example), 197–99

Dollard, J., 202, 204

Drinking patterns: suicide and, 229

Drug dependence: defined, 180–81

Drug dependent behavior, 176–92; alcohol, 181–83 (*see also* Alcohol abuse); amphetamines, 187–88 (*see also* Amphetamines); barbiturates, 181 (*see also* Barbiturates); cocaine, 181, 187; definitions in, 179–81; general considerations on, 176, 178–79; hallucinogens, 186–87, 190; helpful hints on forms of drug abuse other than alcohol, 189–91; marijuana, 181, 187; mild tranquilizers, 181, 188; narcotics (opiates), 185–86, 190

Drug use: defined, 176, 178–79

Drugs: sexual deviancy and, 165; *see also* Drug dependent behavior

Drummond, Edward, 268

DSM–I (Diagnostic and Statistical Manual of Mental Disorders), 75

DSM–II (Diagnostic and Statistical Manual of Mental Disorders), 75, 92, 169

Durham decision, 269

Durkheim, Émile, 221

Eden, Judy (case example), 116–17, 119

Education of police, xi, xii

Ego: defined, 30–31; reactions of, to anxiety and guilt, 44–52

Ego ideal: defined, 32

Eibl-Eibesfeldt, I., 204

Eisenhower, Dwight D., 258

Emotion-producing rumor in riots, 257

Emotions: psychotic disturbances in, 112; *see also* Affective disorders

Environmental factors in development, 27–29
Epicureans, 221–22
Erikson, Erik: and anxiety, 41; and personality development, 27–29
Escape mob: defined, 252
Evil: mental illness as, 56–57
Exhibitionism: described, 159–60, 164–65
Experience: psychopath's failure to learn by, 141
Expert testimony, 272–73
Exploitation: violent behavior and, 214

Failure: unexplained, in psychopathic behavior, 139
Falsehood: inability of psychopath to distinguish truth from, 140–41
Family: incest and, 161
Fantasy: as defense mechanism, 51; in sadism and masochism, 157
Farberow, Norman, 222–23, 225
Farr, Mike (case example), 119–20
Fatigue: suicide and, 228
FBI (Federal Bureau of Investigation), 185
Fear: anxiety distinguished from, 41–42; extreme, as abnormal, 65; and handling mentally disturbed, 69; as normal emotion, 19–20; phobic neuroses, 100–2; among police officers, 288; and suicidal behavior, 228
Federal Bureau of Investigation (FBI), 185
Fetishism: described, 154–56, 163–64
Fight and flight: defined, 44
Flexibility: of behavior, 61; lack of, in personality disorder, 80
Flight: blind, in riots, 259; fight and, defined, 44; of ideas, 111
Freud, Sigmund; and aggression, 38; and anxiety, 41; and anxiety neuroses, 92; and conversion neuroses, 103; and dissociative neuroses, 105; and homosexuality, 153; and normal personality development, 29–33; and obsessive-compulsive neuroses, 97, 99; and secondary gain, 91; and sexuality, 150
Frustration and Aggression (Dollard et al), 202
Frustration-aggression hypothesis, 202, 204
Frustration and conflict, 37–43; anxiety as reaction to, 41–42; concepts of, 37–38; guilt as reaction to, 41–43; and hostility and aggression, 38–40; in sexuality, 38
Frustration-tolerance threshold: defined, 204

Functional mental illness: classification of, 74

Garmire, Bernard L., 6–7
Gerrard, Margaret (case example), 123
Grandiose ideas: abnormal, 63
Grant, Douglas, 279, 281
Guilt: as reaction to frustration and conflict, 41–43
Gustatory hallucinations, 64, 112

Habituation: defined, 180
Hallucinations: auditory, visual and gustatory, 64; psychotic, 111–12
Hallucinogens, 186–87, 190
Harangue: forceful, in riots, 258
Harrington, Alan, 129, 139
Hearing voices (auditory hallucinations), 64
Heath, Neville G. G. (case example), 158
Hebephrenic schizophrenia: described, 117
Heredity: in development, 26–27; id and, 30; in schizophrenia, 114
Heroin: classification of, 181; *see also* Drug dependent behavior
Highway hypnosis, 105
Hippocrates, 74, 118
Hiroshima: bombing of, effects of, 246
Homeostasis: defined, 31
Homosexuality: described, 152–54, 163; transvestitism and, 156, 164
Hopelessness: suicide and feelings of, 229
Horstman, P. L., 214–16
Hostility: and frustration and conflict, 38–40; in handling mentally ill, 67–68
Hormones: schizophrenia and, 113
Hospitalization and commitment, 273–74
How to Recognize and Handle Abnormal People (Matthews and Rowland), 62
Humor: use of, in riot control, 262–63
Hunt, Officer (case example), 45
Hysterial amnesia, 105
Hysterical neuroses (conversion neuroses; conversion hysteria): described, 103–5
Hysterical personality disorder, 83–85

Id: defined, 29–30, 37; guilt feelings and, 42; primary aggression and, 38
Ideas of reference: defined, 65
Identification: as defense mechanism, 50
Identity: sense of, defined, 28
Imitation in riots, 256

Immediate reaction after impact of disasters, 244
Impact period behavior in disasters, 244
Impersonality of group behavior: rioter and, 255
Impulsivity of behavior, 61–62
Incest, 160–61
Individual rioters, 255–56
Individual violent behavior, 204–6
Ineffective behavior: as abnormal, 56
Initiation: sense of, defined, 28
Insight (mimicry of insight): psychopath's lack of, 141–42
Intentional crowd: defined, 252
Interests: suicide and loss of, 228
Internal defense mechanisms, *see* Defense mechanisms
Intimacy: sense of, defined, 28
Intoxication: drug, defined, 179; pathological, defined, 183
Involutional psychotic depression: described, 122–23
Irish Republican Army (IRA), 206
Irritability: suicide and, 228

Janet, Pierre, 97
Jeffers, Officer (case example), 51
Judgment: psychotic disturbances in, 112
Juvenile delinquency, *see* Delinquent behavior

Kahlbaum, 118
Kanner, Officer (case example), 104–5
Kennedy, Robert F., 40
Kierkegaard, Soren, 43
Kinsey, Alfred, 155
Kleptomania, 98
Klineberg, Otto, 55
Kozol, H. L., 208, 209
Kraepelin, Emil, 74, 112–13, 118

La Folie circulaire (Falret), 118
Lawbreaker: psychopath differentiated from, 146
Le Suicide (Durkheim), 221
Learned aggression (compensatory or secondary aggression); defined, 38
Learning: concept of, 20–24
Legal aspects of abnormal behavior, 266–74; commitment and hospitalization as, 273–74; competency to stand trial as, 270; confidentiality in, 271; credibility of witnesses as, 271–72; crim-

inal responsibility as, 268–70; expert testimony as, 272–73
Lesbianism, 152; *see also* Homosexuality
Libido: defined, 30
Lindgren, Larry (case example), 136–39, 141
Lindsay, John V., 254
Loosening of associations, 111
Los Angeles County Hospital, 223
Los Angeles Police Department, 291
Love: psychopath's incapacity for closeness and, 141
Lysergic acid diethylamide (LSD), 178, 181; *see also* Drug dependent behavior

McNaughten, Robert (case example), 268
McNaughten Rule, 268–69
Malingering: defined, 91
Maloney, Sergeant (case example), 45–46
Manic-depressive psychosis: early descriptions of, 118; *see also* Affective disorders
Manic-depressive reaction: described, 119–20
Manipulation of people: described, 138–39
Marijuana, 181, 187; *see also* Drug dependent behavior
Martinez, Gregory (case example), 82
Mask of Sanity, The (Cleckley), 140–41
Masochism: described, 157–59
Matthews, R. A., 62
Megargee, C. I., 210
Memory losses: abnormal, 62
Menninger, Karl, 268
Mental health: as matter of degree, 57–58
Mental health professionals: violent behavior and, 207–9
Mental inheritance: id as, 30
Mental retardation: classification of, 75
Methadone, 186; *see also* Drug dependent behavior
Methadrine, 188; *see also* Drug dependent behavior
Mild tranquilizers, 181, 188; *see also* Drug dependent behavior
Milton, Catherine, 286–87
Mimicry of insight: defined, 141–42
"Mixed" violent behavior, 205, 207
Mobs and crowds: characteristics of, 252
Monroe, Michael (case example), 99–100
Morally insane: defined, 131
Morris, Harry (case example), 134–35, 140, 141
Morris, Hike (case example), 86–87
Motivation (drives): concept of, 20–21; defined, 37

Mott, Lieutenant Colonel, 242
Multiple personality, 105

Narcotic drugs (opiates), 185–86, 190; *see also* Drug dependent behavior
National Advisory Commission on Civil Disorders, 262
National Institute of Mental Health, 223
Necrophilia, 162
Need gratification: defined, 30
Neuroses, 90–109; anxiety, 92–94; battlefield, 19, 242–43, 272; conversion, 103–5; defined, 76, 92; depressive, 94–97; dissociative, 105–6; general considerations on, 90–91; helpful hints on, 106–8; obsessive-compulsive, 97–100; personality disorders compared with, 79; phobic, 100–2
Neurotic anxiety: absence of, in psychopathic behavior, 139–40
New York Police Department, 286
Newton, Hazel (case example), 93–94
Nondiagnostic terms for administrative use, 75
Nonspecific conditions: classification of, 75
Norm enforcing: and violent behavior, 214
Normal behavior: defined, 55
Normal development, 26–53; conflicts and mechanisms of defense in, *see* Defense mechanisms; constitutional factors in, 26–27; developmental factors in, 29–34; ego in, 30–31 (*see also* Ego); id in, 29–30 (*see also* Id); situational and environmental factors in, 27–29; superego in, 31–32; three levels of mental activity in, 32–34
Nostalgia, 242
Novelty: as factor in riots, 256
Numophan, 816

Oakland Police Department, 212
O'Brien, Allen (case example), 82–83
Obsessive-compulsive: classification of, 74
Obsessive-compulsive neuroses: described, 97–100
Odors: smelling strange (olfactory hallucinations), 64
O'Neal, P., 143
Open conflict: as behavior in riot process, 254–55
Opium, *see* Drug dependent behavior
Organic brain syndrome: classification of, 75; defined, 77

Organic mental illness, 74
Organizational climate of police work, 281–82
Overactive reaction to disasters, 245

Panic: as reaction to disasters, 245; in riots, 259
Paranoid personality disorder, 85–86; paranoid state and paranoid schizophrenia compared with, 195; as riot-prone, 257
Paranoid psychoses: amphetamines causing, 188, 190–91
Paranoid schizophrenia: described, 116–17; paranoid state and paranoid personality disorder compared with, 195
Paranoid state, 193–201; described, 64–65, 193; helpful hints on, 199–200; paranoid personality and paranoid schizophrenia compared with, 195; progression of, 195–99; spectrum of, 193, 195
Passive-aggressive personality disorder, 80–83; as riot-prone, 256–57
Pathological intoxication: defined, 183
Patton, George, 19
Pedophilia, 161–62
Peel, Sir Robert, 268
Peeping Tom: defined, 160
People watching and talking about him, 64–65; *see also* Paranoid state
Perception: psychotic disturbances in, 111
Personal involvement: professional attitude and, 17–20
Personality development, *see* Normal development
Personality disorders, 79–89; classification of, 75; compulsive, 86–87; defined, 75–76; general characteristics of, 80; helpful hints on, 88; hysterical, 83–85; paranoid, *see* Paranoid personality disorder; passive-aggressive, 80–83
Persecution feelings: described, 62–63; *see also entries beginning with term: paranoid*
Phobic neuroses: described, 100–2
Phobic object: defined, 100
Phobic situation: described, 100
Physical complaints: unrealistic, as abnormal, 65
Physical conditions: schizophrenia and, 113
Physical crowd, 252
Pima County Sheriff's Department, 285
Pinel, Philippe, 74
Police Foundation, 286
Police officers, 277–93; assaults on, 211–16; behavior to be dealt with by,

xi–xii; broad range of tasks confronting, 6–12; changing role of, 3–13; children of, 291; code of conduct of, for riot control, 264; code of conduct of, and violent behavior, 217; core element of role of, 9–12; danger as stressful on, 283; difficulties of, with bureaucracy, 284–85; dishonest, 285; education of, xi, xii; effect of police work on, 280–81; as enforcer of the law, 3–6, 11–12; environment of, 281–82; fear as stressful on, 288; killed or injured, xii, 10; perception of danger by, 211; policewomen, *see* Policewomen; primary task of, 19; publicity as stressful on, 283; relationship of, with spouses, 290–91; retirement of, 292; scapegoating and, 286; shift work as stressful on, 289; stresses on, 282–92; tunnel vision developed by, 283–84; type of person becoming, 279–80; unrealistic role expectations among, 288–89; *see also* Professional attitude

Policewomen, 286–90; fears of, 288; spouses' relationship with, 290; and "super-cop" syndrome, 289

Polygraph: psychopath and, 145

Postpartum blues, 121–22

Precipitating incident: riot, 253–54

Preconsciousness: defined, 32, 33

Prejudice (discrimination): adverse effects of, 27

Pressure removing: violent behavior and, 214

Preston, George, 21

Primary aggression: defined, 38

Primary drives: defined, 37

Pritchard, James, 131

Prodromal signs: defined, 221

Professional attitude, 17–25; and concept of learning, 20–24; and concept of motivation, 20–21; in operation, 23–24; personal involvement and, 17–20

Projections: abnormal, 64–65; as defense mechanisms, 47

Propaganda: riot, 257–58

Psychedelics (hallucinogens), 186–87, 190; *see also* Drug dependent behavior

Psychiatry for the Curious (Preston), 21

Psychological crowd: defined, 252

Psychopathic behavior, 129–47; case histories of, 131–38; characteristics of, 138–43; and description of violent behavior, 209; helpful hints on, 144–46; historical background on, 131; judging, 65; as riot prone, 257; sadism and, 142, 157–59; underlying factors in, 143–44

Psychophysiological disorders: described, 75, 77–78

Psychoses, 110–25; absence of, in psychopath, 140; affective disorders as, *see* Affective disorders; classification of, 75; common characteristics of, 110–12; defined, 76; helpful hints on, 123–25; schizophrenia as, *see* Schizophrenia

Psychotic depressive reaction: described, 120–22

Publicity: police work and, 283

Rape: statutory and assaultive, 151

Rappaport, Jonas R., 207–8

Rationalization: as defense mechanism, 45–46

Reaction formation: as defense mechanism, 47–48; in obsessive-compulsive, 98

Reactive drinkers: defined, 181–82

Reality: loss of contact with, in psychoses, 110–12

Regression: as defense mechanism, 51; of psychotics, 112

Reiser, Martin, 291

Rep-defending: violent behavior and, 214

Repression: as defense mechanism, 49

Responsibility: criminal, 268–70

Retirement of police officers, 292

Riley, Officer (case example), 51

Riot control, 260–65; alertness for, 260–61; community support for, 261–62; police officers' code of conduct for, 264; police policy in, 263–64; self-control for, 260; use of humor in, 262–64

Riot-prone personality, 256–57

Riots, 250–60; characteristics of crowds and mobs, 252; confrontation in, 254; individual rioter, characterized, 255–56; open conflict in, 254–55; precipitating incident in, 253–54; the riot process, 253–55; riot-prone personality in, 256–57; "Roman Holiday" phase of, 254; techniques of agitators in, 257–60; *see also* Riot control

Rosenberg, Judith (case example), 101–2

Role expectations: unrealistic, among police officers, 288–89

"Role of the Police, The" (Terris), 10

"Roman Holiday" phase in riots, 254

Rowland, L. W., 62

Rumor: emotion producing, in riot, 257

Rutherford, Mary (case example), 85–86

Sadism: described, 157–59; of psychopaths, 142, 157–59

San Quentin (prison), 212

Scapegoating: police work and, 286

Schizophrenia, 112–17; catatonic, described, 117; hebephrenic, described, 117; helpful hints on, 124–25; historical background of, 112–13; paranoid, 116–17; paranoid state and paranoid personality disorder compared with paranoid, 195; simple, 114–16; underlying factors of, 113–17
Schneidman, Edwin, 222–23, 225, 226
Schwartz, Mrs. (case example), 101–2
Secondary aggression: defined, 38
Secondary drives: defined, 37
Secondary gain: defined, 91
Self-control in riot control, 260
Self-defeating behavior: as abnormal, 56; persistence of antisocial, in psychopath, 140
Self-defending: violent behavior and, 214
Self-deprecation: suicide and feelings of, 229
Self-destructive behavior: as abnormal, 56; see also Suicidal behavior
Self-image compensating: violent behavior and, 214
Self-indulging: violent behavior and, 214
Sexuality: deviant, see Deviant sexual behavior; frustration and conflict in, 38; normal, 150; psychopath's shallow and impersonal responses to, 142
Shell shock (battlefield neurosis), 19, 242–43, 272
Shift work: stress of, 289
Show of force principle, 66–67
Sick behavior, see Abnormal behavior
Signal anxiety: defined, 92
Simple schizophrenia, 114–16
Sirhan-Sirhan, 40
Situational anxiety in psychopaths, 139
Situational communications in suicidal behavior, 227
Situational factors in development, 27–29
Sleep: difficulty with, suicide and, 228
Sleepwalking trance, 105
Smith, Charlie (case example), 51–52
Smith, Marie (case example), 50
Social violent behavior (collective violence), 205–7; see also Disasters; Riots
Sociocultural factors in schizophrenia, 114
Sociopath, see Psychopathic behavior
Socrates, 33
Sodomy, 162
Southern Arizona Law Enforcement Institute, 260
Speck, Richard (case example), 206
Special symptoms: classification of, 75
Spectator sports, 39–40
Spouses: police officers' relationship with, 290–91
Starkweather, Charles, 40

Status need: frustration and conflict and, 40
Statutory rape, 151
Sterling, J. W., 5, 10, 211, 279–81
Stimulus generalization: defined, 22
Stocking anesthesia, 104
Sublimation: as defense mechanism, 51–52
Substitution: as defense mechanism, 50–51
Suicidal behavior, 219–39; as abnormal, 56; assessment of resources blocking, 232–33; behavioral clues to, 226–27; case examples of, 235–38; clues to, 226–29; evaluation of suicide potential, 230; helpful hints on, 68, 228–35; historical background on, 221–23; identification and clarification of focal problem in dealing with, 230; relationship established for dealing with, 229–30; rescue operations and referral procedures, 233–34; at retirement, 292; suicide attempter, characterized, 223–25; situational communications in, 227; syndromatic communications in, 228–29; verbal clues to, 226
Suicide prevention centers: growth of, 223
Suicides: age, sex and death rate from, 231; false improvement and, 107; number of yearly, 219; psychopaths and threat of, 143–43; as violent behavior, 205–6; see also Suicidal behavior
Sullivan, Harry Stack, 93
Sullivan, Mary (case example), 158–59
Suggestibility: rioter open to, 256
Superego: defined, 31–32
Syndromatic communications in suicidal behavior, 228–29

Tactile hallucinations, 112
Talbert, Marion, 189, 292
Talks to himself: as abnormal, 63
Tangential thinking: described, 111
Tastes: peculiar (gustatory hallucinations), 64, 112
Teasing, 39
Terris, Bruce, 10
Thinking: psychoses and disturbances in, 111; see also Schizophrenia
Thomas (recruit; case example), 46–47
Thompson, Russell (case example), 135–36, 139, 140, 152
Toch, Hans, 209–10, 212–15
Toledo, Council of (693), 222
Tolerance: defined, 180
Tranquilizers: mild, 181, 188

Transient situational disturbances: defined, 75, 78
Transsexuality: defined, 156
Transvestitism: described, 156, 164
Troy, Helen (case example), 49
Trust, sense of: defined, 28
Truth: inability to distinguish falsehood from, in psychopath, 140–41
"Truth serum": limitations of, 271–72
Tucson Police Department, 290
Tunnel vision: police work developing, 283–84

Unconsciousness: defined, 32–34
Undoing: defined, 98
Urban Institute, 287, 289

Verbal clues to suicidal intent, 226
Vicarious aggression: defined, 38; examples of, 39–40
Victimless crimes, 151–52
Vincent, John (case example), 106
Violent behavior, 202–18; agitators' use of, 258–60; assaults on police officers as, 211–16; definitions and concepts about, 202, 204–7; helpful hints on, 216–18; individual, 204–6; "mixed," 205, 207;

and police officers' perception of danger, 211; predicting front page, 209–10; prediction of dangerousness in, 207–10; social, 205–7; television and movie, 40
Violent Men (Toch), 212
Visual hallucinations (visions), 64, 112
Voyeurism: described, 160

War neurosis (battlefield neurosis), 19, 243–44, 272
Warning-period behavior in disasters, 243–44
Washington (D.C.) Police Department, 286
Washington (D.C.) riots (1968), 254–55
Weight loss: suicidal behavior and, 228
White, R. W., 32
Whitman, Charles (case example), 206
Willis, Victor (case example), 81–82
Withdrawal syndrome: alcohol, 184; defined, 179–80; drug, 189–90
Witnesses: establishing credibility of, 271–72; expert, 272–73

Zoophilia, 162